K₁
R.

Tu. Pkw
473

The Excavation of

Roman and Mediaeval

LONDON

W. F. GRIMES

Professor of Archaeology, University of London

The Excavation of

Roman and Mediaeval

LONDON

LONDON: ROUTLEDGE & KEGAN PAUL

First published 1968
by Routledge & Kegan Paul Limited
Broadway House, 68–74 Carter Lane
London, E.C.4

Printed in Great Britain by
Western Printing Services Limited
Bristol

© *W. F. Grimes 1968*

SBN 7100 2897 0

For my Wife
who, during and since,
endured much in this Cause

Contents

CONTENTS

CONTENTS

Preface

I HAVE indicated elsewhere that this book does not set out to be a definitive report on the series of excavations that the Roman and Mediaeval London Excavation Council has carried out in London since 1947. While providing a summary of the work which incorporates some detailed archaeological information which has not been published before (as well as desultory comments on one or two other matters) it provides an opportunity to acknowledge publicly the generosity of those who subscribed to the Council's funds and gives them some indication of the way in which their money has been spent.

These and other benefactions will be found to be acknowledged at various points in the text. This is the place in which (facing the charge of being repetitious) I must acknowledge personal indebtedness. First, to my colleagues on the Council in general and especially to the succession of officers who as Chairman, Secretary or Treasurer were ever-ready with help and advice: the late Sir Harold Idris Bell, Adrian Oswald, Edward Holland-Martin, John Giuseppi, Jack Head, who started us on our way, the late Sir Ian Richmond, Norman Cook, Alan Woods and Charles Denham, who took over from them. Thanks are due also to Norman Cook as head of the Guildhall Museum and to his colleagues, Ralph Merrifield and Peter Marsden in particular; and amongst their fellow officers in the Corporation's service Francis Forty, until recently City Engineer, and his assistants Messrs. N. G. Hutton and F. Trewin. Amongst volunteers the name of George Rybot figures honourably; and I keep a special place for Walter Henderson, formerly of the London Museum, who continues to shoulder tasks that lay beyond the call of duty even when he worked for the Museum. My former secretary, Jean Macdonald, my present secretary, Marjory Hunt, have shown a forebearance in these activities which only those who have suffered from me can begin to appreciate. I believe that they remain my friends, and I hope that this also goes for my publishers.

W.F.G.

Figures in the Text

With the exception of Figure 40
the drawings are the work of the author

List of Plates

(at end)

Unless otherwise indicated the photographs are the author's

I

Introduction

THIS book is a preliminary record of excavations in the City of London over the fifteen years from 1947 to 1962—preliminary, because a final assessment of the results will not be possible until the mass of material which the excavations have produced has been examined. It is a contribution to the understanding of London's past; but it has a limited purpose and does not attempt to take in all the evidence, whether of recent or more remote origin, on which a complete study of early London would require to be based.

The immediate background to this work was the bombing of London during the Second World War, which led to the destruction of more than 50 of the 350 or so acres that make up the walled city. It was seen that there must be some interval before new buildings could be erected in these areas; for the first time therefore opportunity was provided for archaeological excavation in controlled conditions, free from the cramping limitations of time and builders' needs which had prevailed formerly. Having in 1946 sponsored a short trial season, the Society of Antiquaries of London took the initiative in establishing the Roman and Mediaeval London Excavation Council to organise a more extended programme of excavation. The Council, which is a body widely representative of archaeological and other interests in and beyond London, began its operations in July 1947 and the work went on without ceasing, winter and summer, from then until December 1962. The excavations have been partly financed by such funds as the Council has been able to raise privately: a list of donors is printed on pages 245–51. The general question of financial support for archaeological work in the city is referred to again later, but this is the point at which thanks for these all-important benefactions should be expressed. It must also be added however that the Council's activities would long ago have come to an enforced end but for an annual grant from the Ministry of Public Building and Works as it is now known. The Ministry is often the target of criticism from archaeologists, with varying degrees of justification. This is one of those occasions when the Department deserves nothing but praise for generously shouldering a burden the larger part of which it might reasonably have considered to rest elsewhere.

From 1947, then, the Excavation Council has devoted its attention to the excavation of sites awaiting development and to this extent its programme can be said to have been planned. This work has run parallel with the 'rescue' work on sites where building was already in progress which has long been the responsibility of the staff of the Corporation of London's Guildhall Museum. The Council and the Museum have maintained close co-operation throughout: the Museum has accepted responsibility for the finds from the Council's work and will in due course be the repository for the no doubt relatively small proportion of this material which will require to be permanently preserved.

One essential in enterprises of this sort is money; the other is people. Apart from its small paid labour force, the Excavation Council's officers have all been honorary. It is impossible to emphasise too strongly how much is owing to colleagues who have found time in busy lives taken up with other things to further the Council's work. Too often the wrong names appear in newspapers. The plain truth is that no organisation functioning as the Excavation Council has over this unbroken period, could have survived without either the weekly attention to its affairs of honorary secretaries and honorary treasurers or the thought given to matters of policy and procedure by chairmen and members of committees. Expressions of personal gratitude appear elsewhere; in the meantime the thanks of all interested in London's history should go to the officers and members of the Council for their work on its behalf.

It has already been said that this is a record of excavation. One essential pre-requisite to an appreciation of its results is some account of the conditions under which the work was done if only to remove the fairly widespread misunderstanding of what is involved.

The Roman city of London was established on a portion of the 50-foot or Taplow terrace of the River Thames which consists of sandy-gravel deposits laid down during the Pleistocene Ice Age on the grey-brown London Clay which is found in deeper excavations in the London area. The gravel, of varying thickness, is overlaid by brown loam, the so-called brick-earth, which also varies in depth and in consistency: it is sometimes pre-dominantly clayey, sometimes sandy. The surface of the brickearth is thus the natural surface on which the occupation remains of early man[1] have accumulated.

The gravel terraces of the Thames have long been recognised as favoured settlement areas in prehistoric times—a fact which has been well brought out by air photographs in the Oxford region and elsewhere. Excavation of sites on the gravel outside the built-up area of London has produced evidence of continuous settlement into and beyond the Roman period. From the city area have come numbers of finds of pre-Roman objects which indicate that its twin hills of Cornhill and St. Paul's were frequented before the Romans came; but it remains true that in all the work that has been done since the war no structural remains of settlement, such as hut sites, or rubbish-pits, have been observed. There is therefore nothing to contradict the view that if when they came here the Romans found a settlement on the site which they selected for their own occupation it could have been any-thing more than a small village, a cluster of huts of a type for which there are parallels elsewhere in the Lower Thames valley. It is to be noted in-cidentally that the fact that such huts have not been recorded is not in itself conclusive: their remains would have been slight and in the nature of the brickearth recognisable only to expert eyes.

As to the reasons underlying the siting of London, here also there is no new evidence to contradict the view that the choice was dictated by the convenience of the river-crossing along this section of the Thames. As is well known, the crucial factor was the level of the river in relation to the land: the facts which are taken to show that there has been a submergence of the land of at least 13 feet since Roman times have been fully marshalled

[1] By 'early' man is meant here people from the Middle Stone Age (Mesolithic) period down-wards, a period of roughly 8,000–10,000 years. The gravels also produce the implements of man of the Older Stone Age (Palaeolithic) periods, but these come from the gravel itself and belong to the much more remote time of the formation of the terraces during the Ice Age.

as far as they go.[1] This is not the place to renew arguments on the vexed question of the crossings of the Thames under the Romans. It must suffice to say that much of the evidence that is brought to bear on this subject is of uncertain value and that only the Westminster and City of London (London Bridge) crossings fit the pattern of Roman roads as it survives at the present day. The subject is discussed at greater length below (pp. 40–6).

But to return to Londinium itself. Whether or not it is as true as was once thought that the growth of the settlement area was a simple process of spread across the Walbrook valley from the eastern to the western hill there can be little doubt about the primacy of Cornhill as the centre of the city. It is also true that if depth of deposit is any guide the area on the west of most intensive occupation throughout the Roman period flanked the line of modern Cheapside–Poultry. The result of all recent work has been to show that broadly speaking movement away from these centres is accompanied by a thinning out of the deposits. Leaving out of account the special conditions in the Walbrook valley (p. 93) the greatest depths of the natural surface from which everything starts are of the order of 10–11 feet below cellar floor (17–20 feet more or less below modern street) in the centres of settlement. (Not all of this build-up is Roman of course: the upper deposits are of post-Roman origin.) In the Cripplegate area, on the other hand, the situation goes to the other extreme. Here cellar floors and natural surface frequently coincide, while in the extreme north-west of the walled area even the natural ground to a depth of 3 feet below the surface has been completely swept away. It should be emphasised that this state of affairs is not due simply to the excavation of the ground for cellars. Cellars were excavated in the central areas also. It is quite clear both that the ground level was relatively higher in Cripplegate and that the accumulations upon it were less deep.

The manner of the accumulation of deposits in a city of long standing now requires to be considered both because it is of interest in itself and because it has a bearing on the techniques of excavation employed to elucidate the various features and their chronological and other relationships to one another.

[1] Royal Commission on Historical Monuments (England), *Roman London* (1928), pp. 13–14, hereafter referred to as *Roman London*.

The character of the deposits on a particular site is directly related to the nature of the structures on the area and the activities that they represent. This statement, self-evident for all early settlements, is particularly apposite for London, where the absence of building stone near at hand has led to a widespread use of substitutes wherever possible; and these, of timber, 'cob'[1] and plaster, have each left their mark in their characteristic way (pp. 121, 139). Other things being equal, stone buildings have a longer life than buildings of other materials. But modification and rebuilding may take place for a variety of reasons having nothing to do with the endurance of the actual structure; and even if the changes in stone buildings are less frequent they often have a more drastic effect on their surroundings because of the more massive and more permanent character of the materials used in them.

The history-bearing deposits of a city like London in fact mirror two parallel processes. On the natural surface of the ground once settlement begins there accumulate deposits which are partly constructional (hut floors, roads, etc.), partly fortuitous (occupation débris), the actual nature of the first varying for the kind of reasons that have already been mentioned. But with the building-up process goes a second involving digging out. Each level or floor is accompanied by its own disturbances: pits of more than one kind, wells, gullies and post-holes; and these, being dug from various levels, may cut through one another and through earlier floors. These processes have been at work throughout all time: mediaeval pits, which are often of considerable size, may have been dug from high levels which have now disappeared and penetrate to depths below the deepest Roman deposits; post-mediaeval walls and cesspits behave in the same way; and even quite modern disturbances for foundations, drains and the like may in some circumstances lead to confusion and difficulty. For the archaeologist the chief and most daunting effect of later disturbance is the destruction of the earlier features which may be his main objective: it adds considerably to the difficulties of reconstructing even a partial plan when only a limited portion of a site is available. The pursuit of the southern defences of the Cripplegate fort (pp. 23–4) was a good example of this.

[1] By 'cob' is meant a mixture of plastic material, such as clay, with a coarser backing, such as chalk, as the core for a built wall which is given protection from the weather by a surface-finish of plaster or the like. The technique is common in the stoneless conditions of much of southern and eastern England, but with variations in materials occurs also elsewhere.

The other important point that this interpenetration of elements of different periods brings out is that mere depth below the modern surface is meaningless as a clue to date. Objects of relatively late date from the deeper fillings of pits may be found at the same depth as objects of early date from deposits which have accumulated on the site and through which the pits have been dug. This relationship appears to cut across the stratigraphical succession in which archaeologists accept the principles enunciated by the geologists: according to these the lower layers in a succession are older than the higher; but the pits and their fillings are of course linked with the higher levels which were the surfaces when they were made. Since a deposit is dated by the latest object in it[1] a method of excavation devised in terms of depth (as when a trench is dug in a succession of uniform 'spits') could produce very misleading results, because of the interlocking of the different structures. The same unsatisfactory consequence will follow a failure to recognise the existence of later disturbance, the contents of which may then contaminate the surrounding levels. It becomes essential therefore to identify the various features as soon as possible and to deal with them separately if the different 'periods' are not to be mixed up and the historical sequence of the site thereby confused.

It is perhaps desirable at this stage to digress in order to emphasise this point. The modern archaeologist's main aim is to reconstruct the past in all its aspects. In 'historic' periods such as the Roman and mediaeval he hopes to extend by the study of material remains the information obtained by the historians from documentary sources. The day of 'treasure-hunting', of finds for their own sake, has gone, even if no excavator, however high-minded, can escape the excitement that a beautiful or interesting object may bring. The truth is that for historical purposes a good part of the value of any discovery is likely to be lost if the circumstances attending it have been inadequately observed and recorded. The site and the find are closely linked; the one will often help to explain or to augment the other. Most excavators can recall instances of finds of quite common coins or even of potsherds in circumstances which gave them a value as historical documents far beyond their worth as antiquities because they afforded a date or a 'period' to some element on the site on which they were found. In the City of London the best examples of this are provided by the north-

___

[1] More accurately, the latest object fixes the *earliest* date of a deposit.

western defences (pp. 50–1), for there the dating of the different elements associated with the wall has a wide historical significance. This dating relies everywhere on finds of minor antiquities recovered from significant situations; and if it be argued that this is slender material from which to build, the answer must be, first that the method of excavation adopted was such as to ensure accurate observation; secondly that the results are consistent with themselves and fit into the broad pattern of events as worked out by historians and archaeologists over a much wider area.

This view of the close interdependence of site and find demands a standard of discipline and order in excavation which is completely out of keeping with the treasure-hunt approach and comes with pained surprise to the more romantically-minded volunteers. This was inevitable if archaeology was to achieve full stature as a serious study—a study in which the trained amateur can continue to make a worthy contribution but in which also the methods of Ben Gunn and Long John Silver have no place.

From what has been said it will be seen that the techniques of modern excavation are directed not merely at making 'finds' but at elucidating the structures with which the finds are associated. Here 'structure' means such things as pits and floor-surfaces as well as the more obvious remains of buildings: the digging must follow the pattern that they create and be capable of adjustment as that pattern changes.

Usually therefore a cutting through a typical London deposit is likely to present a curiously untidy appearance, at any rate in its early stages. With the cellar floor removed, the surface is usually dark in colour and obviously made up of artificial occupation deposits. But it is rarely uniform; and careful cleaning will usually reveal variations both in colour and in consistency which are evidence of disturbance and usually indicate pits of some kind— this apart from modern features such as drains, foundations and the like. The obvious first step is the removal of the modern remains. The limits of each disturbance must then be determined—not always an easy task in the soil conditions. Where they impinge on one another their sequence must be established; and they must then be excavated in reverse order to that in which they were originally dug. If the last pit to be made is the first to be cleared there can be no danger of its contents contaminating its neighbours.

The first surface will appear as a level area broken by holes and pits of various shapes and depths; it is the surface of the ground in which these disturbances have been made. This material is then removed over the whole area until a change in colour, consistency or content indicates a new floor. Should the uncovering of this reveal pits or other features which have been cut into it (since they do not appear at the higher level) these also are excavated now; and the process is repeated as the cutting deepens until the surface of the undisturbed natural ground is reached. While the sides of the cutting will be straight—for they preserve the essential vertical record of the sequence of structures on the site—the floor at any given time will almost certainly be an irregular affair, and this for two reasons. It will be broken by the excavated pits that either belong to it or penetrate it from above; it will be uneven on its own account because it has been unevenly laid or compressed. The excavation procedure will have required that its irregularities should be closely followed, in the interests of working to structural divisions rather than according to a formally conceived plan of digging to a uniform level whose deceptive precision conceals its rigid, essentially unscientific character. By this means gradually each structure emerges with its associated objects (recorded as the work proceeds) as a distinct feature. The process is illustrated graphically in the accompanying diagram (Fig. 1: see also Plates 6, 7; 57), but is inevitably simplified by the omission of the wide range of difficulties of procedure and interpretation which most sites present.

The excavation conducted as described here requires to be recorded and for this a plan (or plans) and sections will be essential. As to the former, whether there is one or more must depend upon the number and significance of the floors that make up the deposit. The decision must depend upon the contribution that any given level may make to an understanding of the site at that stage in its development: the layout and alignment of its buildings, their structural character and so on.

The section is the vertical record of the deposits which, correlated with the datable finds, provides the historical picture, as the plan may cover the social or economic aspect by revealing the nature of the building or of the activity on the site. As with plans so with sections more than one may be necessary: on occasion both faces of the cutting have been drawn for some of the London excavations—sometimes to show disturbingly different results, bearing in mind that the faces were generally only a few feet apart.

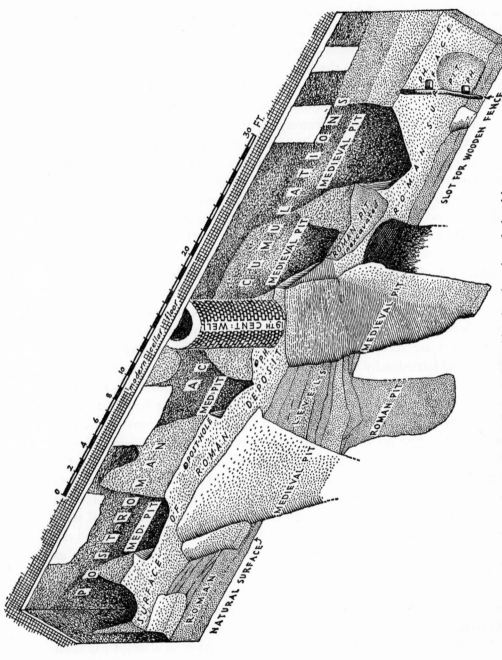

1. Reconstruction of a section at Gutter Lane, Cheapside, showing the relationship of Roman deposits to mediaeval pits and other later features.

(On complicated sites the implications of this for the interpretation of any-thing other than a total excavation are self-evident.)

Here there are two problems of presentation, one of them related to what has just been written. As to the first, structures appear in the cutting itself which are not projected into the section; and will not therefore figure in the record if it is limited to the sides of the trench. This difficulty must be overcome where necessary by drawing separate sections of the structure in question, at the same time fixing its position in the vertical sequence. (It is, incidentally, characteristic of this type of excavation that features like floors that present themselves clearly in the trench as it is being dug are often much less obvious, if not unidentifiable, in the section.)

The second point has to do with the actual manner of recording the section. As a matter of general comment it is worth noting that the pro-blems that attend the presentation of a plan are different from those of illustrating a section. For the former a set of acceptable conventions exists which only rarely and in exceptional circumstances does violence to, or confuses, the facts. Correctness of interpretation and accuracy in surveying apart, there are probably many ways of indicating walls, post-holes, pits and so on which are acceptable because they speak for themselves, with the minimum of intrusion by the recorder. The sections of complicated occupa-tion-sites on the other hand may display a wide range of materials variously disposed and demanding the exercise of judgment and selection in their representation. Archaeologists have on a number of occasions in the past discussed the appropriate techniques for portraying these changes. At the one end of the scale there is an almost total reliance upon convention, at the other something approaching naturalism. Each of these approaches has its disadvantages. The conventionalised drawing tends to over-simplify: the student sees the section only through the excavator's eyes; the use of stan-dard conventions often masks the range of variation in the deposits; and the lines of demarcation between the different layers are often by no means as definite as many drawings would suggest. On the other hand the 'natural-istic' style leads to problems of labelling, which, since it must normally be done on the drawing itself, must lead to loss of archaeological detail. Throughout the excavations described in this book a combination of methods has been used. In drawing the actual section an attempt has been made to record what could be seen, reproducing variations of tone and texture as accurately as possible. In most cases the working drawings were finished in ink on the site. Only on some of the later sites were they completed elsewhere—and by this time there was a considerable body of experience on which to work. By these means the section is presented with a minimum of convention. With the graphic treatment of the section goes an outline version, which in part labels, in part interprets, the deposits. The reader thus sees the section as the excavator saw it and is given the maximum opportunity of exercising his own judgment upon it. For present purposes, however, some sections are presented in simplified form.

The procedures above outlined are essential to the understanding of the remains of early London in all its phases, for only so can the history of each site be established, to make its contribution to the history of the city as a whole. So too the other aim of these operations, to learn the kind of place that London was and to evaluate the sort of life that its citizens lived, will be in danger of being defeated, or at least partly frustrated, by the use of wrong methods. This objective depends for its achievement on the full understanding of finds and structures as such, independently of their value as dating media.

It is assumed frequently that London, like many Roman towns of much less importance, was a place of large houses and other buildings, each elaborately laid out and equipped with all the refinements of Mediterranean culture. That there were such houses is certain enough. But they are known mainly only by uncoordinated fragments: the odd length of wall, the occasional mosaic pavement; and while the Council's investigations and the observations of the Guildhall Museum have added more such fragments, it still remains true that it is not possible to reconstruct one complete building as the typical house of a Roman citizen.

The distribution of such houses seems to have been largely restricted to the area centred on Cornhill with the extension westwards along the line of modern Cheapside to which reference has already been made: this had also been the extent of the early city which was destroyed by Boudicca in A.D. 60 or 61.[1] Over large areas much slighter buildings were the rule and they

---

[1] For the extent of the damage done to London at this time see G. C. Dunning, 'Two Fires of Roman London', *Antiquaries Journal*, XXV (1945), pp. 48–52; and for a general account of Boudicca, D. R. Dudley and Graham Webster, *The Rebellion of Boudicca* (1962) with on pp. 144–5 a note on the date of the rising.

must frequently have been mingled with those of stone even in the more central zones. The contrast in building practice is in essence a reflection of the stoneless condition of the London area already mentioned.

In the conditions in the city the varied character of these less permanent buildings can only be deduced from scraps of evidence widely dispersed over a number of sites. Floors, to begin with, are of different kinds. Sand, gravel or clay are the commonest materials; more rarely 'concrete' (*opus signinum*) or timber occur. There is one instance of a tessellated pavement associated with a timber building (p. 149). The floor surface may be sunk below the general level: plank floors are sometimes set in a shallow hollow resembling a modern carpet-well (p. 140). Timber-framed buildings were anchored to posts driven into the ground: the surviving evidence is then that of the post-holes, which are often massive and deeply driven; but the evidence from Walbrook (p. 96) suggests that prefabricated framed buildings may also have been used. The buildings must have varied in scale. Some were mere shacks and huts with light walls of wattle and daub and roofs of thatch, as on the west side of Walbrook (p. 97). Others, to judge by the scale of their posts, were more massive and may have been roofed with normal baked-clay roofing-tiles (p. 148). The difficulty about such remains is that they rarely or never contribute to a plan. With stone buildings even the shortest piece of wall has at least direction. Post-holes, even when several can be recognised as being of the same date, are much more difficult to interpret. With larger areas uncovered than was usually possible the outlines of the buildings of which they formed part might have been traced; but this is to take no account of the frequently extensive later disturbance, which might have left too little untouched.

But while the combined effect of the use of perishable materials in the absence of stone and of later obstruction and destruction is such that Roman London could never have been as well known as many much smaller provincial towns and cities, the evidence, fragmentary as it is, continues to have a bearing on the nature and history of the city. As to the latter this book has little to say that may not require to be modified when the related finds have been given the detailed study that has now begun. As to the former, Londinium, like most big cities at all ages, presents a full range of contrasts in wealth and the absence of it: at one end of the scale stone-built houses with hypocausts, mosaic pavements and the rest, provincial modifications of the Roman town-house; at the other, wooden thatched-roof shacks and huts not very different from the huts in which the Iron Age people had lived, along the banks of the Thames and elsewhere,[1] before the Romans came. And in between, houses of a 'semi-permanent' nature which partook a little of each.

Throughout, the inhabitants at their different levels enjoyed the same kind of possessions and equipment. There is some evidence of 'native' pottery forms in the early stages, but pottery and domestic appliances generally are essentially Roman. The *graffiti* left by workmen and others show that Latin was in common use and that many were sufficiently educated to write it. There is no indication that the contrasts in house-forms reflect distinctions between native and Roman: in any case, such distinctions would not have outlasted the early years of the occupation. Whether there was any zoning of habitation on a social-economic basis is less clear. It has already been said (p. 4) that there was evidently a concentration of the finer buildings in the Cornhill–Mansion House district. This was unmistakably the hub of London; and inevitably within easy reach of it would have been gathered the prosperous houses. But stone houses are not limited to the central area, though elsewhere they seem to be either on street-frontages or dispersed as isolated buildings. The building beneath St. Bride's Church in Fleet Street actually lies well outside the western wall, beyond the River Fleet (p. 182).

Two other general matters deserve mention. The first is the light, limited as it is, that has been shed on the Roman street plan. The St. Swithun excavation (*48*)[2] established the fact that some part at any rate of Cannon Street overlies a Roman street and that here the two follow the same direction, though whether they are of the same width cannot be said. So too with Cheapside in the neighbourhood of St. Mary-le-Bow Church the mediaeval/modern road has a Roman predecessor. With Cheapside, however, a larger body of evidence presents greater difficulty which is discussed at greater length later (pp. 41–3). Further west also there must have been

---

[1] For huts on the foreshore of the Thames at Tilbury see RCHM, *Essex S.E.*, pp. 38–9; for Old England, R. E. M. Wheeler, ' "Old England", Brentford', *Antiquity*, III (1929), pp. 20–32. And for an earlier period, F. H. Worsfold, 'A Report on the Late Bronze Age Site excavated at Minnis Bay, Birchington, Kent', *Proc. Prehist. Soc.* IX (1943), pp. 28–47.

[2] Numbers in brackets after site-names identify the positions of sites on the map, Fig. 2.

another change, since from the evidence of the Newgate Street site (*26, 27*) the course of the road to Newgate must have approximated to that of Newgate Street. But the difficulties that attend the recognition of gravel-metalled roads in Roman London are notorious. Such variations may be more apparent than real, or may embody changes over a period of time.

The second matter is the evidence that supports the view that the early history of the city was one of movement westwards from the Cornhill area towards St. Paul's. Both in Queen Victoria Street (*31*) and in the Paternoster Row area (*29*) there were indications of extensive disturbance of the natural surface for the excavation of brickearth. It seems unlikely that this would have been going on if the area was much occupied. It is tempting to associate this activity with the potters whose kilns were found at St. Paul's in 1672.[1] At the same time, it should be noted that in the area of the Cripplegate fort there was at least sporadic occupation before the fort was built in the early second century (p. 32).

[1] *Roman London*, p. 140.

II

The Roman Fort of Cripplegate

---

1. INTRODUCTION: THE POSITION IN 1947

THOUGH the bombed areas of the city (Fig. 2) were indiscriminately distributed both within and beyond the walls, the largest single zone of destruction was in the western half of the city, behind St. Paul's Cathedral, from Barbican and Moorgate on the north to Thames Street on the south. Scattered buildings had indeed survived in this region: nevertheless, from at least one position on the north wall of the city it was possible looking southwards to see the church tower of St. Mary Somerset, which must be near the Roman river frontage.

On the north the bomb-damaged area took in a very considerable length of the line of the Roman city wall: practically from Moorgate on the east to St. Giles Cripplegate on the west; and thence southwards to Falcon Square and St. Anne and St. Agnes' Church in Gresham Street, the last point being the inner angle of the Aldersgate re-entrant (p. 20). By no means all this expanse was available for investigation: many of the cellars still contained bomb-rubble, or were otherwise obstructed. In 1947, however, there were no priorities dictated by the building-programme, which had not then really started; and the Council decided that its first excavations should be undertaken in the comparatively unencumbered Cripplegate region, with the particular aim of learning more about the city wall, its date and structural features. This decision was not of course governed entirely by the practical requirements of the immediate situation. In the nature of things, the defences of a city are not normally as productive of occupation-material as are the actual dwelling-sites and it is upon

15

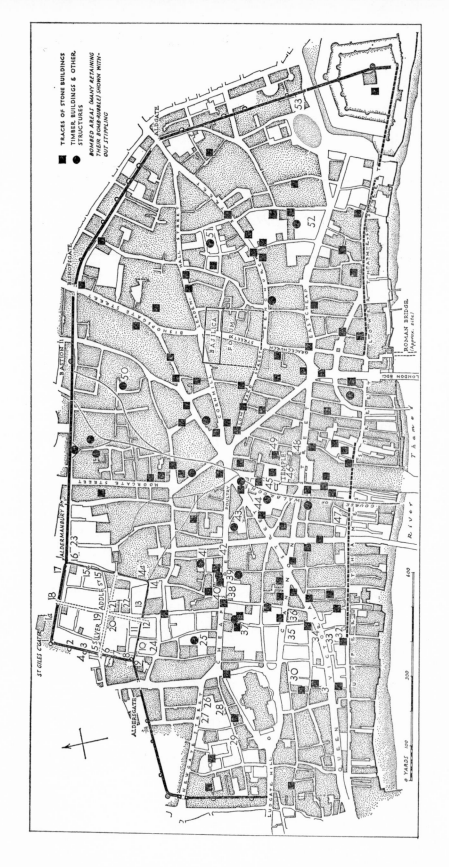

2. Map of the walled city of London showing areas devastated by bombing, with sites excavated by the Excavation Council numbered 1 to 53.

occupation-material that the dating of the different elements depends. Even so, apart from their own intrinsic interest, the defences of a walled city may provide particularly sensitive pointers to the history of their period, pointers which may have significance, not merely for the city, but for the province of which it is a part. For in times of peace—or of disorganisation—the citizens tend to neglect their walls and allow them to fall into decay; in times of war or of uneasiness they restore and maintain them: the dating of the work resulting from such activities may have therefore a more than local importance.

2. THE DISCOVERY OF THE FORT

The area chosen for the first cuttings, in July 1947, was in Windsor Court (3), just north of Falcon Square and near Bastion 14, the choice being dictated by the absence here of basements of full depth, so that the early deposits would be more completely preserved below the modern floor. In these early days the excavators had yet to learn how thoroughly the superficial promise of a site could be dissipated when the modern floors were removed. In Windsor Court a series of massive concrete foundations drastically reduced the area available for examination. Much of the site was also taken up with the extensive chalk foundations of a mediaeval house, not to mention a number of rubbish-pits and other disturbances of similar or later date. In spite of these handicaps, however, sufficient of the Roman wall remained here and just to the north, behind Bastion 14, to give a first picture of the wall and its related features on this side and to set the investigators along the road which led to the recognition of the fort.

The natural ground surface in Windsor Court was about 6 feet below the modern street, so that 4–5 feet in depth of the early deposits had survived for examination. Internally the features of the Roman defences followed the normal pattern. Behind the wall there was a bank of clean brickearth, the upcast, no doubt, of the external ditch or ditches: the bank was quite slight compared with those met with in the defences of other Roman towns—here about 12 feet wide and 4–5 feet high. Beneath the bank in Windsor Court and subsequently elsewhere were several mortar-mixing pits (Plate 1) associated with the building of the fort wall, one at Windsor Court retaining its mix intact. Behind the bank was a gravel road, here only partly preserved, but remaining in places to a depth of about 12 inches. The gravel was hard-rammed; the road had a width of about 17 feet and was flanked by drainage gullies cut into the natural ground.

Study of the wall itself in the southern part of the area was rendered difficult by destruction and by the fact that the outer face was not at that time available for examination. But these disadvantages were not present behind Bastion 14 (4), where the wall, standing to a height on the outside of just under 4 feet, was well preserved and its outer face readily accessible.

The wall behind the bastion was examined as part of the process of removing the contents of the bastion and this subject belongs to a later section of this account. Two facts immediately presented themselves, however (Plates 2, 3). In the first place, the wall was in two parts built lengthwise against one another in a straight joint, the outer somewhat narrower and set more deeply than the inner, the base of which did not penetrate through the bank to the natural surface (Fig. 3). These features in themselves provoked a good deal of discussion at the time. But the true explanation of them could not be forthcoming at this stage, for the wall had undergone a late repair which was the possible explanation for the straight joint; and the precise relationship of the two parts could not have been determined without destroying a large part of what still survived.

The second and more immediately significant fact was that the external face of the wall had been given a treatment which had not been met with anywhere else in the Roman city. The Roman town wall of London has been seen at many points on its circuit and its features have been consistent. Though showing a variation in width from about 7 to about 9 feet, its base is always marked by a chamfered external plinth, usually though not invariably of purple sandstone; and at vertical intervals of four to six courses (2–3 feet) in the stonework occur bonding or levelling courses of tiles whose purpose is to provide a new, stable bed for each successive 'lift' of the wall (Fig. 9).[1]

None of these features was present in the wall-face exposed behind Bastion 14: there was no plinth to demarcate faced wall from foundation and although the height of the former was sufficient to incorporate the lowest

---

[1] The photograph which best illustrates the features of the Roman wall is the well-known one reproduced as Plate 25 (facing p. 85) in *Roman London*, taken during the destruction of the wall north of Tower Hill in 1882.

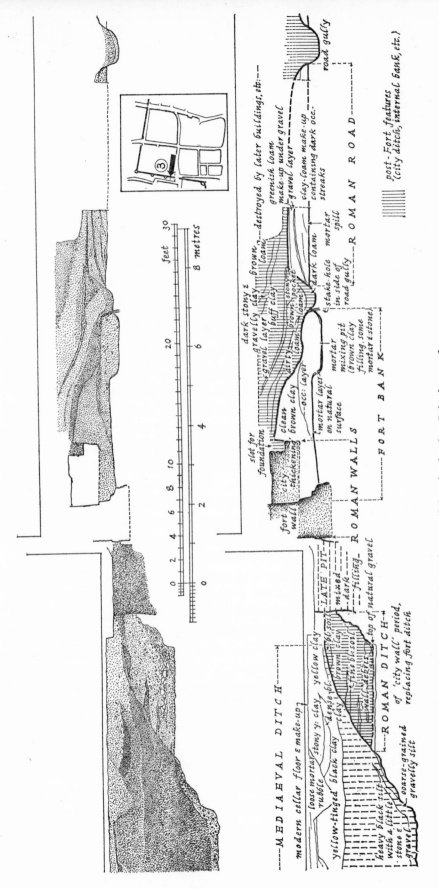

3. Composite section through the defences of the city in the Cripplegate fort area south of Bastion 14 (site 3).

tile course this also was absent. Whatever the meaning of the unusual features observed on this site, the one clear fact to emerge was that there was some variation in the history of the city wall in this area as compared with elsewhere; and the next objective was therefore to be to determine the extent of the structural differences and to try to date them. It should be noted that throughout this investigation, which was continued at intervals over a period of some months, the face of the wall and the other external elements of the defences were not accessible because of obstructions of one sort or another; and it was not until a quite late stage that the external features were seen anywhere other than behind Bastion 14.

The programme therefore took the form of a succession of cuttings behind the wall and at right angles to it. The work to the north of Bastion 14 can be dismissed briefly. The relative depths of the modern cellars and the degree of rebuilding along the line of the city wall were such that nothing at all had survived. The only exception to this statement was the site of the Barber Surgeons' Hall near the north end of Monkwell Street (2): there the deposits had survived to modern street-level. The evidence from the Hall did not, however, help with the immediate objectives though it made its contribution in other ways.

A detailed account of the features of each of the cuttings to the south of Bastion 14 is not called for here. Suffice it to say that the wall retained its double construction throughout, with a straight joint defining the two parts and the inner consistently let into the artificial bank and not penetrating to the underlying natural surface. In the cellar of the building which was originally no. 33 Noble Street (8), however, the investigators met with a surprise. No. 33 was just north of the angle of the Aldersgate re-entrant, the point at which, from a number of earlier observations, the city wall is known to have turned westwards in its course for the second north-western angle at Newgate (p. 52); and the wall now being examined might have been expected to show some signs of accommodating itself to this change. In fact, it was found to behave in a completely contradictory fashion, departing from its original straight course and curving inwards, to the east, and towards the interior of the city (Plate 4).

The meaning of this conduct became clear in the next basement southwards, that of no. 34 (9). Here there had been much disturbance in the eighteenth and nineteenth centuries, but a good fragment of the outer 'half'

20

of the double wall had survived and was found to be continuing the eastward curve of the wall in the basement of no. 33. The really significant feature of the cellar, however, was the presence of a small sub-rectangular turret, built against the inner face of the wall on the crest of the curve. Taken in conjunction with the rest, it was immediately recognisable as the quite typical corner turret of a Roman fort (Plate 4).

Before continuing the account of this investigation three points require to be noticed for future reference. First, the curve of the Roman wall in no. 33 Noble Street was sufficient to bring the face into the basement, clear by about 2 feet of the modern party wall, and therefore to expose the junction with it of Bastion 15 (8). Secondly, the inner 'half' of the double wall was not continued southwards into no. 34 Noble Street but stopped short of the corner-turret. And thirdly, a break in the inner 'half', where it had been cut by a modern wall, made it possible for the first time to see the true relationships of the different parts—and this without any destruction of the already much-reduced remains. From the section thus exposed it could be seen that the outer 'half' of the wall was the earlier. This, which must now be called the *fort* wall, had a partly-battered inner face with an offset foundation. The internal bank, of clayey brickearth, overlay the offset and rested against the inner face of the wall: wall and bank were clearly of the same period. The inner 'half' of the double wall had on the other hand been let into the bank, as previous cuttings had suggested. The inner wall, or more truly foundation (for as seen today it is (with one exception: p. 48) buried in the bank), is therefore an addition to the fort wall. Its date and significance are better discussed later.

To eyes opened by these discoveries it was now easy to see the shape that this unexpected fort might take; and since so much of the area was devastated by bombing the pursuit of its main elements was in theory at least a simple matter. It has long been recognised that the Cripplegate angle of London Wall, by St. Giles Cripplegate Church (1), is a right angle; and although the wall itself has been destroyed the line of its modern successors must reflect the original and is typically that of a fort corner. The existing north-east side of the Aldersgate re-entrant, therefore, a wall some 260 yards long, must represent the west wall of the fort; its north wall must have been some part of the city wall that runs eastwards along the south side of St. Giles Cripplegate churchyard and beyond. Here two features are significant: the gate of Cripplegate itself; and a change in direction made by the wall on the east side, somewhere in the neighbourhood of Aldermanbury Postern (*16*).

As to the former, Cripplegate, though its remains have never been seen, has long been accepted as a Roman gate on the strength of a mention in the Laws of Ethelred of *c.* A.D. 1000.[1] A gate at this position does not fit into the recognised pattern of Roman roads approaching the city, but need not have done so if it was part of the standard layout of a fort.[2] As to the wall-alignment: the course of the wall is fixed by the St. Alphage stretch to the west of Aldermanbury Postern (*17*), and by the London Wall stretch to the east (*23*). Observations made in 1857 show that the London Wall alignment must have been carried as far as Aldermanbury Postern.[3] The change in direction, therefore, though variously shown on plans of the Roman city, must have taken place within the space of a few yards on the west side of Aldermanbury Postern, about 230 yards east of the Cripplegate corner. The final significant point in this preliminary survey of the possibilities is that Cripplegate itself is midway along this dimension, occupying therefore the appropriate position for a gate if this should prove to be the shorter side of the 'playing-card' that is the normal outline for a Roman fort. This tentative conclusion carries one further corollary. Wood Street, which passes through Cripplegate, is approximately parallel with the west wall and divides the 260 by 230-yard enclosure just defined along its main axis. A feature of the internal layout of most Roman forts is their main streets linking opposed gates, which are prevented from intersecting at the centre only by the presence of the headquarters building, athwart the long axis, with its main frontage on the short axis, or *via principalis*. Wood Street therefore has claims to Roman ancestry; and at or near the point at which it crossed the south wall of the fort, yet to be found at this stage, should be the remains of the south gate. In fact, the likely position for this gate was to the west of Wood Street (*12*), for as with most ancient roads Wood Street had not been able to retain its original straight course throughout its history and as it went southwards had taken on a curve to the east.

It will be seen presently that these prognostications followed fairly closely the results obtained by excavation. But they are set out here neither as the outcome of a species of second sight nor as a demonstration of wisdom

---

[1] *Roman London*, p. 97. [2] See further below, p. 41. [3] *Roman London*, p. 90.

after the event, but as an example of the kind of 'field-work' that every excavator is obliged to do before beginning to explore his site. The problem presented by a continuously occupied area like the City of London is that later activities mask (when they do not actually destroy) the earlier. Yet the earlier features have frequently left their mark (p. 55) and the difficulty that confronts the archaeologist working in such conditions is to recognise the signs and appreciate their possibilities.

Working, then, from the hypothesis that the course and extent of the north and west walls and the position of the north gate were known, the course of the south wall was pursued on the assumption that it would run parallel with the north wall, beginning from the south-west corner in Noble Street (9). As has been said, practically all the buildings along the supposed line of the south wall had been destroyed and in theory at least the investigation should have been simple enough. In practice there were the inevitable complications springing partly from disturbance of the ground, partly from low cellar levels, which were frequently only a few inches above the original surface, so that practically all the accumulated deposits had already been removed. While therefore the main objective was the wall (or, more usually, its foundation) too often it had been destroyed or was too mutilated for its behaviour to be determined. It was then necessary to concentrate on the ditch as a pointer to the line and direction of the wall, with which it would have run more or less parallel.

Returning now to the account of the remains, the south-west corner was completed by the discovery of the wall on the opposite side of Noble Street in what was then Honeypot Lane (10).[1] Here, having turned through a right angle, the wall began its straight run eastwards. It survived to a height of three courses beneath a seventeenth-century floor: stone steps relating to the floor, which was perhaps that of a cellar, rested directly upon it. From this point eastwards across Staining Lane and for some distance the results were not satisfactory, but the line was confirmed by the finding of a short length of foundation-trench in a much-mutilated area on the east side of Staining Lane (11).

The course set by these features showed only too clearly that if the south

[1] Throughout this book sites are described in terms of the older street names. Many of these streets have disappeared in the reconstruction but this seems to be the only way of fixing the sites precisely.

gate had indeed stood where expected on the west side of what is now Wood Street, little of it was likely to have survived. As it neared Wood Street the Roman wall converged at a very acute angle from the north on a massive nineteenth-century wall-foundation (*12*); and while it was likely that in due course it would emerge on the south side the levels and the scale of the modern foundation were such that nothing of the Roman work could be expected to survive for some distance. These forebodings were only too thoroughly fulfilled when the area came to be excavated. By some extraordinary chance a small fragment, less than a foot square, of the foundation of one gate-jamb had survived on the south side of the modern wall: that it was the east jamb of an opening was shown by the fact that it ended on the west against solid brickearth; its Roman date was established by the characteristic use of a sticky grey-yellow clay as a bonding material. But the degree of disturbance and destruction on the north side in particular was such that all other traces of the masonry of the gateway had vanished apart from a few stones, no longer *in situ*, some of which still had sticky clay adhering to them.

But if the masonry had gone, other features relating to the gate had survived. Within the *enceinte* of the fort—to the north, that is, of the wall—traces of the north-to-south road remained as a thin much-broken gravel layer immediately beneath the cellar floor. More important, outside the wall not only was there a further piece of the road, here a very compact gravel surface, but the ditch across the gate-approach had survived undamaged for a length of about 19 feet (Plate *5*). The ditch was a remarkably slight affair, V-sectioned and a mere 5 feet wide by 4 feet deep, but it had been necessary to carry the road across it on a bridge which had been provided with timber supports let into the sides of the ditch. Not enough had survived to enable the complete arrangement of these timbers to be worked out. They occurred sometimes singly, sometimes in groups of three, and most of them had been at least roughly squared. An interesting feature was the use of one or two obliquely-set struts which gave support to the middle of the bridge from the underside.

Immediately to the east of Wood Street a short stretch of the wall foundation was recognisable (*13*). From this point on the line was masked by obstructions. Fortunately the crucial area, that of the cellars on the west side of Aldermanbury, was clear; for here, if the preliminary reading of the evidence was correct, should be the south-eastern angle of the fort, where the wall should turn northwards, parallel with the already established west side. The relevant cellars were those of nos. 70A and 71 Aldermanbury, 70A being to the north (14).

Once again, the wall in no. 70A, though not completely destroyed, was seriously mutilated. Both masonry and foundation had survived, but nowhere sufficiently to enable the actual line to be made out. Recourse had therefore to be had to the ditch; and since the purpose of this particular investigation was to establish the *course* of the ditch and not merely its existence the whole cellar was cleared to enable it to be seen in plan as well as in section. The removal of the cellar floor and its modern make-up revealed an area of completely artificial deposits which was obviously composed of a number of separate elements, mainly pits of mediaeval date. The identification and removal of these features along the lines already described, however, revealed the Roman fort ditch as it were between and amongst them (Plates 6, 7). The ditch was a good deal larger than further west, 12 feet wide and nearly 6 feet deep with well-cut convex sides; and a real obstacle. Its important feature, however, was its course. For some feet it ran straight; but as it approached the eastern side of the cellar to pass under the modern street it began to take on a pronounced northward curve, anticipating unmistakably the presence of the south-east corner of the fort beneath the roadway of Aldermanbury.

At this stage, then, excavation can be said to have confirmed in a general way the outline of the fort as suggested by the evidence above ground; for the position of the south-east angle beneath Aldermanbury corresponds neatly with a north-east angle beside Aldermanbury Postern (16). But the exact location of the east wall of the fort remained a matter of some uncertainty. All the indications were that it should lie just within the cellars on the west side of Aldermanbury, north of Addle Street. An attempt to find it here (15a) came up against the problem of levels: all trace both of wall and of ditch had vanished and it must be assumed that they were removed when the basements were dug. At the north-east corner itself there was a similar state of affairs, except that where the early features had not been destroyed by deep floors they had been replaced by massive modern walls or foundations. About 30 feet west of Aldermanbury Postern, however, in much disturbed ground (16), were the slight remains of the fort ditch curving in from the south to merge with the U-sectioned ditch that is characteristic of the City defences (p. 15). Here, therefore, must have been the north-east angle of the fort—a fact which can now be seen to be reflected in yet another surface detail. The angle in the frontage of London Wall[1] where it is—or was (for this area is now completely altered)—entered by a small court which is nameless on recent maps is not an accident but owes its existence to the disposition of the Roman defences of London 1,700 years or more ago (Plate 8).

Since the above was written further discoveries at the south-eastern corner have established the position of the east wall of the fort. Here on the east side of Aldermanbury the demolition of buildings as a preliminary to the re-development of the Guildhall area exposed ground which had not previously been available for examination. In 1965 a group of volunteers under Messrs. Peter Marsden and N. Farrant exposed a 40-foot length of the foundation-trench of the wall with its accompanying ditch. The foundation-trench, which had been almost completely robbed lay just within the western margin of the area available; the ditch as it passed under the road had begun to turn westwards to make the corner, which as already noted must lie under the street, but somewhat further to the east than was originally thought from the evidence of the ditch at 71 Aldermanbury.[2]

With this valuable information the overall dimensions of the fort can now be fairly accurately stated as about 760 feet north-south to 710 feet east-west—'fairly' accurately because in the conditions it has not been possible to relate individual structures directly to one another for surveying purposes, particularly when (as here) discoveries are made over long periods of time. As plotted, also, the outline is not quite a true rectangle, but the variation is very slight and again may be due to the same factor.

Before 1965 there was little to say of the north wall of the fort. Of the part west of Cripplegate a considerable stretch towards the corner had been completely destroyed and replaced by modern brick: it was tested in the cellars on its inside in a couple of places in 1947–8. Further to the east, more or less opposite the east end of St. Giles Cripplegate church a small fragment of post-Roman wall was recognisable above the modern surface but

[1] The original street of that name, of course, not the new London Wall (Route 11).

[2] Thanks are due to Messrs. Marsden and Farrant for permission to incorporate their discovery in the fort plan which could not be completed without it.

did not appear to be extensive. Since the cellars here contained much bomb-rubble no attempt was made to pursue it.

The lowering of the level of the churchyard as part of the Barbican development and the removal of obstructions on the south side showed that appearances on this site (*1a*) had been deceptive. As this is being written much work remains to be done, but the base of the fort wall appears to survive (and serves as a foundation for its multi-period successor) over a distance of something over 100 feet. Here as elsewhere the face remains to a maximum height of only 3–4 feet on the outside; internally in the one place where it can be clearly seen the face survives to 6–7 feet and displays the usual batter in its lower part. The depth of the cellars against the back of the wall was such that the 'city thickening' had completely disappeared. At the extreme western end of the surviving wall, about 175 feet from the centre-line of Cripplegate Buildings (the site of the north gate of the fort, recognisable by the hump that it makes in the modern road) a fortunate chance has preserved the stump of the east wall of an internal turret. This is not only a valuable addition to the plan: its siting seems to help to account for that of the turret on the west wall (*7*) which is further discussed below (p. 34).

Another completely unexpected find on this site is that of a bastion which does not appear to figure in any of the records. More is said of this in the appropriate place later (pp. 71–5).

East of Cripplegate the fragment in St. Alphage Churchyard (*17*) is noteworthy for the later periods; but the base and foundation of the wall are Roman, and although the outer facing-stones have gone the back shows all the features met with on the west side of the fort. The inner face of the fort wall is battered, and built against it but at a higher level is the internal addition, the inner 'half' of the double wall. The evidence from this site is valuable in that it shows that on the north as on the west there had been a double wall.

Apart from the very recent discoveries on the north wall which have been fitted into their place above, the investigation of the Cripplegate Fort has been described so far in the order in which work proceeded, though with other demands on the excavators' attention the individual excavations did not always immediately follow one on the other. In establishing the outline of the fort, with its four angles at St. Giles Cripplegate, St. Anne and St.

LONDINIVM · CRIPPLEGATE FORT

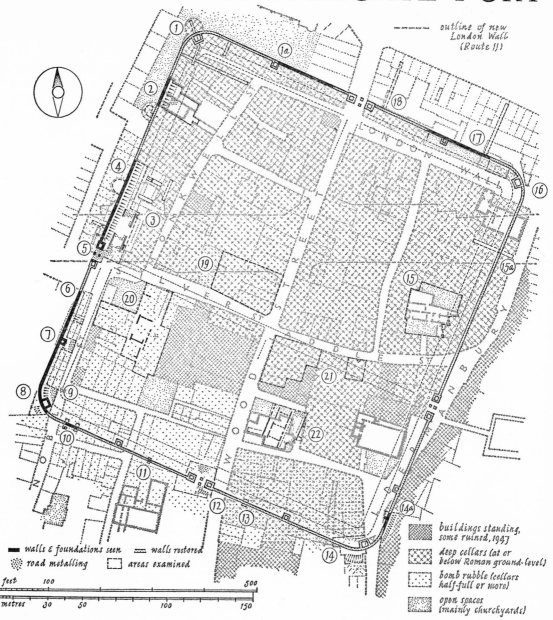

outline of new
London Wall
(Route II)

walls & foundations seen · · · walls restored
road metalling ☐ areas examined

buildings standing,
some ruined, 1947

deep cellars (at or
below Roman ground-level)

bomb rubble (cellars
half-full or more)

open spaces
(mainly churchyards)

0 feet   100   500
0 metres   30   50   100   150

4. Plan of the Cripplegate Roman fort.

Agnes, Aldermanbury and Aldermanbury Postern, other features of the defences were of course observed and studied; but for the moment it is worth while to leave these details and turn to another important element in the plan, though to do so is to lift it out of the order in which it was actually uncovered. This is the west gateway of the fort, in Falcon Square (5).

3. THE WEST GATEWAY

In the rectilinear 'playing-card' plan of the normal Roman fort the position of the gates in the longer sides is not always easy to determine exactly since it is usually to one side of the mid-point. But here again the modern street plan provides the clue. The dominant element, recognisable in the light of much later knowledge, in the layout of the fort area as it was at the time of the bombing was the irregular cross-pattern made by Wood Street with the east-to-west line of Addle Street and Silver Street (with Falcon Square) (Fig. 4). There are of course abundant analogies for the survival, inevitably distorted, of the features of Roman forts or settlements in the plans of the towns or villages that have succeeded them; and it has already been demonstrated that Wood Street is the descendant of the north-to-south street of the fort. It was not unreasonable to guess therefore that Addle Street–Silver Street might be its east-to-west equivalent, though Addle Street at its east end must have moved a good deal off its original course. If this were indeed so, hope of finding the east gate was foredoomed to disappointment, for the cellars where the street crossed the line of the east wall were too deep for anything to have survived. At the west end on the other hand what was known of the relative levels suggested that some part of the gate might survive there. When these possibilities were being deliberated conditions on the site were such that they could not be put to the test because all the relevant cellars were full of bomb-rubble. The matter had therefore to be postponed until 1956, when the City Engineer kindly agreed that as part of the preliminary work of site-clearance for the building of the new Route 11 (later named London Wall) from Aldersgate Street to Moorgate Street the obstructions should be removed in sufficient time to enable an excavation to be conducted before the road-works in this area commenced.

The result was to confirm the above diagnosis in the most satisfactory fashion. It is not too much to say that the Roman remains were wrapped about with modern brickwork: their solid quality was such that the modern builders had not thought it necessary to remove them but had wherever possible incorporated the earlier work in their own. Much therefore of the northern half of the gate had survived within the area available for excavation and it had not suffered unduly from the presence of one or two stone- or brick-lined cesspits of the eighteenth–nineteenth century, which had not destroyed the Roman work at any significant point.

The gate followed one of the normal patterns for a fort gate (Fig. 5 and Plate 10). It consisted of a double roadway of hard-rammed gravel divided by a central 'spine', made up of two detached piers. These piers carried the arches which spanned the roads and supported the gallery over them to provide access to the wall-walk from each side without descending to street-level. The roads on each side of the spine were $8\frac{1}{2}$ feet wide. The roadways were flanked to the north and south by square turrets. The northern turret was available for excavation at this stage; that to the south lay under Falcon Square, but part of its north side became accessible later when the Square was cut back to make way for new works. The face of the north turret was set slightly in front of that of the fort wall and its lower part at least was built of massive blocks of purple sandstone, some of them as much as 4 feet long: the generally rugged appearance of the frontage would have been enhanced by the heavy rock-dressing of the stone faces. The walls were fairly uniformly about 3 feet thick but the foundations of the front and back walls were deeper than those on the sides. A curious feature of the rear wall was that it did not rest conformably on its foundation, oversailing it by several inches externally, while the foundation was offset from the faced wall by a corresponding amount on the inside. The variation was presumably due either to a mistake in laying the foundation or to a change in plan while building was in progress. The turret is about 15 feet square overall. The doorway, at the south-east angle—that is, at the inner end of the gate-passage—had had its sill renewed at least once, probably as an adjustment to the raising of the road-level, and the stones showed signs of much wear. The floor of the turret was made up of mixed materials, but displayed no special features and produced no finds of significance.

In the rebates of the outer arch both on the turret and on the spine the sockets for the door-pivots had survived, that on the turret being the better

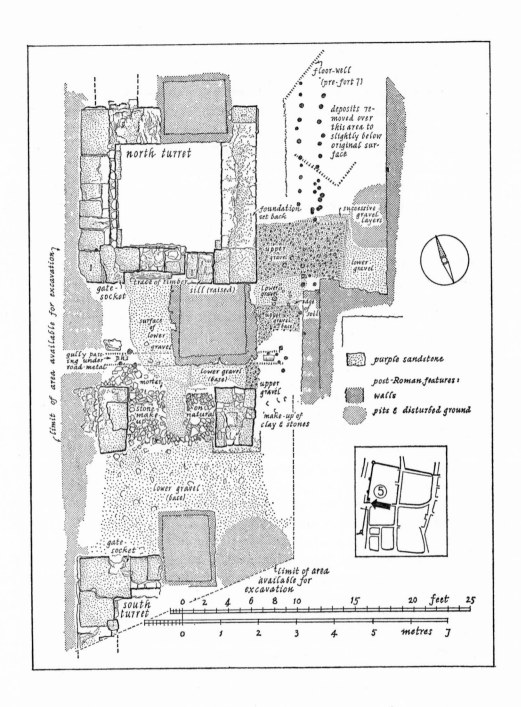

The following labels appear on the plan:

floor-well
(pre-fort ?)

deposits re-
moved over
this area to
slightly below
original sur-
face

north turret

foundation
set back

successive
gravel
layers

upper
gravel

lower
gravel

gate-
socket

trace of timber

sill (raised)

lower
gravel

edge
of soil

surface
of
lower
gravel

upper
gravel
(at base)

gully pass-
ing under
road-metal

pits

lower gravel
(base)

upper
gravel

mortar

'make-up' of
clay & stones

stone
'make-
up'

on
natural

limit of area available for excavation

lower gravel
(base)

purple sandstone

post-Roman features:

walls

pits & disturbed ground

gate-
socket

south
turret

limit of area
available for
excavation

0 2 4 6 8 10   15   20 feet 25

0   1   2   3   4   5   metres

5. The Cripplegate fort: plan of west gateway (5) as excavated.

preserved and retaining the remains of the horizontal borings for keeping the lining in place. Of the complicated features of the roadway mention must be made of a small timber-lined gutter beneath the gravel surface and there were indications also of a stone building earlier than the gate and evidently quite independent of the fort. From the surviving deposits the road had been made up twice: the gravel layers combined were up to 2 feet thick: but later additions may well have been removed when the cellars were excavated.

The intriguing feature about the gate, however, was that both openings had been blocked, putting it out of action. A wall of rough masonry, based on a somewhat inadequate foundation sunk in the gravel of the roads, had sealed the outer arches. Since the front of this wall had been cut away by a modern wall its adequacy as a blocking to the gateway is uncertain: it can only be said that what remained did not suggest any great strength (Plates 65–6). It is also unfortunately undated; its part in the later history of the site can only be a matter for speculation.

4. ROMAN FEATURES WITHIN THE FORT

The framework of the Cripplegate fort plan was thus established with the discovery of the west gate, but enough had been seen in the excavations to suggest that there could be little hope of filling in much of the detail. There were some particularly deep cellars in the central part of the fort where nothing would have survived even if the deposits had been as thick as they are in such areas as that of Cheapside.

North of the Silver Street–Addle Street line basement floors of normal depths, 7–11 feet below street, were usually well below the original natural surface; south of the same line the depth tended to increase southwards: at Addle Street cellar floor and natural surface coincided; near the south-west corner accumulations might be as much as 3–4 feet deep. But the variation in cellar-floor levels was such that these variations could not be constant. In dealing with internal structures, such as they were, it will be convenient to start with those relating to the defences: they were well preserved in the cellars of Noble Street, south of the west gate, where they had not suffered the same degree of mutilation as in Windsor Court, for all that the modern floor of the latter was at a higher level. The arrangements at Cripplegate were identical with those of other Roman military sites. The internal bank has already been mentioned (p. 17). It varied both in size and in profile, but was always slight, reflecting the character of the external ditch as the quarry for its raw material. Within the bank was a gravel road flanked by side-ditches, the full width of which was determined in Windsor Court at about 17 feet (Fig. 3). The road had been made up on a number of occasions. Behind the north turret of the gateway the second addition had filled in and sealed the original side-gully. At no. 29 Noble Street (7) the total thickness of the gravel was just over 2 feet and the margins of the successive layers varied in their distance from the bank: the inner edge of the road here lies under the modern street and has not therefore been seen. The variation in the position of the road in relation to the wall was not entirely accidental, since, as will be seen, it was at least partly related to changes in the wall itself. Nevertheless, the different elements showed an unusual amount of fluctuation between one part of the fort and another, though in general the story that these changes tell is the same throughout.

An interesting feature of the side-gullies of the *intervallum* road was that in the neighbourhood of the gates (but apparently only there) their sides had a wickerwork or similar lining. Both at the west and at the south gate the gullies had a row of stake-holes driven vertically into their sides (Plate 9). The purpose of the stakes, which were usually up to 2–3 inches in diameter, must have been to anchor a revetment; but though carefully looked for they did not appear to be present everywhere. To the north of the west gate stake-holes were recognised for a distance of about 80 feet in the western gully of the *intervallum* road; they could not be recognised at all in the eastern gully in those places where the ground had survived. The gullies of the main streets within the fort of which a small part remained had been similarly treated near the gates, but whether their whole length was revetted cannot now be known.

The other discovery, the work of a group of volunteers under Mr. G. V. D. Rybot, F.S.A., to be noted in connexion with the defences was that of an internal turret on the wall rather more than half-way between the gate and the south-west corner (7: Plate 11). The turret is small, 11 (N–S) by 10 (E–W) feet externally. Its side walls stood to a height of 3 feet; its inner wall had been neatly removed, probably at quite a late date, in mediaeval or post-mediaeval times. To the underside of the cellar floor its interior had been filled with a clean yellow-brown brickearth resembling that of the bank behind the wall. This material had the appearance of having been deliberately inserted. It suggested that the ground-floor level was not intended for use.

The discovery of this turret made a more general contribution to the plan of the fort, but raises a minor problem of planning to which the fragmentary internal turret on the north wall (*1a*: p. 27) perhaps makes a contribution. Since the actual position of the north gate has not been established it is impossible to think in precise terms, but the indications are that the north turret may be half-way between the centre-line of the north gate and the north western angle. This measurement corresponds quite closely with that between the west gateway and the turret in the forward part of the fort (*praetentura*) to the south of it, so that for the shorter sectors of the defences this may have been the unit that was adopted in siting one turret in each length of wall. In the longer rear part of the fort, made up of the central administrative division and the *retentura* to the north of it, some different system must have been followed. It would be possible to accommodate two turrets there; but it so happens that along the west wall those areas in which the turrets should have appeared have survived in a relatively undisturbed condition (the northern part of Windsor Court (*3*) and the Barber Surgeons' Hall (*2*)) and there was no sign of them. The provision of internal turrets in Roman forts varies very much from one fort to the next and uniformity is not to be assumed. It seems likely that at Cripplegate only a single turret was allocated to the longer sectors of wall as to the shorter ones. If this had been set about half-way between gate and corner it would have been in an area of deeper cellars and would not have survived.

The search for internal buildings and above all for datable evidence which might shed light on the history of the fort in its later periods, has not been very fruitful. The new London Wall (Route 11) crosses obliquely the area of the headquarters building (*principia*) which, as already stated, would have straddled Wood Street on the north side of the Silver Street–Addle Street frontage (*19*). Clearance for the new road presented an opportunity for the exploration of the ground along its line and it was hoped that since the buildings of the central block at least would be likely to be constructed in stone, some part of their foundations might survive below the destruction level of the cellar floors. This hope again was frustrated: the only remaining antiquities were the lower parts of mediaeval rubbish-pits, one or more Roman pits and a few post-holes. So, too, on the east side, but still in the central block, the site of the Brewers' Hall (*15*), though ostensibly preserved to street-level, produced a complicated series of mediaeval and post-mediaeval pits and cellars which were of interest in themselves but had penetrated to levels which involved the complete destruction of all Roman features apart from one or two scraps of possibly Roman masonry.

In Windsor Court also post-Roman destruction had removed most of the Roman deposits; but here at least were the bases of Roman foundations belonging to a long narrow building running with the *intervallum* road of which traces were found further south, nearer the gateway (Fig. 3). The hope of evidence bearing on the fort's later history therefore steadily recedes and there are few if any places now which can be said to be even potentially valuable in this respect.

Another area within the fort lay on the south side of Silver Street (*20*) and was therefore in the *praetentura*. The cellars were comparatively shallow and about 4 feet of deposit had survived beneath the modern floor; but there had also been much downward disturbance and the effective depth available over the parts of the site that could be examined was usually 2 feet or sometimes less. As elsewhere (above, p. 32) there were already occupation deposits on this site before the building which was its main feature was erected. In the limited area available only a small part of the plan could be recovered: the recognisable feature of it appears to be a comparatively narrow building, or perhaps a range of rooms, with its long axis north to south and a corridor along part of the east side. The arrangement suggests a barrack-block; but the rooms were too big for this purpose, as far as their sizes could be determined, and the relatively high standard of furnishing scarcely supported such a purely military function. Not only had the walls been plastered, with much fragmentary plaster surviving in the overlying deposits, some of it in large pieces: remains of a mosaic floor of plain red tesserae were still *in situ*. In legionary fortresses a somewhat similar position was occupied by the tribunes' houses. It may be that in the special circumstances of the Cripplegate fort as the military depot in London accommodation of superior quality was provided within the fort for staff officers or others whose military duties brought them to or kept them in London.

The remaining site was that of St. Alban Wood Street (*22*), lying in the

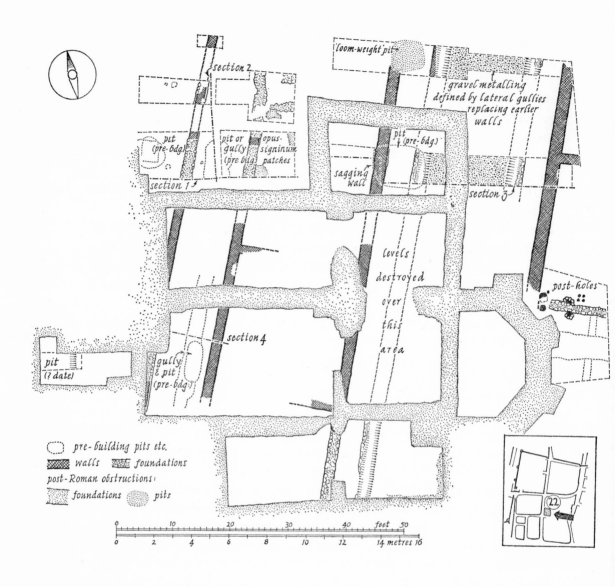

Labels within the figure:

section 2

loom-weight pit

gravel metalling
defined by lateral gullies
replacing earlier
walls

pit
(pre-bdg)

pit or
gully
(pre bdg)

opus-
signinum
patches

pit
(pre-bdg)

sagging
wall

section 1

section 3

levels

destroyed

over

this

area

post-holes

pit
(? date)

section 4

gully
& pit
(pre-bdg)

pre-building pits etc.

walls   foundations

post-Roman obstructions:

foundations   pits

0   10   20   30   40   feet   50

0   2   4   6   8   10   12   14 metres 16

22

6. The Cripplegate fort: buildings in the area of the church and
churchyard of St. Alban Wood Street (22).

praetentura immediately east of the north–south street. The area comprised the site of the church and churchyard and impinged on the north on the Addle Street site (*12*) which from the Roman point of view was unproductive. (Much of the ground to the east was taken up with very deep cellars.) Here the Roman deposits had survived to a thickness of not more than 2 feet: within the church and churchyard burial disturbance had often penetrated below this level.

As with the Silver Street site this area produced buildings with long axes north–south: evidently two elongated ranges facing one another with corridors or verandahs looking on to a 13-foot-wide gravel road (Fig. 6). When first seen the remains had the appearance of barrack-blocks, with fairly uniform rooms (21–22 feet each way) and this is probably the best interpretation for them. The area had been occupied sporadically before the stone buildings were erected: amongst the remains of this phase were pits and gullies which produced quantities of pottery broadly of late first–early second-century date. The post-holes met with did not make a coherent plan and there was nothing to suggest that the stone buildings may have had timber predecessors.

The walls of the buildings survived to a maximum of three courses above the foundation offset, but with the building the general level was raised by the laying-down of a deposit of clean red-brown clay. The floor which this clay must have carried had not survived because of destruction. In the limited area available the buildings showed no sign of later alteration apart from the fact that the slight verandah or corridor walls had been removed and replaced by shallow gullies defining the road. In the western range a main wall had subsided into one of the earlier pits. Reused building material was found in its reconstruction. Amongst a quantity of tiles with pink mortar still adhering to them was one with a fragmentary blurred stamp which Mr. R. P. Wright has identified as belonging to the PR BR LON series.[1]

The value of the evidence from this site is that at the moment it gives more clearly than any other a date early in the second century (and therefore in the reign of Trajan) for stone buildings within the fort.

[1] For which see *Roman London*, p. 176; *London in Roman Times*, pp. 50–1.

5. THE HISTORY OF THE FORT

Fragmentary as knowledge of the fort must always be, its discovery must be regarded as perhaps the outstanding event in the twentieth-century archaeological study of London. For not only is it new in itself; it sheds light on other aspects of the Roman city, and it had an important bearing upon subsequent developments. But so far little has been said about its date. The time has now come when its position should be assessed in relation to the history and development of London as a whole.

The first point to be made is that this discovery has no bearing on the status of London as a military site at the time of the conquest just after A.D. 43. Limited as the amount of datable evidence is, it is quite definite on the point that the fort could not have been constructed until at least some time about the end of the first century A.D.: the earliest possible date is provided by the finding of a coin of Vespasian in a pit beneath the rampart-bank of the fort a few yards north of the west gateway. The coin is somewhat worn, but appears to be of the emperor's third consulship, dating therefore to A.D. 71: in any case, its condition suggests that it had been in circulation for some time. The fort bank can hardly have been erected over the pit before about A.D. 80; other evidence from the defences—as with that referred to above for the internal buildings—indicates a rather later date, in the early second century.

The association of the Cripplegate fort with the other military event to affect London's early history—Boudicca's rebellion in A.D. 60–1—is also ruled out by the same chronological difficulty, though here the interval between the two events is almost halved. A crucial element in the success—from the native point of view—of the rising was the fact that no Roman troops were close at hand: they were away in the west and north, in remote theatres of war from which it was not possible to get them back in time to prevent the destruction of the cities of the south-east. Had the dates been right it would have been possible to argue that the fort was built to house a garrison as an insurance against a repetition of the Boudiccan incident.

However this may be, London in the early second century A.D. must now be visualised as made up of two parts. Centred on the eastern hill but spreading gradually from it was the redeveloping city, perhaps replanned after the Boudiccan destruction. Away from the civil settlement, though the houses were creeping towards it, and apparently occupying an area which had previously carried some civilian occupation, the fort took up the slightly higher ground to the north-east. Fort and city reflect the separateness of military and civil which is a feature of Roman organisation in the frontier provinces, but the fort was so placed that it was within easy reach both of any part of the city and port, and of the most important roads that fanned out from the crossing of the Thames towards the interior of Britain. There are indeed hints that the axes of the fort were aligned on Ermin Street and Watling Street: but since the exact courses of the trunk roads are not known it is impossible to be certain on this point (p. 41).

Of the many problems relating to the fort that are likely to remain unsolved one of the chief is that of its later history. It has already been observed that the higher levels in the deposits which might have been helpful here have nowhere survived. It is not therefore possible to say whether the fort continued a separate existence after it was incorporated into the city's defences (p. 47) or whether its east and south walls were removed and its area made one with that of the civil settlement. The second of these alternatives is unlikely on general grounds and such evidence as there is seems to be against it. This relates entirely to the survival in modified form of the street plan of the fort (p. 29) which might be expected to have suffered more drastic alteration if it had gone out of use before the end of the Roman period, to reappear when after the lost years of the early dark ages the city was reoccupied. Only the fort ditch has so far yielded datable evidence that can be said to cover the full period of its effective existence. The filling of the ditch at the south-east corner (*14*) produced material ranging down to the late second or early third century suggesting that by this time this part of the fort's defences at any rate had gone out of use. But the problem is to know whether the fort wall suffered in the same way. It may not be coincidence that the evidence from the ditch is consistent with the late second/early third century date which at present holds the field for the construction of the city wall (pp. 50–1). The new wall robbed the fort ditch on the east and south sides of any value that it ever had as a defensive obstacle, but its disappearance need not have affected the fort wall, which may have continued to separate military from civilian London, even while they were enclosed in the common defence of the city wall.

The later Saxon association with the area of the fort is referred to below (p. 204).

6. A NOTE ON SOME EARLY ROADS IN AND ABOUT LONDON

Since the account of the Cripplegate fort was written the Viatores in *Roman Roads in the South-east Midlands* (pp. 185 ff., with maps on pp. 389–92, 475) have produced suggestions for a system of roads linked with the west and north gates of the fort. From the former they show a road running north-westwards by way of the modern King's Cross station area to Hampstead and beyond (their road no. 167); from the latter road no. 220 is represented as running more or less due north by way of Canonbury and Southgate.[1]

It must be said at once that whatever the antiquity of these routes over their more northerly courses there is no real evidence for their existence in the long built-up areas that enclose the city itself. The lines proposed cut arbitrarily across streets many of which are represented in maps of London from the sixteenth century onwards. Where the conjectured course and existing streets coincide the coincidence appears to be nothing more than accidental.

It would seem to be in the highest degree unlikely that had these roads existed they would have disappeared as completely as they have. The continuing importance of the other gates of London is reflected in the relationship of trunk roads to them. Having been created by the Romans they have continued to the present day with such modifications as time has rendered inevitable. That such continuity could apply to matters of detail is well shown by a comparison of the sixteenth- and seventeenth-century panoramic maps, Hogenberg, 'Agas' and the rest,[2] with modern maps: nowhere is this more marked than in the districts of Clerkenwell and Farringdon through which the proposed roads would have passed.

[1] Mr. Merrifield's map, *Roman City of London*, fig. 2, appears to give some support to these proposals. In the interests of accuracy it should be added that the Viatores' account of Cripplegate (*op. cit.*, p. 187) is confused and misleading since they attach to Cripplegate as the *north* gate of the fort observations which relate to the south gate. The Roman version of Cripplegate has not been seen, but there is every reason to believe in its existence and to accept its siting.

[2] Some are conveniently illustrated in Darlington and Howgego, *Printed Maps of London circa 1553–1850*, Pl. 2, ff.

With two external gates to the Cripplegate fort the Viatores were constrained to find roads for them; but as a study of the layout of many a Roman fort will show, the four gates reflect standard (though not constant) Roman military practice. By no means all had roads of importance issuing from them, though they may have provided ready access to parade or exercise grounds, bath-buildings or other centres of literally extra-mural activity. Cripplegate therefore need not have had its long-distance road and it would seem to be a profitless exercise to strain the evidence in the effort to produce one. Although in this and many similar matters certainty is precluded by lack of precise knowledge of the alignment everything seems to point to the fort having been laid out at right angles to the Newgate Street sector of the Bucklersbury–Newgate Roman street. But there is some inconsistency in the available evidence. As the plan (Fig. 7) shows, 'Roman Cheapside' appears to have been in three lengths. The eastern (Bucklersbury) and western (Newgate Street) portions seem to be on the same or nearly the same alignment but when prolonged do not meet smoothly; this alignment cuts obliquely across present-day Cheapside. The middle portion near St. Mary le Bow church, is parallel with the modern street, with its south edge running with the south frontage of Cheapside.

Only a tiny fragment of the street was seen at this point (*38*: p. 134), but it was accompanied by its side-ditch and there was no doubt about its direction. About 100 feet to the east is the tower of St. Mary le Bow church, under which, as is well known, Wren observed the metalling of the Roman street. Wren did not record the direction taken by this metalling, which may not in any case have been determinable in the area uncovered; so this evidence, while acceptable as indicating the presence of a street at this point, cannot be used one way or the other to define its alignment. The only other evidence bearing on the problem seems to be the direction taken by the fragmentary buildings on the north side of the modern street at Honey Lane (*40*; p. 136) and Lawrence Lane (*42*; pp. 146–8). The former appears to be more or less at right angles to the middle sector as described above; the latter again appears to be at right angles to the eastern sector in Bucklersbury. But this evidence cannot be pressed. The buildings along Roman street frontages are often by no means regular in their layout and in all cases these particular remains were very imperfectly seen.

The answer to this problem if it now survives at all, is under the roadway

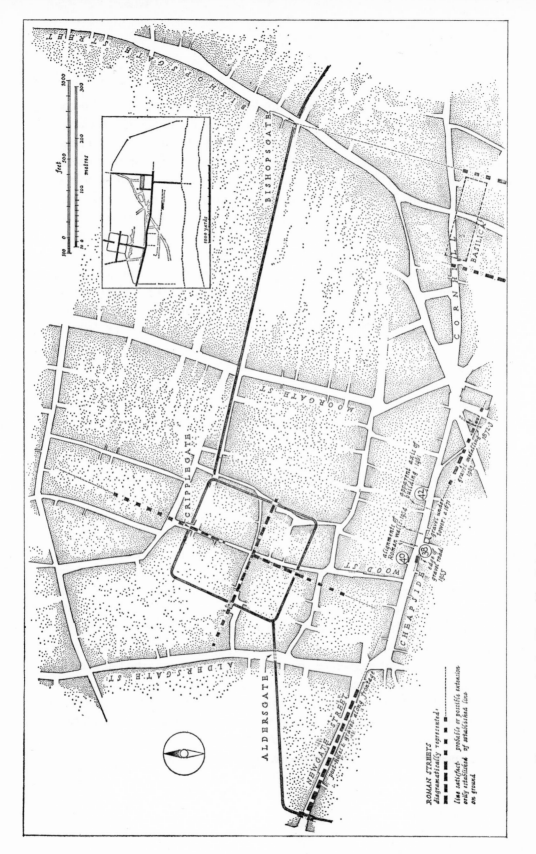

7. Roman streets in the Cheapside–Cripplegate area.

of Cheapside. Its very existence as a problem reflects, as only too often, the imperfections of present knowledge in both its extent and its precision. One possibility, however, is that the change in direction of the middle stretch of the street related to a chequer-pattern of insulae on which the remainder of the street to east and west impinges unconformably. It is perhaps worth noting that the east–west axis of this middle stretch is parallel with that of the basilica on the city's eastern hill. The inset in Fig. 7 makes the point. It should be taken, not as representing a firmly-held view (which would in any case contradict the many 'seems to's' and 'perhaps' 'that pepper this section) but as an effort to keep the subject open. An immediate and obvious argument against it is its untidiness, which hardly seems in keeping with the beginning of one of the great trunk roads of Roman Britain, later to be called Watling Street.

The uncertainties attending the internal street-system here can thus be seen to be such that even the course of the road southward from the south gate of the fort may not have prolonged exactly the line of the *via praetoria*, its main north-bound road. It is reasonable to suppose that there was such an extension, whatever its actual direction; and similarly that both on the west (Falcon Square—now London Wall (Route 11)) and on the north (Cripplegate itself) there were direct links with the road that issued from Aldersgate on the one hand, and with the Old Street road (here less than half a mile away to the north) on the other.

But there is equally no reason to suppose that these extensions became trunk roads in their own right. Apart from the Ermin Street which left the city at Bishopsgate two roads have claims to be regarded as ancient and continuous links with the north. From Aldersgate the first is represented by Aldersgate Street and Goswell Road to Islington, and then by alternative ways to Holloway, Highgate Hill and so to High Barnet, Potters Bar and beyond. The second lies more to the west and goes from Newgate or Aldersgate (by way of Little Britain), West Smithfield, St. John Street, King's Cross, Maiden Lane (now York Way and Brecknock Road) and so up Dartmouth Park Hill to unite with the other near the top of Highgate Hill.

The topography of the city and of the land immediately to the north of it is nowhere very emphatic[1] and does not present itself clearly on a map even

---

[1] A condition which in itself would have made for difficulty by the creation of areas of bad drainage which would have been obstacles to movement.

when contoured at 25-foot intervals. The behaviour of both of these roads in relation to it is quite un-Roman. They leave the city on the back of the broad but gentle ridge which divides the River Fleet on the west from the Walbrook and other streams that flow (in a general sense) eastwards. Con-

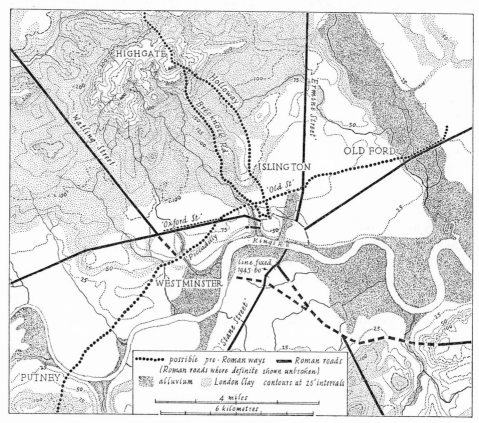

8. Map of Roman and other roads around London.

sistently they hold to such higher ground that there is: the map (Fig. 8) is not large enough to show every detail, but 'Maiden Lane' in particular can be seen negotiating ridges and spurs between streams on the climb up to Highgate in a manner completely characteristic of a primary road. It is of course impossible to give these roads a date, but their significance for their area is brought out by the way in which other roads converge upon them. Typologically 'Maiden Lane' looks the earlier; its relation to Newgate must remain uncertain since clearly Newgate's main purpose was to receive the Watling Street approximately along the line of what is now High Holborn. The situation of the eastern road is clouded by the problem of Aldersgate itself, where some years ago Mr. Adrian Oswald observed that the structure of the Roman gate as he saw it appeared to be later than the city wall, suggesting that it was an insertion.

Nevertheless, the possibility that these roads are of pre-Roman origin deserves to be borne in mind; and they are so presented on the map, again, as with the Cheapside situation, as a warning against a tendency to oversimplify the problems that the early human settlement of the London area presents. It is widely accepted that the siting of the Roman city along the stretch of the river known in later times as the King's Reach was due to a combination of circumstances which made it at that time the easiest crossing-place. This is speculation, but the same conditions may have operated to the same effect at any rate in the Iron Age. The Aldersgate roads may relate to a pre-Roman crossing and it would probably not be difficult to isolate their counterparts on the south side of the river at least to the point at which they would have become merged in the Roman road system converging on the south end of the first London Bridge.

The other road on which further attention should probably be given is Old Street, by which is meant an approximately east–west line of communication having the present long-named Old Street as only a small part of its total length. On the early maps 'Old Street' does not appear as a continuous feature, but in spite of breaks in the Bethnal Green area it appears to be generally accepted that to the east it made for the crossing of the River Lea at Old Ford (which also took the Roman road from Aldgate: Fig. 8). To the west the course of the road seems also to have suffered various vicissitudes. Its present course in Clerkenwell and Farringdon is apparently a relatively recent development. One seventeenth-century version by way of Long Acre, Kingsgate (the equivalent of the northern part of modern Kingsway), and Theobalds Road was used by King James I to by-pass the city on his way to his country seat at Theobalds, near Cheshunt.[1] Another version of it appears to have joined Watling Street (modern Oxford Street) to the north-west of St. Giles-in-the-Fields.

The link with the Roman road has led to the identification of 'Old Street'

[1] N. G. Brett-James, *The Growth of Stuart London*, p. 165.

itself as a Roman road, though the fact that it ignores the city and may therefore have been in existence before the Roman occupation has also been noted on more than one occasion.[1] But the tendency when roads are under discussion to adopt an *omne antiquum pro Romanum* approach has led to no further exploration of the pre-Roman possibilities. 'Old Street' is therefore often regarded as a branch of 'Oxford Street', on the assumption, presumably, that together they may have formed a prehistoric route which was taken over by the Romans and developed a more southerly branch along the line of Holborn with the foundation of London.

Whatever the origin of 'Oxford Street', which does in fact lie on the 50-foot terrace of the Thames throughout its length, there is some justification for the view that there may have been an extension of 'Old Street' more to the south-west. For such a road there would be some uncertainty in the eastern part, about the St. Giles—Seven Dials area: here only a generalised course can be suggested for the link between points in Holborn and the eastern end of Piccadilly, ranging between Shaftesbury Avenue (a modern street) and Long Acre, the latter part of King James' private road referred to above. The line represented by Piccadilly, Knightsbridge, Old Brompton Road, Fulham Road to the south-west is however continuous to the Fulham/Putney crossing of the Thames.

At the crossing on each bank there is gravel, making for an easy approach with no intervening alluvium. This stretch of the river is one of the richest in finds of early antiquities.[2] The indications are that the crossing has always played a significant part in the communications system of the area; it may well have been a determining factor in the siting of the riverside settlements of Fulham and Putney at each end of it: there are many parallels for such an arrangement elsewhere. 'Old Street' thus might seem to have a more honourable purpose than that of serving as a relatively unimportant alternative to a Roman trunk road. Linking two important river-crossings, Putney and Old Ford, across the London area it becomes part of a land route between the area to the north-east and east of London and that to south-west and south. Its period of origin, of course, remains uncertain; its period of use, as with other early tracks, would have taken it into the Roman period whether or not it was 'Romanised'. 'Old' here may really mean what it says.

[1] I. D. Margary, *Roman Roads in Britain*, I, pp. 47, 51.
[2] G. F. Lawrence, *Journ. Roy. Arch. Inst.* 86 (1930), pp. 89–90.

III

London Wall

I. THE ROMAN CITY WALL

THE character of the city wall has already been described (Fig. 9): its chamfered plinth and levelling courses of tile have been noted as features not present in the wall of the fort, but constant elsewhere. Putting on one side for the moment questions of date, the building of the wall, whenever it happened, had the effect of uniting city and fort by incorporating them in what was virtually a single defensive ring. When it was decided to enclose the occupied area it was natural that the fort should be brought into the new arrangement. On the northern frontage the wall was carried from the east (the Tower) to the north-east corner of the fort, to create the change of alignment at Aldermanbury Postern the diagnostic value of which has already been noted (p. 26). On the west the wall was taken away from the south-west corner of the fort at something more than a right angle. This wall ran westwards for about 1,200 feet before turning southwards near Newgate to make towards the river. It formed, therefore, with the west wall of the fort, the Aldersgate re-entrant, which must now be recognised as the outcome of a logical development on the site rather than as an accident or freak of planning, determined as it might have been by some feature in the topography which is no longer apparent.

The effect of these developments was to turn the outward-looking north and west walls of the fort into part of the defences of the city. It is at this point that the 'double' wall first noted behind Bastion 14 (p. 18) becomes significant. The original wall of the fort was comparatively slight in build, as befitted the offensive character of first/second-century forts in Britain:

with a width of under 4 feet it compared unfavourably with the massive city wall, whose width at the base, as already noted, was anything up to about 9 feet. The purpose of the addition, the inner 'half' of the double wall (Fig. 10; Plates 3–14), seems to have been to bring the fort wall up to the same

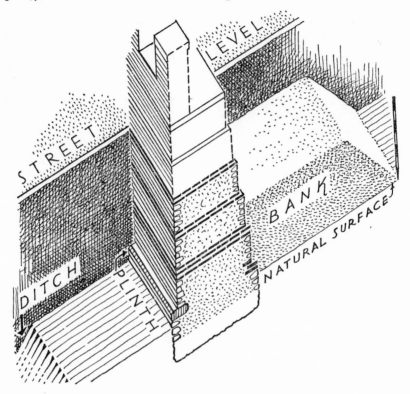

9. The Roman city wall with its attendant features as revealed below modern street-level, with a suggested reconstruction above the street. (*Scale of feet.*)

strength as the city wall; and it is significant that the thickening is confined to those parts of the fort's defences which were incorporated in the defences of the city as a whole.[1] More accurately, it should be said that the thickening

[1] Since the above was written the removal of the modern facing of the early wall at no. 23 Noble Street (*6*) has revealed the core of the thickening surviving to a height of some feet above the plinth level. Its face has gone, but it can be seen to rest against the back of the fort wall. Its construction—alternating obliquely-set courses laid dry on horizontal beds of mortar—is that of the city wall proper. It lacks the tile bonding courses of the city wall.

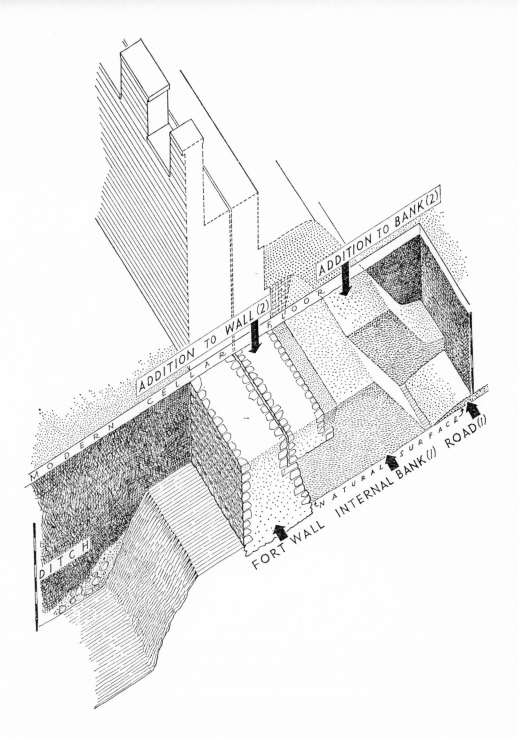

ADDITION TO WALL (2)

ADDITION TO BANK (2)

MODERN CELLAR

FLOOR

NATURAL SURFACE

FORT WALL

INTERNAL BANK (1)

ROAD (1)

DITCH

10. The Roman defences in the Cripplegate area (with a suggested reconstruction above street-level) showing the fort wall and bank with the additions made to them when the city wall was built. (*Scale of feet.*)

is *known* to have existed on the west and north: it does not *appear* to have been added on the east and south, and it could be argued that in the conditions such absence may be due merely to subsequent destruction. In fact, however, the evidence of the south-western corner (*9*) can be taken to be fairly conclusive. Here the addition to the fort wall was carried up to the corner turret on the west wall, but did not start again beyond the turret on the south wall; nor did it appear across Noble Street in Honeypot Lane, where the depth of the remains was probably sufficient to have preserved some indication of it. In other words, the thickening ended here at the point where the fort wall ceased to be part of the city's external defences, as has already been said; and it seems reasonable to assume that it behaved similarly at the north-east corner.

2. THE DATE OF THE ROMAN WALL

Acceptance of this interpretation carries with it the valuable corollary that evidence for the dating of the internal thickening of the fort wall can be applied to the city wall proper. It is not necessary here to review the various theories that have been advanced for the date of the Roman wall. Suffice it to say that the evidence that has accumulated since the position was reviewed in 1927[1] has tended to move this event ever further from the time of the first foundation of the city. In 1935, Mr. Cottrill was able to show from his observations on Tower Hill that the wall there could not have been built before A.D. 120–30, the significant discovery being a fragment of Samian pottery of that date which came from beneath the internal bank which is of the same date as the wall.[2]

Assuming the relationship already stated between the internal addition to the fort wall and the city wall, the evidence from the former has consistently favoured a later date. In 1950 a coin of Aelius Caesar was found in the mortar of the internal thickening at Windsor Court, fixing its construction after A.D. 140; and pottery from the later additions to the internal bank which *preceded* (or perhaps accompanied) the thickening is of the Antonine period. More recently an accumulation of mixed soil which also preceded

[1] *Roman London*, pp. 69–82.

[2] F. Cottrill in W. G. Bell, F. Cottrill and C. Spon, *London Wall through Eighteen Centuries* (Council for Tower Hill Improvement, 1937), pp. 9–21.

the construction of the thickening just north of the west gate produced a coin of Commodus of A.D. 183–4. This coin is in worn condition and may well have been in circulation for twenty years or more before it was lost. It fixes the insertion of the thickening, and therefore the building of the city wall proper, to at least the end of the second century A.D. and cancels out the other evidence on this subject so far obtained.

While it must be emphasised once again that this date should not be regarded as immovable—further examination of the material from the later internal bank may well alter it—it has at least the merit of conforming more closely with the period of the fortification of other of the Roman cities in Britain.[1] It is now possible to assert that the second recognisable phase in the history of London's defences cannot have begun before about the end of the second century A.D., with the building of the city wall and the incorporation into the city's defences of the reinforced walls of the Cripplegate fort.

3. THE ROMAN CITY WALL: SOME FURTHER OBSERVATIONS

The investigations covered by this survey have not otherwise involved any noteworthy change in ideas about the character of the city wall. Though it displays minor variations in structural features from one place to the next such variations are normal to Roman defensive works, in which gangs building separately, and without close co-ordination of their individual efforts, did not always build to the same pattern. A fragment of wall seen and partly preserved beneath the new London Wall (Route 11) (23) is identical in general character with lengths exposed on the eastern side of the city at the Tower of London. Here also there was the internal bank, standing no more than 3 feet high, and—as with the fort bank—reflecting in its slightness the small size of the contemporary ditch. The latter was slightly bigger than the fort ditch, but even so was only 14 feet wide by 5 feet deep, with a weak U-shaped profile—a token, rather than a true defensive feature. A build-up of gravel layers behind the bank suggested an internal road; but because of modern destruction not enough had survived to establish its complete character (Fig. 20 below).

[1] P. Corder, 'The Reorganisation of the Defences of Romano-British Towns in the Fourth Century', *Arch. Journ.* CXII (1955), pp. 20–42; A. L. F. Rivet, *Town and Country in Roman Britain* (1958), pp. 90–7.

More interesting is the small fragment of the city wall which has survived at its junction with the south-west angle of the fort in the Aldersgate re-entrant (9). Here too the Roman work has been mutilated by modern disturbance—in particular by a lift-shaft which had been sunk directly over the junction. The wall at this point is about 10 feet wide. The internal bank is not made of brickearth as elsewhere, but appears to be composed mainly of gravelly material: its full width cannot be seen. The wall is not built up against the fort wall in a straight joint but has been incorporated in it by means of a solid tongue of masonry which projects beyond the inner face of the fort wall into the turret, the lower part of which by this time (if not from the beginning) had been at least partly filled with a mixed brickearth which appeared to have been deliberately introduced. The purpose of this arrangement was no doubt to ensure that the two walls did not part at the joint. Also noteworthy is a tile-built culvert which passes through the city wall above the filled-up fort ditch (Plate 13). There was no space in the angle outside the wall to see what happened to the culvert at its outer end; internally it opened on to a U-shaped gully which continued the line of the fort ditch towards the interior—but here again the restrictions of the site prevented its being pursued for more than a few feet. All these provisions for drainage suggest that the fort ditch—here as elsewhere a slight, V-shaped affair, $6\frac{1}{2}$ feet wide by 4 feet deep—had functioned as a drain before the city wall was built; and the builders of the city wall evidently thought it necessary to provide for a continuance of this arrangement, although the building of the wall and the general raising of levels must drastically have changed the conditions in the area. The bottom of the later gully is above the bottom of the fort ditch.

As to the wall in the south-western angle of the city, comparison of Mr. Merrifield's newly published map with that of the Royal Commission shows how uncertain the position is with regard to its course in this sector. Two discoveries are thought to provide evidence for the wall here: one in Playhouse Yard (RCHM W40a: Merrifield W60), the other 'under the *Times* office' (RCHM W40b; Merrifield W61). On the maps in question RCHM W40a is shown about 30 feet west of Merrifield W60. RCHM W40b is about 70 feet south-west of Merrifield W61. The uncertainties both in dating and in location of these fragments are of course generally acknowledged, and no useful purpose will be served by going into all the

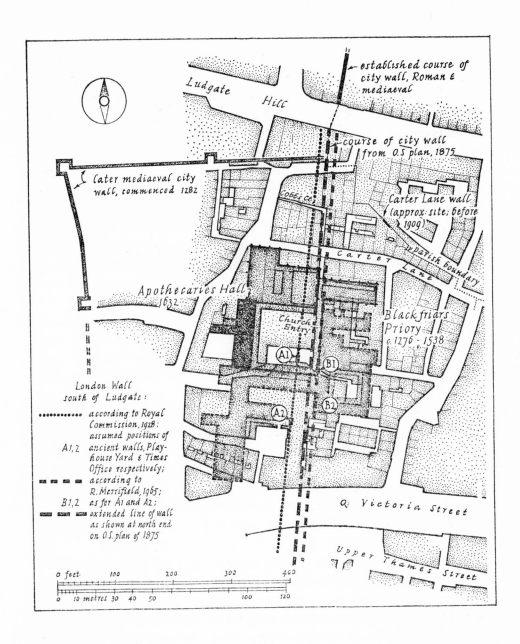

The map contains the following labels:

established course of city wall, Roman & mediaeval

Ludgate   Hill

course of city wall from O.S. plan, 1875

later mediaeval city wall, commenced 1282

Cobb's ct.

Carter Lane wall (approx. site; before 1909)

Carter Lane

parish boundary

Apothecaries Hall 1632

Church Entry

Blackfriars Priory c.1276 - 1538

A1

B1

A2

B2

London Wall south of Ludgate:

•••••••• according to Royal Commission, 1928;

A1,2   assumed positions of ancient walls, Playhouse Yard & Times Office respectively;

▬ ▬ ▬ according to R. Merrifield, 1965;

B1,2   as for A1 and A2;

▬ ▬ ▬ extended line of wall as shown at north end on O.S. plan of 1875

Q. Victoria Street

Upper Thames Street

0 feet   100   200   300   400

0   10 metres 30 40 50   100   120

11. London Wall south of Ludgate: possible alternative courses.

variations here.[1] The siting of the walls is an entirely arbitrary matter: Merrifield's version at its south end is well to the east of the Commission's, whose line appears to be that of the *VCH London* (I, Plan C, nos. 58, 59). The relationships are set out in Fig. 11.

That the mediaeval city wall of London passed through the Blackfriars precinct in close proximity to the church is shown by the licence granted in 1282 to the founder to 'breake and take downe a part of the wall of the Citie from Ludgate to the river of Thames' 'for the enlarging of the blacke Friers Church'.[2] The new wall was then built along the bank of the River Fleet to the west. It would be expected that the original early mediaeval wall here as elsewhere, would have followed the Roman line: this is probably, in view of all the uncertainties and contradictions, the best piece of evidence for a more or less southward prolongation of the wall from Ludgate.

As to its *actual* course, the fact appears not to have been noticed that as presented on the earliest accurate large-scale plans available (as, for instance, the 88 feet-to-the-inch Ordnance Survey plan for 1873–5) the line of the wall on the south side of Ludgate does not precisely prolong the line to the north of it: the southern part is set forward of the northern and varies its alignment by a matter of about five degrees. It is of course true that the southern line is that of the mediaeval wall and there is no certainty that it follows the original course exactly. In addition, only a short length of the wall at the northern end, from Ludgate to Pilgrim Street—the point, that is at which the thirteenth-century wall turned off to the west—is actually recorded. The fact remains that it is the extension of this line southwards that best fits the mediaeval layout of the area as far as it is known, and that is (or was) still reflected in the modern plan.

The late Sir Alfred Clapham's reconstruction of the Blackfriars Priory used as its basis the precise measurements for the monastic church and cloister which had been set out in a survey of 1550, and started from the premise that the Apothecaries' Hall exactly replicates in outline the original west range of the cloister.[3] Whatever the uncertainties of detail the location of the church in relation to surviving features can be closely determined. A point more immediately relevant to the present subject is that the prolonga-

---

[1] They are dealt with by Norman and Reader in *Archaeologia*, 63 (1911–12), p. 305.

[2] Stow, *Survey of London* (ed. Kingsford, 1908), I, p. 9.

[3] *Archaeologia*, 63 (1911–12), pp. 57–84.

tion of the northern line from Ludgate described above coincides as nearly as can be judged with the east wall of the church and the cloister wall to the south of it, along the west side of Church Entry.

But as already observed the wall has left its mark in other parts of the area. North of Carter Lane the eastern arm of the alley known as Cobb's Court coincides with it and property boundaries follow it closely. In Carter Lane itself a change in the alignment of the frontage and a projecting angle on the north side (as shown on the 1873–5 Ordnance plan) appear to coincide with the intersection of the Lane with this version of the wall. South of Carter Lane the part played by Church Entry has already been noted; and further south again the line is prolonged by the east side of the *Times* printing office with a narrow yard and other open spaces beside it to the east.

In comparison with the course here described the Commission's interpretation of the evidence suffers in that it bears no relation to the post-Roman elements. Mr. Merrifield's proposal uses the priory plan and in following the east side of Church Entry runs parallel with the more westerly version. Mr. Merrifield's line has the merit of aligning with the south end of the sector between Newgate and Ludgate; but it seems slightly less satisfactory than the other because it shows less coincidence with later boundaries. It must however be emphasized that at the present time neither of these alternatives is supported by positive evidence in the form of structural remains of a wall accurately located and of city wall character. It has already been said that both the dates and the positions of the earlier discoveries are completely uncertain—this in spite of the fact that a writer in *The Builder* of 1855[1] accompanies his note by a plan which shows the more southerly fragment following the frontage of the east wing of the *Times* building. The plan in question is too unreliable in detail, though according to Roach Smith the wall fragment was of more than one period with the bottom part possibly Roman.

However that may be, until the situation is clarified by future discoveries the early mediaeval wall can be thought of as having followed one of at least two alternative courses running almost due south towards the river from Ludgate. This investigation brings out the element of continuity over the centuries which has been seen to be a feature of other cities besides London, but the question remains of whether the early mediaeval wall overlies the

[1] *The Builder*, 13 (1855), pp. 221, 223 (fig. 4), 269.

Roman wall. The presumptive evidence that the two would have coincided is sufficiently strong to rule out the Carter Lane fragment (also shown on Fig. 11), which has been claimed as part of an alternative line for the city wall running in a south-easterly direction to Upper Thames Street from just south of Ludgate. This wall, which was found a few years before 1912, was also not accurately recorded apart from the statement that a parish boundary for a short distance agreed with it.[1] It would seem likely that it could only be regarded as part of Roman London's defences if there had been some drastic re-planning of the city on this side.

4. THE RIVER FRONTAGE IN ROMAN TIMES

The nature of the riverside works of the Roman city has been the subject of much discussion in the past. Various observations have suggested the existence of a river wall which followed a somewhat erratic line—if all the features recorded really belong to the same structure—along Lower and Upper Thames Streets. The fact that these remains lie under the actual roadway over most of their course has added to the difficulties of interpretation. The tendency now is to believe that there was no continuous defence along the river in Roman times and it is certainly the case that the fragmentary walls so far observed differ in character from the city wall on the landward side. Some of them also appear to be relatively late in date, if the presence in them of re-used architectural fragments is any criterion.[2]

A further complication is the uncertainty that attaches to the relationship of land-and-river levels during the Roman period. At East Tilbury to the east of the city[3] and at Old England, Brentford, to the west[4] Romano-British living-sites occur in situations which would not be available for continuous occupation with present day tide-levels. It has been pointed out that

---

[1] *Archaeologia*, 63 (1911–12), pp. 305–6. The plan, Pl. LXIV, shows the alternative 'Carter Lane' line for the Roman wall.

[2] The facts are set out in *Roman London*, pp. 92–4 and in Merrifield, *The Roman City*, pp. 221–223.

[3] RCHM (England), *Essex, South-east*, p. 38; also *Roman London*, pp. 12–14 for a general discussion.

[4] Wheeler, *Antiquity*, 3 (1929), p. 20.

to make these positions habitable for more than a few hours at a time would involve raising the land by a minimum of about 13 feet compared with the present day: only so could the huts escape flooding by high tides. The evidence from the margin of the river is confirmed in a more general way from Southwark, where Thomas Codrington concluded in 1915 that 'refuse deposits of Roman and later times [lay] on an old land surface as much as 12 or 14 feet and more below high-water level'.[1]

Whatever the figure for this change the fact of its existence requires to be borne in mind when the features of Londinium's river-side are under discussion. If, for instance, timber structures like those in Miles Lane near London Bridge[2] are to be thought of as wharves it must be demonstrated that their level was such that they could have been used, not in relation to the present stream but to one very much lower, with a high-water-mark probably somewhat below Ordnance Datum Newlyn. In Thames Street Ordnance Datum is in general 20 feet or more below the modern road-surface. In all this the problem is one of obtaining precise figures in highly variable circumstances.

In 1962 an investigation was undertaken of cellars on the east side of Lambeth Hill, between Queen Victoria Street and Upper Thames Street (32, 33). The most southerly of the series of cuttings (32) revealed at its north end the surface of the London Clay almost immediately beneath the cellar floor (Plate 64; Fig. 12). The surface was followed downwards to a depth of 8 feet over a horizontal distance of 26 feet, when further excavation became impossible because of standing water. The feature had the appearance of the inner slope of a large ditch and for a time this was the accepted explanation for it. The filling as far as it was visible consisted of Roman building debris (stones and mortar and fragments of wall-plaster and the like) overlying a dark brown silt with finer mixed material above that. A few scraps of pottery included a fragment of bead-rim which came from the building material and may imply a relatively early date, though this cannot be certain. The building debris was tightly packed and had the appearance of having been deliberately introduced.

There seems to be little doubt, however, that the slope is not that of a

---

[1] *Surrey Arch. Colls.*, 28 (1915), pp. 111–63.

[2] *Roman London*, pp. 132–4. No levels that can be related to any fixed datum appear to have been published for these timbers.

man-made ditch, but the edge of the immediately pre-Roman version of the River Thames. On the landward side, up the slope, it is impossible to reconstruct the original conditions because the modern cellar floors have been

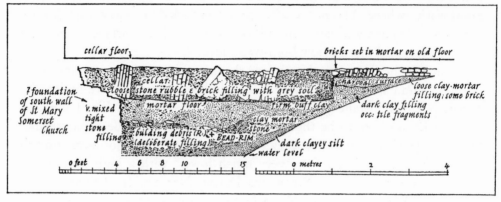

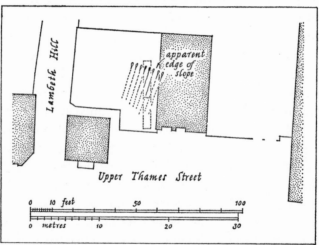

12. *Above:* section showing natural clay slope with Roman filling near the junction of Lambeth Hill and Upper Thames Street; *below:* plan showing apparent alignment of slope.

terraced into the ground—as, seemingly, were the Roman buildings before them—removing not only most of the occupation material but also some part of the natural deposits as well. In the cellar immediately above site 32 the surface of the natural gravel was met at a depth of a little over 4 feet below the cellar floor—about the same distance above the lip of the clay slope to the south (Figs. 13a, b). The significance of this evidence was not appreciated at the time. As usual, the excavation stopped on 'natural' and no effort was made to find the junction of the gravel with the underlying clay. It will however be clear that the junction must lie between the clay surface on Site 32 and that of the gravel to the north of it at 16–18 feet above Ordnance Datum.

The limited picture provided by the excavation can be extended by the information that has come from engineering borings in the neighbourhood, though this must be used with caution (Fig. 13b). Again, to the north, borings on the site of the new *Financial Times* building in Cannon Street (*35*) revealed London Clay consistently at 16–17 feet above O.D., suggesting that here and near Site 32 there was evidently the same London Clay surface at a fairly constant level, overlaid by gravel and (in places) brickearth, which together on Site 35 attained thicknesses of 15 feet or more. Both the clay surface and the overlying deposits are phenomena of late phases in the Pleistocene Ice Age; the former appears to be Bench N of Zeuner's classification of these features,[1] which in this part of the valley has a mean value of about 17 feet O.D. It carries here the gravel of the Upper Flood Plain, the surface of which as surviving on Site 35 is at about 38 feet O.D. where best preserved. But this may not be its total height, for some part of the gravel may have been removed with the brick-earth which formerly overlay it.

On the river side it is necessary to press into service the evidence from more than one site in order to create a composite picture of the conditions (Fig. 13c). The picture will obviously only be in general terms; it suffers in particular from the handicap that an important part of it is effectively hidden from view beneath the surface of Thames Street.

In the first place, a series of borings in the area of what is now the Public Cleansing Depot in Dowgate provides an excellent set of profiles of the inshore deposits that lay beneath the modern surface between Upper Thames Street and the present river frontage.[2] Though this site lies about 1,100 feet to the east of Site 32 (Fig. 13c) it seems reasonable to suppose that it reflects very similar conditions. The succession presented in Figs. 13a, b, is based on borings along the western edge of the Depot area, thus minimising as far

[1] F. E. Zeuner, *The Pleistocene Period* (2nd ed., 1959), pp. 356–62 and Fig. 78.
[2] Thanks are due to Mr. H. K. King, the City Engineer for making this information available

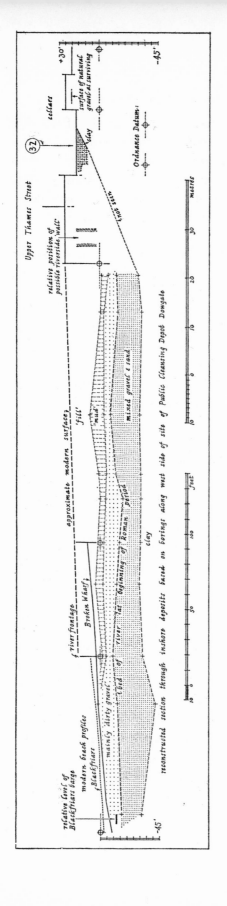

13a. Composite section through inshore deposits at Broken Wharf and Dowgate, related to Lambeth Hill cutting (32).

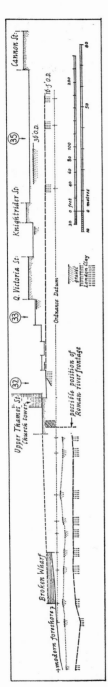

13b. Composite section showing relationship of river deposits at Broken Wharf to London Clay terrace and overlying gravel to north (Queen Victoria Street–Cannon Street).

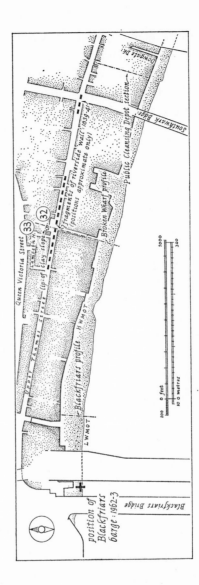

13c. The north bank of the River Thames between Blackfriars and Dowgate, showing the relationship of sites illustrated in Figs. 13a and b.

as possible the effects of the Walbrook outfall at Dowgate. The observations have been amalgamated using the south frontage of Thames Street as datum for horizontal measurements. The justification for this procedure is the assumption that Thames Street marks approximately the Roman river frontage; its effect, since the distance between the Roman and the modern frontage is greater by more than 100 feet at Dowgate than further west, is to carry the Dowgate section out under the present river when the two are combined.

There are inevitable minor variations in the individual borings and since they were not made nor described for the purposes of this study no information bearing upon the date or origin of the deposits revealed by them is directly available. The vertical succession itself, however, seems to be uniform; and the layers cover the full width of the site. The events that they represent are thus to be seen as parts of a single process affecting at least the immediate area as a whole.

The sequence is as follows:

(1) at the base: brown *London Clay*, except in one place appearing at a fairly uniform depth of 28–30 feet below Ordnance Datum;

(2) a *gravel-and-sand* layer, varying in character and ranging in thickness from a maximum of 25–28 feet, its surface lying between extremes of about 18 and about 5 feet below Ordnance Datum, with the mean at 10–12 feet;

(3) *'dirty gravel'*, containing other material besides gravel, 10–12 feet thick, its surface at or a few feet below Ordnance Datum;

(4) *'mud'*, to a maximum of 8 feet above Ordnance Datum, but generally rather less and not everywhere present; and

(5) *'fill'*, or made ground to the modern surface, 16–24 feet above Ordnance Datum.

The broad distinction lies between (1) and (2) and the rest. They appear to be 'natural', while the 'dirty gravel' seems to owe something to human activity (being the product partly of natural silting partly of dumping in the river), and marks the presence of man as a dominant in the locality from then on. The London Clay is the 'solid' geology. Its surface is that of one of the floors or benches cut by the river at a time when the sea-level was low; and one of three such benches belonging to the last phases of the Pleistocene Ice Age, for which there is abundant evidence elsewhere along the Thames. At a depth of 28–30 feet below O.D. here it would appear to be part of the bench labelled R by Zeuner, and linked by him with the final stage of the last (Würm) glaciation.[1] The 'sand-and-gravel' layer (2) then, lying on the London Clay, would be of post-Glacial date, the so-called valley drift which in archaeological terms would be equated in its lower part at least with the mesolithic age. Its surface is that of the river-bed at some time in the post-Glacial period; but its *actual* date is uncertain and could only be determined by detailed study of its character and by the recovery from it of archaeologically or scientifically datable objects. Nevertheless, that the surface is unlikely to be different by more than a foot or two from that of the river-bed in Roman times is shown by the other recent discovery in the area: that of the Roman boat or barge found off the mouth of the River Fleet at Blackfriars in 1962–3.[2] The boat lay 'in coarse river-gravel on a stratum of stiff grey silt at 11·79 feet below O.D.'—a figure which falls within the range of variation for the surface of layer 2 as revealed in the Dowgate depot borings.

Without more evidence it would be misleading to press the conclusion further, with the early Roman river-bed at 10 to 12 feet below the modern and carrying an accumulation of gravel containing Roman material in some quantity.[3] Amongst much that it is required to know the outstanding need is to learn more both about the Roman river-works and about the behaviour of the river itself. The sloping clay surface in site 32 can now be seen to be a natural feature, the upper part of the step demarcating two benches in the Pleistocene sequence of the river. It may be guessed that the Romans built their river wall or their wharves in advance of this slope, filling in the hollow behind it with building-debris as the section shows; but the structure itself lies under Thames Street and apart from the use of timber in

---

[1] F. E. Zeuner, *The Pleistocene Period* (2nd ed., 1959) as above. It should be added that on the evidence of a well-boring at Fishmongers' Hall the levels at London Bridge are very similar: London Clay at the equivalent of about 32 feet O.D., the 'valley drift' surface at about 12 feet O.D.: Whitaker, *Geology of London*, II, p. 102.

[2] P. R. V. Marsden, *The Mariner's Mirror*, 51, i (1965), pp. 59–62. Thanks are due to Mr. Marsden for additional information and in particular for allowing the use of the hitherto unpublished figure for the depth of the boat.

[3] See Merrifield, *The Roman City*, pp. 269–70 (no. 262) for a summary of Mr. Marsden's observations made during the contractor's excavation of the Cleansing Depot site. It does not include measurements of depth, but presents evidence for two distinct layers of Roman gravels, succeeded by 'river silt', presumably the 'mud' of the borings, which produced pottery of early mediaeval date.

its foundation little enough is known about it. The only figure of significance for its relation to its surroundings is that in Lower Thames Street near Fish Street Hill the foundation rested upon ballast at a depth of 24 feet below the street; but in the absence of any precise relationship to a common datum even the value of this figure is uncertain. More helpful is the statement that the foundation rested upon 'ballast', which presumably means the 'valley drift', layer 2 at Dowgate. If this somewhat protracted note has shed some light on the general setting of the frontage works of Roman London and perhaps also on the Pleistocene features of this part of the Thames valley it has also demonstrated the urgent need to lose no opportunity to observe and record as precisely as possible any feature, artificial or natural, that may present itself along Thames Street, Upper or Lower. The deposits here are as important as the constructions.

5. THE LATER HISTORY OF THE ROMAN WALL AND THE BASTIONS

The next phase in the history of London Wall is a period of decline when in some places at least the wall had degenerated into a decayed state. This change had already taken place by the time that some of the later bastions were built. When Bastion 19 near Newgate was exposed in 1909 it was found that the city wall was standing to a height of only 5 feet above its plinth.[1] Its top as surviving appeared to be toppling over outwards—a fact which can be observed today. The end of the bastion, butting against the wall, fits the curve of its upper courses and there can be little doubt that when the bastion was built the wall could not have been standing to any appreciably greater height than it does now. The external situation at Bastion 14 in Castle Street is still (in 1965) not yet clear: investigation here must await the removal of modern obstructions. Behind the bastion itself, however, the wall had been reduced to a height of only just over 2 feet above its foundation level (Plate 3): here a rebuilding in random rubble very similar in character to that of the bastion had taken place: whatever the position with the internal thickening the original wall had been completely rebuilt from this low level.

So, too, at St. Alphage (but not at the neighbouring London Wall site,

[1] *Roman London*, pp. 104–6 and Fig. 28.

nor, apparently, further east again at All-Hallows-on-the-Wall[1]) the Roman wall-face seems to have been renewed in its lower part at some remote date in the past. The original core is covered by a random-rubble face set on a very irregular line well behind the original Roman face (Fig. 19); and there is some hint that the body of the wall as a whole may have required reconstruction from a very low level.

It is impossible to say at present when these repairs were carried out and it seems likely now that no further evidence on them will be forthcoming apart from what may result from the stripping of Bastions 13 and 14. Though they display a certain similarity they need not be of the same date; the same sort of repairs had to be done to the wall in places away from the north-western area, for instance on the eastern side. It can at least be said, however, that the wall was not everywhere maintained in its original state throughout the centuries; and that some parts of it were in a decayed condition when the bastions were built. It has already been observed that the workmanship of the repair behind Bastion 14 is very similar to that of the bastion itself.

It is now time to consider the bastions. They are semi-circular or horseshoe-shaped towers, here as in most other places structurally later than the city wall. Their ends usually, but not invariably, abut on the wall; but Bastion 15, across the angle of the Aldersgate re-entrant (8), is toothed into the wall at its surviving north-east end (Plate 14). Down to recent times there has been no completely reliable evidence on which to base a close date for the bastions of London. Twenty-one are known or recorded,[2] and they fall into two groups according to their construction: the one involving the reuse of stones from other buildings or monuments and having its lower part built solid; the other hollow-based and constructed in random rubble. These differences may well imply differences in date, but there is no evidence on which this question can be decided. The first group is often spoken of as the eastern series, the others as the western, but it is doubtful whether the distinction can be completely maintained. On the whole, however, the 'eastern' series appears to have been better built than the 'western', whose walls are frequently of very irregular construction, with uneven offsets and other indications of a low level of building skill.

The eastern salient of the Aldersgate re-entrant, between St. Giles

[1] *Roman London*, pp. 103–4.   [2] *Ibid.*, pp. 99–106.

Cripplegate and St. Anne and St. Agnes churches, is noteworthy for the possession, complete or in part, of four of the small number of bastions that now survives. Bastion 12 is the well-known Cripplegate bastion; 13 was

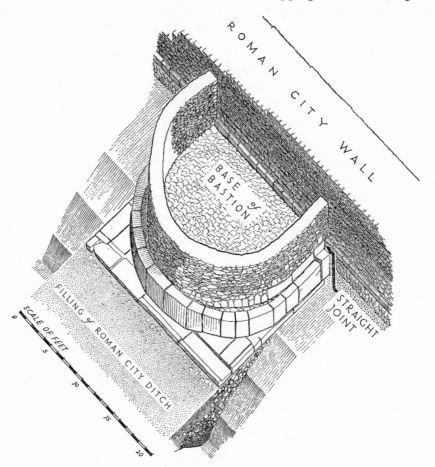

14. Bastion 11 (All Hallows on the Wall): its relationship to the city wall and Roman city ditch.

once part of the courtroom of the Barber Surgeons' Hall in Monkwell Street (2); 14, in Castle Street, is the best preserved of the group; 15, already mentioned, is represented only by a small fragment of the bastion which originally covered the re-entrant angle itself.

The area around Bastion 12 was examined during the last century, when it was established that the deposits against it had already been much disturbed by, amongst other things, the seventeenth-century brick culvert which has been seen recently elsewhere: the exposed part of the bastion was drastically refaced at the end of the nineteenth century.[1] Internally, the levels are such that part of the offset foundation is exposed, though it has been given a protective rendering. The remainder of the bastion also has a modern finish which largely masks the original masonry, but where visible this appears to be of the random rubble characteristic of the 'western' bastions as a whole.

Bastion 13 (2) survives only to the level of St. Giles' churchyard and has suffered extensive mutilation in other ways.[2] Recent investigation has shown that on the north externally it ends on the city wall (Plate 20); to the south the junction has been destroyed. Internally, the ends of the bastion have been cut away or underpinned by modern foundations. In spite, however, of the low level of the cellar enough remained to show that the foundation, a little over 2 feet deep, was set in the floor of the Roman city ditch, the base of which had survived. The level of the offset of this bastion no doubt marks the surface level of the ditch-filling when the bastion was built, so that by that time the city ditch had silted up to rather less than half its original depth in this sector. Excavation of the area outside the bastion may in due course shed fresh light on these relationships, though the depth of late disturbance nearby does not encourage much hope of this.

It would have been instructive to have seen more of Bastion 15, but the greater part of it was destroyed in 1922 and only a foot or two of its wall had survived where it joined the city wall. This bastion is (as already noted) the exception to the rule that the bastions mostly rest against the city wall and are not bonded into it; for here a slot had existed, or been created, in the wall and the bastion was toothed into it. The slot was wider than the bastion wall, so that for a foot or two behind the bastion there was a shallow recess, the face of which was set back behind the original city wall face. At this point also the foundation was not deep and rose over a wedge-shaped deposit of occupation-material (Plate 23) from which came a few

[1] J. Terry, 'On a Bastion of the Wall of London in Cripplegate Churchyard', *Trans. London and M'sex Arch. Soc.* VIII (1889–1903), pp. 356–9.

[2] The Commission (*Roman London*, p. 104) say that the building of which it was a part had been destroyed: but the bastion itself survives below churchyard level.

sherds which are unfortunately indeterminate as to their form, though in general appearance they look to be of late Roman date.

From the bastions so far described, therefore, all the evidence is of a somewhat inconclusive kind. With Bastion 14 the position is rather better, though problems enough remain. Bastion 14 has had a chequered career. The Royal Commission refer to it as if it no longer existed in 1927.[1] But it had in fact survived within the buildings in Castle Street, escaping German bombs, and being more seriously threatened by the activities of a squad of Pioneers, who were prevented from demolishing it as an unsafe structure by the fortunate intervention of an architect who recognised it for what it was.

As this is being written, therefore, Bastion 14 still stands to a height of 9–10 feet above the modern surface level of Castle Street. Externally, at this height, it is of mediaeval construction (below, p. 84); internally it is masked by a modern skin of brick that prevents its character from being seen. Fortunately, the modern floor-level within the bastion provided only for a half-cellar, with the consequence that a depth of deposit was preserved to open up the possibility that datable material might be forthcoming.

It is rarely possible to date a featureless wall or other stone construction without the aid of evidence derived from some source other than its own masonry; and since the dates of the bastions that are a feature of many Roman towns are of considerable importance in the elucidation of the history of the towns it was hoped that any datable levels within Bastion 14 could be shown to be closely related to its construction and use. With these problems in mind the interior of the bastion was emptied with the greatest care. A trench dug along its main axis was widened by cutting back its faces a foot at a time, each new section thus exposed being cleaned and studied until finally all the filling had been removed. The result was to show that, like the neighbouring bastion (13), this had been carried out across the Roman ditch, the inner slope of which had survived beneath the later filling (Fig. 15). The bastion wall, behind and below the modern lining referred to above, was of random rubble, most of the stones being small and thin and poorly coursed, with no definite demarcation between foundation and faced wall.

Within the bastion at a depth of $2\frac{1}{2}$ feet falling to 4 feet below the cellar surface was a floor of hard-rammed gravel (Plate 21). On the inside the

[1] *Roman London*, p. 104.

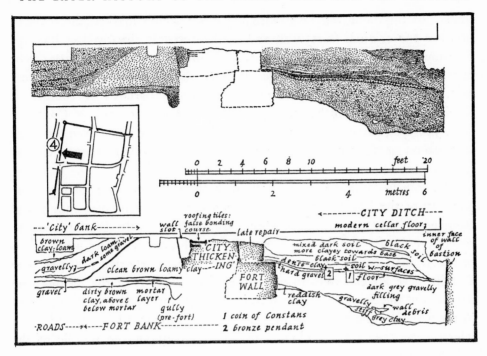

15. Bastion 14 (4): section through deposits associated with the bastion and with the combined city and fort wall.

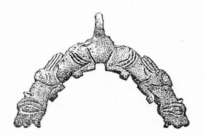

16. Bastion 14: bronze pendant from surface of gravel floor within the bastion. ($\frac{1}{1}$)

69

surface of this floor was level with the offset which marked the division between the original (fort) wall and the later repair already described (p. 64); toward sthe outside the floor sloped downwards over the city ditch, now filled up. Both above and below the floor the deposits were a featureless dark soil. Two finds of great importance but apparently of conflicting significance came from the gravel surface. The first was a coin of Constans (A.D. 346–50), partly buried in the floor. Barely a foot away from the coin, and also on or very near the surface, was found a small bronze pendant (Fig. 16).

The coin is completely consistent with the accepted date for the great majority of the bastions which are attached to the walls of a number of Romano-British towns. The bastions are assumed, with good reason, to reflect the uneasy conditions of the third and fourth centuries when much of the Roman Empire was subjected to external barbarian pressure. For Britain these attacks were in effect the first invasions of the Saxons: the defences of the Saxon Shore, begun in the late third century, were created to repel them. The town bastions, however, are somewhat later, and those which have been dated belong consistently to about the middle of the fourth century.[1]

But the pendant seems to be much later. Its zoomorphic ornament of hares and (apparently) dogs' heads places it in the period of the eighth/ ninth century: if the evidence of its ornament means anything therefore it is late Saxon rather than Roman in date.

The value of the pendant as a dating medium for the bastion clearly depends on whether bastion and floor go together. It seems quite certain that the pendant did not find its way down to the gravel surface as a result of some later disturbance of the covering deposits; and it is most unlikely that the surface could have remained open through the four centuries or so that must have elapsed between the loss of the coin and the loss of the pendant. The lack of distinction between foundation and faced wall in the bastion (p. 68) precludes complete certainty as to the relationship of wall and floor; but whatever the truth about this the pendant provides a reminder that for some at any rate of London's bastions a Roman date should not be too readily assumed. The possibility of some variation in date is hinted at in the constructional differences which have already been noted (p. 65);

[1] For surveys of the evidence see the references given in the footnote on p. 51 above.

but the difficulty of defining dates will always be that none of the significant deposits has survived for investigation by modern methods of stratigraphical excavation.

6. NEW EVIDENCE ON THE DATE OF SOME OF THE BASTIONS

The foregoing paragraphs on the London bastions were written some time ago. In many respects they have been rendered obsolete by the recent discovery (in 1965: Plate 18) of a hitherto unrecorded bastion in Cripplegate churchyard. The original account has been retained unaltered because with what follows it well illustrates the manner in which a situation may be resolved by fresh evidence; and reiterates the point already made that in times of doubt it may be misleading to rely on the latest object in a particular deposit for the date of that deposit.

The 'new' bastion is situated about half-way between Cripplegate and the north-western corner of the fort (Bastion 12): it was exposed during the lowering of the surface of the churchyard of St. Giles Cripplegate as part of the Barbican Redevelopment Scheme. The bastion survives as two curving stumps built against the city wall (Fig. 17): the outer part has been cut away by the seventeenth-century sewer which follows the line of the city ditch in this area. The existing masonry is all foundation work: grave-digging has probably been the chief cause of the destruction of the superstructure, but late re-cutting of the ditch may also have had something to do with it. It is remarkable that in spite of all the activity and disturbance not only the wall but also the internal features of the bastion should have survived. The indications are that throughout the length of the churchyard on this side the Roman berm at 7–8 feet below the modern surface was not broken by burials, though further out, over the city ditch, burials went to depths of as much as 14 feet. It is possible that the zone before the wall may have been avoided to begin with because burials too close to it may have been thought to threaten its stability. Later on, burials were actually made close to the wall-face, but by this time the surface had built up quite considerably. The deepest of these burials were about 6 feet down.

As remarkable as its survival is the fact that the bastion does not figure on the sixteenth-century panoramic maps which are one of the sources of

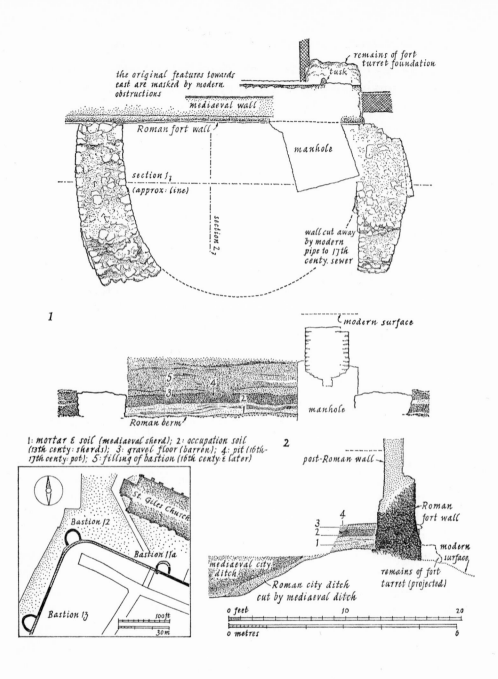

the original features towards
east are masked by modern
obstructions

remains of fort
turret foundation

tusk

mediaeval wall

Roman fort wall

manhole

section J_1
(approx: line)

section 2_2

wall cut away
by modern
pipe to 17th
centy. sewer

1

modern surface

5

4

3

2

manhole

Roman berm

1: mortar & soil (mediaeval sherd); 2: occupation soil
(13th centy: sherds); 3: gravel floor (barren); 4: pit (16th-
17th centy: pot); 5: filling of bastion (16th centy: & later)

2

post-Roman wall

St. Giles Church

Bastion 12

Bastion 11a

3
2
1

4

Roman
fort wall

modern
surface

mediaeval city
ditch

Bastion 13

100 ft

30 m

Roman city ditch
cut by mediaeval ditch

remains of fort
turret (projected)

0 feet   10   20

0 metres   6

17. Bastion 11A: plan and sections.

information on features of London's defences that no longer survive. This presumably means that it had vanished from view by about the middle of the sixteenth century; but there has been no opportunity of checking the possibility that it may be shown on unpublished manuscript maps, which might enable the date of its disappearance to be more closely fixed. In the numerical sequence by which the bastions of London are identified this bastion stands between Bastion 11 at All-Hallows-on-the-wall on the east and Bastion 12 on the Cripplegate corner. It has seemed better at this stage to call it 11A, rather than to disturb the long-established numbering of the bastions that follow it westwards, at any rate until it is certain that no further bastions remain to be discovered.

In the condition in which the bastion was made available for archaeological investigation the remains consisted of the stumps of the wall already mentioned with between them the full depth of the deposit from the modern surface of the churchyard to the Roman berm, here a matter of about $7\frac{1}{2}$ feet. In the western (internal) angle of the bastion there was a large brick-built inspection chamber which penetrated the natural gravel and had destroyed everything in that corner.

The removal of burials in the surrounding area had left a more or less vertical section face, east to west along a chord of the bastion and about 4 feet out from the city wall. The most noticeable feature of the section was a layer of tightly packed gravel about 9 inches thick and 18 inches above the feature that appeared to mark the original berm. There was a break about half-way along it which indicated a small pit of some kind. The gravel layer was exactly like that in Bastion 14 (Plates 21, 22) and its potential significance for dating purposes was therefore considerable.

Above the gravel surface the very mixed accumulation of soil and other materials showed no burials on the face though there was a number of relatively shallow ones nearer the city wall. All this material can be dismissed very briefly for it produced fragments of bellarmine and even later pottery, to show that it had been disturbed certainly down to some time well into the nineteenth century.

The break in the face of the gravel proved as expected to be a small pit. The purpose of the pit was not obvious nor could the level from which it had been dug be recognised. In it were found the fragments of one pot, a red-ware bottle with a large key-hole-shaped opening cut in its base before

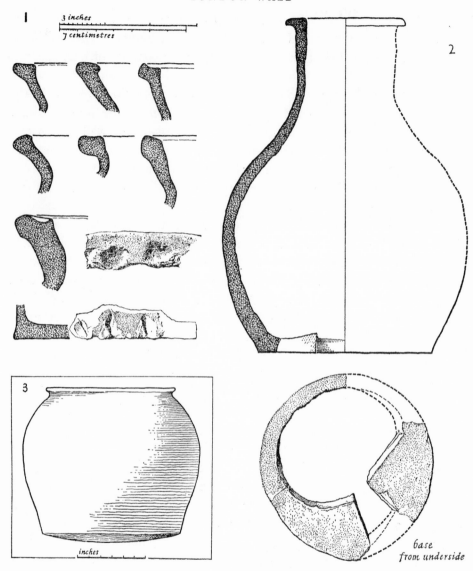

18. Bastion 11A: pottery associated with the bastion, 1 antedating the foundations (with 3 illustrating the complete form represented by the rims); 2 from pit in gravel floor.

74

firing (Fig. 18, 2). (Since the front part of the pit had been cut away it is possible that the remainder of the bottle was removed at that time.) The purpose of the curious opening in the base of the pot can only be guessed at, though other examples are known. On the authority of Mr. John Hurst the bottle is of sixteenth- or seventeenth-century date. It provides therefore a *terminus ante quem* for the gravel floor.

The floor itself was homogeneous and quite hard. It produced no finds. In the east-to-west section the floor appeared to be continued beyond the bastion wall, which gave the impression of having been set in it. But appearances here were deceptive: the gravel outside the bastion seems to have formed a floor or surface-rendering of the berm which had suffered some mutilation by burials but was in fact continuous as far as could be seen in the area exposed.

Beneath the gravel layer was an accumulation of dark loamy soil which produced evidence of occupation though it was not simply an occupation deposit. Scattered through it, but not at any particular level were animal bones and some oyster and other shells, scraps of charcoal, tile-fragments and potsherds. This deposit was continued beyond the bastion on the east; it has been destroyed by burials on the west. The foundation of the bastion had been dug into it and it was clearly older than the bastion. The potsherds and some of the tile-fragments were recognizably mediaeval; the datable fragments were mainly cooking-pot rims (Fig. 18, 1) of the thirteenth century. Below the thirteenth-century deposit were mortary layers with in places dark soil between them: they were continued westwards to the limit of the undisturbed ground but not apparently to the east. These layers also had been cut through by the bastion foundations. Their mediaeval date was established by one potsherd. Between them and the brick-earth surface which formed the berm between city wall and ditch in the Roman period was a hard rammed gravel and stone surface.

The facts are set out in some detail because here for the first time is unequivocal evidence based on stratigraphical excavation for the date of one of the London bastions. Bastion 11A, having been dug into pre-existing thirteenth-century deposits, must be thirteenth century or later. It does not of course affect the possibility that some of the other bastions are late Roman, but it does demand a re-examination of such evidence as exists.

In the first place, the situation with Bastion 14 is now resolved. Bastion 14's gravel floor was identical with that of Bastion 11A; there can be little doubt that it also is mediaeval.[1] The bronze pendant is thus as much an 'accident' as the coin of Constans (p. 70): they are survivors from earlier periods which have drifted into a later setting—a common enough happening on long-occupied sites like London, though it is a rather remarkable coincidence that the date of one of these chance finds should fit the pattern of events for which there is good evidence in other places. King Alfred thus disappears from the scene, archaeologically speaking; but the consolation for having lost one of English history's more romantic figures is the partial clarification of a position over which doubt has hung for a very long time. Unless further unrecorded bastions await discovery (which is very unlikely) Bastion 14 and its neighbours 13 and 12 are now the most hopeful source of further information on the general problem of the London bastions. As the redevelopment of the Barbican area proceeds the removal of the modern obstructions that now conceal them should be watched with the closest attention.

While it seems wise to suspend judgment on Bastions 12 and 13 until they can be completely seen,[2] the small surviving fragment of Bastion 15, in the Aldersgate angle (p. 67) must surely be of the same date as 11A. It has already been observed that the butt of the foundation of this bastion was found to rise on the inside over a wedge-shaped deposit of occupation soil instead of resting on the natural brick-earth, its base overlying the ledge that had been created for it in the fort wall. This feature occurs also in the east foundation of Bastion 11A (Plate 24). It is so distinctive that the two bastions must be of the same date and were no doubt built by the same hands.

Three of the surviving bastions along the Cripplegate sector of the city wall, 11A, 14 and 15 must now be regarded as mediaeval and more precisely as of post-thirteenth century date. It seems to be impossible to say how many more of the known bastions belong to this time and it would probably be dangerous to regard all of the so-called 'western' group (to which these

---

[1] It should be added that in a report on the mortars which will be published in due course Dr. Norman Davey expressed the view that the mortar from Bastion 14 is of post-Roman character.

[2] Bastion 12, the corner bastion, may well be completely exposed and available for detailed and complete study before this book is published.

three belong) as contemporary. Even amongst this group there are note-worthy structural variations. Bastion 11 which is hollow and therefore presumably belongs to it, is very different from 11A and the others, as comparison of Fig. 14 with Fig. 17 here will show. Of two of the recorded bastions that have been claimed to be mediaeval, number 10 in Camomile Street is one of the 'solid' variety, which produced a number of Roman worked stones. The evidence supporting the later date was the handle of a green-glazed pitcher, which was found beneath the bastion;[1] but since the Romans also made green-glazed ware the mediaeval date of this fragment is not certain. The sherd has not apparently survived but if it had indeed been mediaeval the consequences for the group of 'solid' bastions would be serious. On the other hand, the second bastion, 16, near King Edward Street[2] might more readily go with the dated mediaeval examples. Here the bastion is hollow and the evidence takes the form of pieces of worked stone from the foundations which showed 'traces of Norman mouldings and of foliage of the Early English Period'. These stones also have not apparently survived.

The difficulty in all this is of course the usual one of the uncertain value of the statements of early observers often operating in conditions of great difficulty. It must be admitted that the dating of Bastion 11A, while it has disposed of the Saxons, adds to the curious features of the London bastions as a whole. It confirms in the first place the evidence of the best of the early maps that the number of bastions could at one time have been much larger than now appears, for many could have vanished without record. The addition of missing bastions would do something to even out the discrepancies in their spacing which is a feature of the London plan at the present time, but considerable differences in the distances between many of them would still remain. Indeed, only in the Cripplegate sector is there any semblance of consistent spacing, with Bastions 11A to 14 50 to 55 yards apart centre to centre. The removal of any or all of them from the Roman defensive system renders the Roman distribution more uneven as between east to west than it was already, though a similar unevenness is found at some other Roman towns and is usually explained as due to the greater vulnerability or exposure to attack of some parts of their periphery as compared with others.

The archaeological date for the mediaeval bastions is too imprecise to enable their construction to be ascribed to any particular event or set of

---

[1] *Roman London*, pp. 102–3.   [2] *Ibid.*, p. 104.

circumstances. The only hope of progress here would seem to rest on a chance discovery in the records.[1]

7. LONDON WALL IN THE MIDDLE AGES AND LATER

The general relationship of the mediaeval city wall to its Roman predecessor has long been known. The late wall follows the line of the first wall everywhere on the landward side, departing from it only at the south-west, where below Ludgate the line was moved outwards to practically the east bank of the River Fleet. These events have been discussed in connexion with the siting of the Roman wall in this area (pp. 52–6).

But while the two walls run together with the mediaeval wall overlying the other and using its remains as a base the actual manner in which they were joined does not appear to have been as straightforward as the well-known reconstruction in the Roman London volume of the Royal Commission would suggest.[2] The evidence has of course only come to light since that volume was published and it has shown that at any rate in the north-western sector the later work does not always rest tidily upon the Roman.

At St. Alphage (*17*) the outer part of the Roman wall had evidently completely collapsed. It was refaced at an uncertain date on an irregular line which lay behind that of the original wall (Fig. 19). At both the east and the west ends of this sector the straight joint between fort and city 'thickening' survives only to a height of about 6 feet above the original plinth-level. Above this the double wall is replaced by solid post-Roman masonry and the junction between the two is irregular and not easy to define precisely.

At Falcon Square (*5*) on the other hand, an entirely new wall had been built on the outer wall of the south turret of the fort gateway. Its face was set back behind the Roman face which remained to a height of only 2

---

[1] Stow's comments (*op. cit.*, I, pp. 8–9) on the subject of the towers on the wall appear to be contradictory. He quotes fitz Stephen for the statement that the wall is 'wel towred on the North-side, with due distances betweene the towres'. Later he says: 'In the yeare 1257. *Henrie* the third caused the walles of this Citie, which was sore decaied & destitute of towers, to be repaired in more seemely wise than before, at the common charges of the Citie'. The second statement could be taken to mean that Bastion 11A and its fellows were constructed at this time.

[2] *Roman London*, Fig. 9.

feet above the foundation. The rebuild was a good deal wider than the Roman wall and projected behind it for at least 7 feet, its rear part resting upon a mixed clay filling in the lower part of the turret. It seems fairly certain that this wall is of mediaeval date, though no significant mediaeval material was associated with it.

The relationship of the mediaeval to the Roman wall in the north-western part of the city is even clearer at the Barber Surgeons' Hall. Within the hall the rear face of the wall is largely masked by later walls which have sometimes destroyed the internal thickening: it would appear, nevertheless, that on the inside the fort wall survives to a height of at least 4 feet. Externally, on the other hand, the Roman wall has been completely refaced from plinth-level to modern surface. Only in the angle of wall and Bastion 13, where the structure has been protected by the projecting bastion, does any Roman face-work survive at all; and there it remains to a height of only four or five courses over a horizontal distance of about 5 feet. This refacing does not resemble the random rubble of uncertain but possibly post-Roman date which has already been described both at St. Alphage and behind Bastion 14 (pp. 65, 64): the rubble is squared, but entirely without regular coursing, and most of the material has the look of being reused (Plate 20).

In the Cripplegate region therefore little of the Roman work on the wall can have been visible during the Middle Ages. Not only was the damaged front of the wall renewed, perhaps at more than one period, but its height also was made up, no doubt to replace the collapsed upper part of the original wall. These additions are thinner and slighter than the original wall on which they are carried. Their distinctive feature is a series of tile or brick courses at intervals of three or four courses of Kentish ragstone which might at first glance be mistaken for Roman work. In fact, however, the courses are too closely set and they are not continuous, quite apart from the un-Roman character of the bricks themselves. A small fragment of this type of construction still survives at the north end of Noble Street (6) where also recent work has revealed that the mediaeval masonry, which is uncoursed in the core of the wall, is closely bonded to the Roman masonry at irregular heights. Until 1958 there was another to the north which had an interest for the final phase in the wall's history (p. 90).

The actual date of the brick-coursed fragments remains uncertain, but the work bears a sufficient resemblance to datable remains presently to be

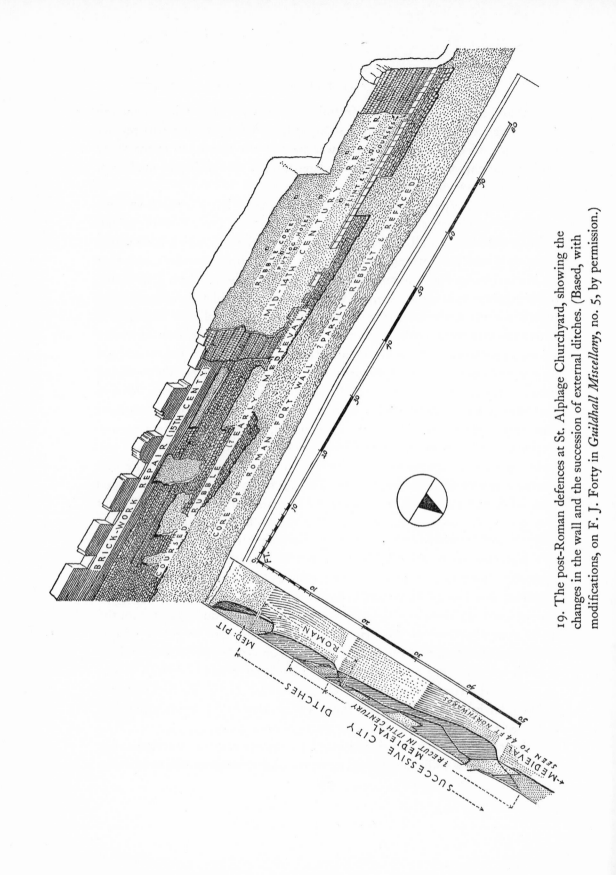

19. The post-Roman defences at St. Alphage Churchyard, showing the changes in the wall and the succession of external ditches. (Based, with modifications, on F. J. Forty in *Guildhall Miscellany*, no. 5, by permission.)

described to suggest that they may be of the mid-fourteenth century. It should be noted that the courses are present only on the face: the core of the wall is made up of compacted rubble, often containing much chalk and showing none of the structural method of the Roman wall.

From the documentary evidence it has long been clear that the wall was at various times repaired or reconstructed. One such rebuilding in Cripplegate also has long been well known: it is the brick wall of which a portion now survives in the churchyard of St. Alphage, though until into the last century it had been more extensively preserved. The distinctive feature of this wall, which survives to almost its full height, is its diaper-pattern of dark brick, now made more obvious as a result of recent cleaning. Its outer face had been covered by modern buildings on the north side, and with the destruction of these buildings, the City Corporation have taken the opportunity of preserving the wall so that it is now visible on both faces.[1] Its total height is about 25 feet above the Roman foundation and most of this height must have been exposed in mediaeval times. Only the top 6 feet of the wall are taken up with the later brick-work, the core of which appears to merge with the earlier structure.

This work is generally ascribed to Mayor Joceline who in 1477 was responsible for a large-scale repair of the wall between Aldgate and Aldersgate.[2] The exposure of the external face of the St. Alphage wall revealed that Joceline's work abutted on the west a rebuilding which seems to be nearly a hundred years earlier (Fig. 19). The distinctive facing of this wall survives, with breaks, over a distance of about 50 feet. The masonry consists mainly of small close-jointed ashlar in which there are at narrow vertical intervals courses of knapped flints or of tiles set in the face (Plate 25). Masonry of identical character is to be seen at Westminster Abbey in the transept-like additions to St. Katherine's Chapel (the Infirmary) built in the mid-fourteenth century (Plate 26).[3] The resemblance is so close, even to the presence of occasional deeper courses, that the two structures must have

---

[1] The Excavation Council suggested that the wall might be treated and preserved as part of the City's commemoration of the 1951 Festival and this suggestion was finally taken up. The scheme had long been in the mind of Mr. F. J. Forty, then City Engineer, who took a close personal interest in the work and published a fully illustrated account of it in *Guildhall Miscellany*.

[2] Stow, *Survey of London* (1908 ed.), I, p. 10.

[3] RCHM, *London I, Westminster Abbey*, pp. 90–1 and historical ground plan.

been built by the same hands. London Wall in Cripplegate is thus brought into close relationship with another important London building. This type of work does not appear to have occurred throughout the full length of the Cripplegate salient, for there is evidence that the wall confronting Cripplegate churchyard (*1a*) was part of Joceline's reconstruction.[1] The tile-coursed wall in Noble Street (*6*) presumably was part of the work done in Joceline's time under the aegis of the Goldsmiths' Company, who accepted responsibility for repair between Cripplegate and Aldersgate. But the repair was no doubt piecemeal, and (as has appeared in the case of St. Alphage) not all the work in the same length need be of the same date.

On the whole it would seem that the Roman wall outside the area of the Cripplegate fort is better preserved than in the parts just described, so that away from Cripplegate there would have been more Roman work visible in the later wall. At Coleman Street, for instance (*23* above, p. 51), the faced wall survived in places to a height of only one or two courses above the plinth; but here, no doubt, it had suffered from being on the frontage of the old London Wall. Further east, at All-Hallows-on-the-Wall and elsewhere, the wall-face had survived to as much as 10 feet. This sort of variation may be due to the differences in construction between the fort wall and the city wall proper, the latter being much more massive and provided with levelling courses. On the other hand the poor state of the city wall at the Newgate angle when the bastion was built has also been noted (p. 64); so that the conditions were evidently not uniform.

No mediaeval masonry capping the Roman work had survived at Coleman Street, but this length of the wall was notable for the presence behind it of a series of massive brick arches (Fig 20; Plate 27), backed against its inner face and evidently intended to reinforce the wall and carry some considerable superstructure. A first reaction was to regard this work as being of the Civil War period, for as will be seen (p. 88) some refurbishing

---

[1] See the drawing by J. T. Smith of the wall as it was here in 1793. W. G. Bell *et al.*, *London Wall through Eighteen Centuries*, Fig. 64. The unexpectedly long piece of the wall exposed in the churchyard in 1965 is not available for detailed study as this is being written and it is not yet possible to say whether any of the fifteenth-century work has survived the early nineteenth-century rebuilding. At Bastion 11A a patch in the later wall immediately above the eastern foundation of the bastion suggests that at this level the bastion was bonded into the city wall; but even if this part proves to belong to one of the dated reconstructions it may not give a date for the actual building of the bastion (Plate 19).

of the defences on this side of the city must have taken place in the seventeenth century. When the arches were examined, however, no datable material of this period was found. It seems safer therefore to conclude that they are of late mediaeval date, perhaps being part once again of Joceline's

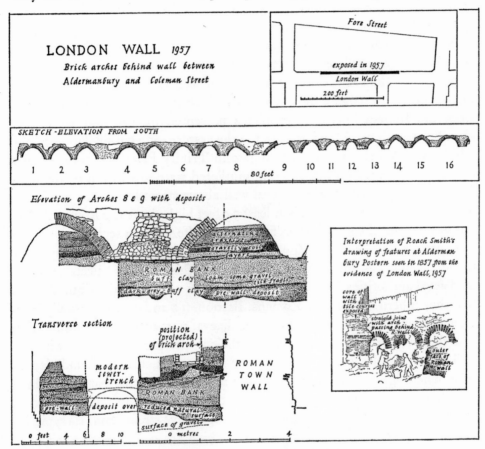

LONDON WALL 1957

Brick arches behind wall between Aldermanbury and Coleman Street

Fore Street

exposed in 1957

London Wall

200 feet

SKETCH-ELEVATION FROM SOUTH

1 2 3 4 5 6 7 8 80 feet 9 10 11 12 13 14 15 16

Elevation of Arches 8 & 9 with deposits

ROMAN BANK
buff clay loam, some gravel, tile frags.
dark grey buff clay pre-wall deposit

Interpretation of Roach Smith's drawing of features at Aldermanbury Postern seen in 1857 from the evidence of London Wall, 1957

core of wall with tile courses exposed

straight joint with arch passing behind R.wall

outer face of Roman wall

Transverse section

position (projected) of brick arch

modern sewer-trench

ROMAN BANK

ROMAN TOWN WALL

pre-wall deposit over reduced natural surface
surface of gravel

0 feet 4 6 8 10 0 metres 2 4

20. London Wall (23): brick arches behind the Roman city wall between Aldermanbury and Coleman Street.

restoration. The arches were built into the ground, their ends resting on the top of the internal Roman bank. This discovery explains the curious feature recorded by Roach Smith at Aldermanbury Postern, a few yards to the east in 1857.[1] Here there were some blind arches which Roach Smith

[1] *Roman London*, p. 90; and for Roach Smith's drawing, Plate 23.

interpreted as part of the Roman wall. His interpretation was accepted by the Royal Commission. His drawing shows, however, that the arches were on the road-frontage *behind* the wall, the broken stump of which, with bonding courses, appears on the right of the picture (Fig. 20). The bonding courses are in the same relative positions in the Roach Smith illustration as in the sector exposed in 1957.

No additional information has been forthcoming about the surviving stretches of the wall on the western side of the city, and the conditions prevailing on the south side of Ludgate Hill as this is being written make it impossible to investigate the one area in which the mediaeval wall departed from the Roman line. The problems presented by the wall there have already been discussed (pp. 52–6). On the eastern side consolidation by the Ministry of Works of the postern-gate in Trinity Place (53) revealed also that the Roman wall is preserved in mutilated state to a height of about 14 feet and again carries the mediaeval wall above street-level. The mediaeval wall retains its wall-walk and is at least 25 feet high above the Roman plinth, but has none of the structural refinements of the western sector.[1]

It has already been seen (pp. 71ff.) that some of the bastions have now to be accepted as mediaeval in origin and this might indicate that the mediaeval authorities felt obliged to extend the unequally distributed series that they inherited from the Romans. Bastions 12 and 14 have usually been quoted as examples of adaptation to mediaeval purposes, on the assumption that they were added to or rebuilt in their upper parts, which as with the wall were thought to use the surviving Roman structure as foundation or base. The original date of Bastion 12 is uncertain and that part of it which has long been visible above ground has been tidied up in relatively recent times. Bastion 14 can be seen to be mediaeval above street-level. Its typically varied stonework contains arrow-loops which are contemporary with the rest, as well as a single-light window, at present blocked, which looks late mediaeval (Plate 15). But the upper work in its present condition looks very different from that exposed at the lower level when the bastion was excavated

---

[1] Since the above was written the well-known stretch of wall to the north, formerly in Barber's Warehouse, Coopers Row (*Roman London*, Plate 23), has been re-exposed and consolidated. It is now the most impressive surviving portion of the wall in the City and Messrs. Sunley, who undertook the work at their own charges, are to be thanked for their public spirit and congratulated on the admirable appearance that these remains now present.

in 1947 (Plates 16, 17). The probability is that when the masonry is stripped of the modern brick and other obstructions now masking it it will be seen to be a structure of two building 'periods', both of them mediaeval.[1]

Opportunities of examining the city ditch have also been restricted. In Castle Street, just north of the fort gateway (5), the inner slope of this ditch was seen to cut across the shallow ditch, here flat-bottomed, which was associated with the Roman city wall. The mediaeval ditch went to a depth of about 10 feet below basement-level (19 feet below the street) but owing to obstructions could not be followed for more than a few feet (Fig. 3). At Cripplegate Buildings (18: where now stands Roman House) the evidence of a complicated section is more difficult to interpret. The post-Roman ditch-filling had been cut through by later disturbance and there were the remains of a massive timber framework supported on large square-sectioned piles. These constructions were of late mediaeval date and had the appearance of some kind of wharf or landing stage. Stow records that in 1569 a 'warf of tymber' was made 'from the head of the *Posterne* [i.e. Moorgate] into the towne ditch'.[2] It would appear that the same arrangement was provided at Cripplegate (Plate 28).

In 1965–6 changes in St. Giles Cripplegate Churchyard in connexion with the Barbican Redevelopment Scheme exposed partial profiles of the mediaeval ditch. It has not so far been possible to study a complete section and it seems likely in any case that here as elsewhere its outer part will have been destroyed by the fairly massive foundations of modern buildings which run with it along the inner side of the lip (see below). The general character of the ditch appeared however to be fairly consistent. It had a flattened-V section, with a width of 30–35 feet from a berm about 9 feet wide; its depth from the offset of the Roman wall (which seems to mark approximately also the base of the mediaeval wall hereabouts) varied between about 6 and about 9 feet. To a depth of 11 feet or more from the graveyard surface the ground

[1] The *Illustrated London News* drawing reproduced by the Royal Commission (*Roman London*, Plate 33) shows what appears to be a bonding course at a high level above the blocked window. It is doubtful whether there was such a feature and in any case it could not have been Roman. It has not survived. It should be added that it is most important that this bastion should receive the most detailed and careful examination when the time comes for its final treatment and consolidation. It would appear to be the last possible source of information; and its relationship to the wall, which is masked at the present time by modern brick, should receive particular attention.

[2] *Survey of London* (1908 ed.), I, p. 20.

was completely disturbed by burials; below this the filling of the ditch was a dark clayey silt with some dumped building rubbish and other debris. There was practically nothing in the way of small finds. The only significant piece was a sherd of 'bellarmine' ware which came from the black silt within 18 inches of the bottom of the ditch: since this was below the burial level it must be taken to indicate that the ditch was open to almost its full depth until (presumably) well into the sixteenth century. Also set in the bottom of the ditch, but towards its outer side were several upright stakes about 4 feet long, at intervals of about 6 feet, all leaning slightly westwards. These were squared timbers of about 5 inches scantling. Their purpose was not obvious and they showed no sign of having formed part of a single structure.

The observations at St. Giles have proved valuable for the interpretation of features observed in a 100-foot cutting that was made near Aldermanbury Postern (St. Alphage: *17*) in 1949–50.

Unfortunately-sited later obstructions here had destroyed the junctions of the surviving features in this cutting, so that not only was it impossible to see exactly how they were related to one another but also their original dimensions remain vague (Fig. 21). In spite of this, the profile of the Roman city ditch, its width 12–13 feet, was nearly complete. Beyond it were a broad U-sectioned ditch, apparently of two periods; and to the north of that a flat-bottomed expanse the full width of which could not be determined because it continued under Fore Street: its visible width was about 45 feet. The Roman ditch had a depth of about 6 feet below the probable level of the Roman berm, which would have been at or near the present cellar floor; the deeper U-sectioned ditch a depth of $9\frac{1}{2}$ feet; and the shallow flat bottomed area beyond a depth of 6 feet. (The last two may have been rather more if their contemporary surface was at all raised above what seems probable.)

From the evidence of the Cripplegate sections the conclusion is justified that the U-sectioned ditch here is at any rate one version of the mediaeval city ditch though its measurements appear to differ somewhat. The filling was in two parts: the lower dense and clayey and wet, particularly towards the base, but producing very little in the way of finds; the upper, defined at the base by a light sandy layer, somewhat similar but containing streaks of sand and yielding much seventeenth-century pottery (Plate 29). The upper part of the ditch had the appearance of a late re-cutting. Its scale did not make it a very effective obstacle, though its surviving depth of only $6\frac{1}{2}$ feet

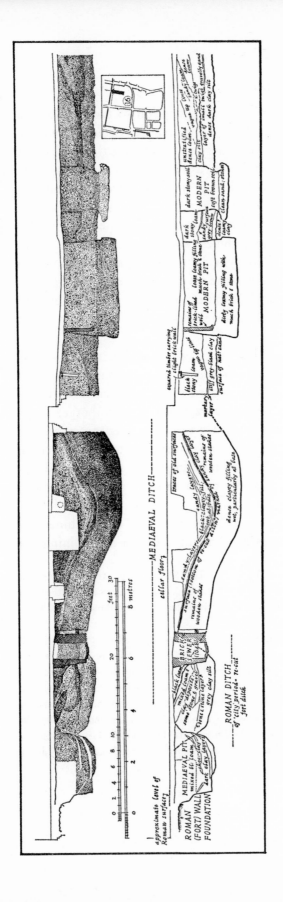

21. St. Alphage (17): section through the external ditches from the wall northwards to Fore Street.

may have been a good deal less than its original depth if by the seventeenth century the general surface of the ground in the area had risen as would be expected. A feature having a further bearing on its date was the brick-built sewer which appeared in this section as well as further west in Cripplegate churchyard to run more or less parallel with the wall: the sewer has been seen in the course of the recent work in the churchyard and was recorded outside Bastion 12 in 1901.[1] The contact between the sewer and the upper ditch-filling is not a very good one; it nevertheless suggests that the ditch was already in existence (and partly filled) when the sewer was constructed in 1648. A ditch open into the early part of the seventeenth century suggests a connexion with the Civil War; and while to the west there is no evidence of re-cutting the ditch south of Bastion 12 also seems to have been open at this time.

Although it is well established that in 1642–3 London was encircled by defences (with forts at intervals) to protect it from the threat of attack by the king's forces, the situation with regard to the original ditch fronting the city wall would seem to be still unresolved. Contemporary maps show that while in the mid-sixteenth century the ditch was preserved and open throughout the whole of its length from Aldersgate to the postern on Tower Hill,[2] by the following century buildings and gardens had encroached upon it in the Minories and Houndsditch sectors and the ditch is not shown at all.

Returning now to the St. Alphage section, it is this encroachment of buildings upon the ditch that makes for difficulty both in determining the

---

[1] J. Terry in *London and M'Sex Arch. Soc. Trans.*, VIII (1889–1903), p. 356; *Roman London*, Pl. 33. The fact that the sewer has lost its vault at St. Alphage, having been truncated by the cellar floor, is in itself an indication that the ground was higher by at least 3 feet in the seventeenth century and the ditch correspondingly deeper.

[2] On the Braun and Hogenberg map (*Civitates Orbis Terrarum*, 1st ed.), 1572, the ditch is shown unobstructed from Aldersgate to the Tower Hill postern. Newcomb's *An Exact Delineation of the Cities of London*, etc. (engraved by William Faithorne), 1658, has buildings confronting the ditch from All Hallows-on-the-Wall eastwards; houses have begun to encroach on the west from Cripplegate to St. Alphage, but from there to Bishopsgate is clear. On the other hand by 1666 (Hollar, *Map or Groundplot of the City of London*: cf. also Morden and Lea's map of 1682) the only exposed stretches of the wall on this side are the southward extension of St. Giles Cripplegate churchyard in front of Bastions 12 and 13 and the piece immediately confronting Moorfields: the rest is entirely houses and gardens.

size of the ditch itself—as in Cripplegate churchyard—and in relating it to other features in the section. The modern foundations are likely to be the more massive successors of the earlier walls which no doubt reluctantly respected the ditch while moving as far across its outer lip as their builders dared. At St. Alphage the modern foundation cuts the section at the point where the mediaeval ditch would have made contact with the flat expanse to the north: it is impossible therefore to say what their relationship was; to decide (for instance) whether the mediaeval ditch had been dug through the filling of the broad hollow or vice versa.

Until the evidence of Cripplegate churchyard became available it was thought likely that the broad hollow represented the original mediaeval ditch, which was 'begun to be made' according to Stow, '. . . in the yere 1211 & was finished in the yeare 1213'.[1] Stow goes on to say that the ditch was then made 'of 200. foot broad'; and while this dimension cannot have been constant there was the possibility that the St. Alphage feature might be part of the exceptionally broad stretch that according to the early maps fronted the wall in the Moorfields area. This possibility still remains and if it could ever be demonstrated as a fact would involve a rapid narrowing of the ditch on the west before Cripplegate is reached. On the other hand, the hollow may have been part of the waterlogged area of Moorfields, frequently referred to by Stow and other early writers from fitz Stephen (*ob.* 1191) downwards. The conditions are generally thought to have been due to the impeding of the natural drainage by the city wall, which acted as a dam, in spite of culverts left for the Walbrook and its tributaries. The sandy floor of the hollow was overlaid by nearly two feet of dense clay silt, dark grey in colour, which was completely barren of finds. The site was covered by mixed materials which looked as if they had been deliberately dumped in order to raise the level. Over the moor in general this activity went on into the sixteenth century; of it Stow said sceptically '. . . if it be made leuell with the Battlements of the Cittie Wall, yet will it bee little the dryer, such is the Moorish nature of that ground'.[2] The St. Alphage section suggests natural or semi-natural marsh conditions alleviated by the artificial raising of the ground level.

The encroachment of buildings upon the city ditch already mentioned, which took place at varying rates in different parts of the defences, marks

---

[1] *Survey of London* (1908 ed.), I, p. 19.   [2] *Op. cit.,* I, pp. 32–3.

the beginning of the final phase in the history of London Wall and its associated features. Stow, again, writes of the ditch 'now of late neglected and forced either to a verie narrow, and the same a filthie chanell, or altogither stopped vp for Gardens planted, and houses builded thereon, euen to the verie wall, and in many places vpon both ditch & wall houses to be builded, to what danger to the Citie, I leaue to wiser consideration: and can but wish that reformation might be had'. Buildings not only crossed the line of the ditch but were built up to and incorporated the wall in their structure. The Barber Surgeons' Hall in Monkwell Street, rebuilt by Inigo Jones in the year 1636,[1] used the city wall as its west wall and the brick-turned openings of Jones' windows still survive in damaged state: the neighbouring bastion (13) provided the dais for the Company's court-room. Further south, towards Falcon Square, the wall became simply a party wall. Here and elsewhere it suffered in response to the demand for increased space within the buildings. Sometimes the results were curious. They were best illustrated just south of Bastion 14 in a piece of the wall which unfortunately no longer survives (Plate 30). Occupiers of the buildings along the wall evidently set themselves to cut back or remove entirely the massive stonework, replacing it where necessary with a slighter wall of brick. But the process of replacement was often incomplete. In the stretch referred to, the older wall had been entirely replaced at ground-floor level by a modern brick wall. Above, the original wall, here of mediaeval date, had survived, to provide the unusual spectacle, contrary to the normal archaeological succession, of the earlier, mediaeval masonry above and supported by later, nineteenth-century, brick. The effect of cutting back and similar treatment may also be seen in the inner face of the mediaeval wall at the west end of the St. Alphage stretch, beyond the churchyard; and the probability is that the irregular behaviour of the modern wall in Noble Street is due to similar erratic treatment of the city wall.[2]

[1] Roy. Com. Hist. Mons., England, *London (The City)* (1929), pp. 115–16.

[2] Perhaps the most striking example of this was uncovered in 1965 at the east end of the Cripplegate churchyard sector. The city wall here was cut back from both sides so that about a foot of its core survives between facings of modern brick.

8. NOTE ON THE NORTH-WESTERN SECTIONS OF LONDON WALL
PRESERVED AS A RESULT OF THE BOMBING
IN THE SECOND WORLD WAR

As the outcome of the investigations above summarised, the Corporation of the City of London has been able to extend its modern policy of conserving the city wall wherever possible. A fortunate combination of circumstances has resulted in the preservation to view of elements covering all the phases represented in the Moorgate–Cripplegate area and they are listed below in order from north-east to south-west.

(a) *The city wall near Moorgate* (*23*). A piece of the city wall about 37 feet long, standing 11 feet high, is preserved in the underground car park of London Wall (Route 11) about 400 feet west of Moorgate.

(b) *St. Alphage* (*17*). This stretch of wall, long visible on the inside in St. Alphage churchyard, is now visible on the exterior also and displays at least two phases of mediaeval reconstruction, resting upon the refaced earlier Roman wall. The relationship of the two phases of the Roman wall, fort wall and addition of city-wall 'date', can be seen in section at cellar level at the west end of the churchyard.

(c) *Cripplegate churchyard* (*1a*). The remains of Bastion 11A and the stretch of Roman and mediaeval wall to the east, with the fragment of an internal turret on the fort wall behind the bastion. Awaiting treatment as part of the Barbican Scheme with (d) below. These features were exposed for the first time within living memory in 1965.

(d) *The Cripplegate–Castle Street bastions*. Bastions 12–14, in 1965 awaiting (with the adjoining surviving lengths of wall) full exposure and treatment as part of the replanning of the area.

(e) *The west gate of the Cripplegate fort* (*5*). Preserved in the underground car park at the west end of London Wall (Route 11).

(f) *The Noble Street sector*. This consists of the double Roman wall, still carrying in one place at its northern end a mediaeval fragment (*6*); an internal-turret of the fort (*7*); and the south-west angle, with its turret, the junction with the Aldersgate length of the city wall and the surviving portion of Bastion 15 (*8, 9*). Final consolidation of these remains awaits the completion of redevelopment schemes in the area.

IV

The Temple of Mithras and its Surroundings

---

1. INTRODUCTION

THE Temple of Mithras lay in one of the largest single bomb-damaged areas at the City's centre. Here the block bounded on the west by Sise Lane, on the north by Queen Victoria Street and Bucklersbury, on the east by Walbrook, on the south by Cannon Street had been almost completely destroyed, $1\frac{1}{2}$ acres in all (*44, 45*). The site as a whole was one on which the excavators had long cast covetous eyes, for in relation to the early city it was one of great potential importance; but it was deeply covered with bomb-rubble and other obstructions and there was very little room in which to work. In 1951, Mr. Owen Campbell Jones, the architect, whose firm had long taken a practical interest in the antiquities of Roman London, very kindly informed the Council that plans were being prepared for a new building for the area. A beginning was then made on a series of cuttings east-to-west across it in such vacant spaces as were available (Fig. 22).

2. THE WALBROOK VALLEY

The primary aim of this operation had originally been a study of the valley of the Walbrook stream, about which little of an exact nature is known, though it has figured frequently in discussions of the City's past. Unlike the Fleet River, Walbrook has not survived as an underground watercourse. It has been lost to the sight of Londoners for a very long time, though its traditional (and no doubt actual) outfall to the Thames can still be seen in the small Dowgate Dock, a little to the west of Cannon Street railway bridge. For the rest, the stream survives in the name of the narrow street (not in 1965 as narrow as it was) linking the Bank area with Cannon Street; and in the records of its course, real or supposed, that have been left by observers hampered by the difficult conditions of the past.

These observations are conveniently summarised in *Roman London*.[1] They have led to various conclusions about the size and character of the stream towards which the writer of the introduction to that inventory displayed a scepticism which is fully supported by the results of work in recent years. These conclusions appear to have been inspired, partly by misunderstandings of the nature of the deposits, most of which, even where they were 'river silt', do not appear necessarily to have defined the course of the stream, partly (apparently) by confusion of the width of the valley with the width of the stream. The sections cut across the southern part of the Walbrook valley in the months before the temple was identified showed that about 400 yards inland from the present river-frontage the main watercourse itself could not have been more than about 14 feet wide and was comparatively shallow withal. The main stream flowed fairly directly to the Thames along a line which hereabouts was towards the east side of the valley; but there were subsidiary rivulets to the west and at the beginning of the Roman occupation the valley floor had been comparatively wet, with some flooding beyond the limits of the streams themselves.

The sections completed after an interval in 1953–4 revealed this part of the Walbrook valley as a shallow basin 290–300 feet across (Fig. 23*a*): on the west its edge coincided generally with Sise Lane, on the east with the Walbrook street. The process of raising the levels by the artificial dumping of material began at an early stage and was particularly well illustrated on the west side of the main channel, directly opposite the temple.

Sections here (Fig 23*b*) presented a succession of artificial deposits with their associated timber elements, preserved because of the waterlogged nature of the area as a whole. The deposits consisted of layers of mixed and variable material, often containing much clay, put down to provide fresh

[1] pp. 15–16.

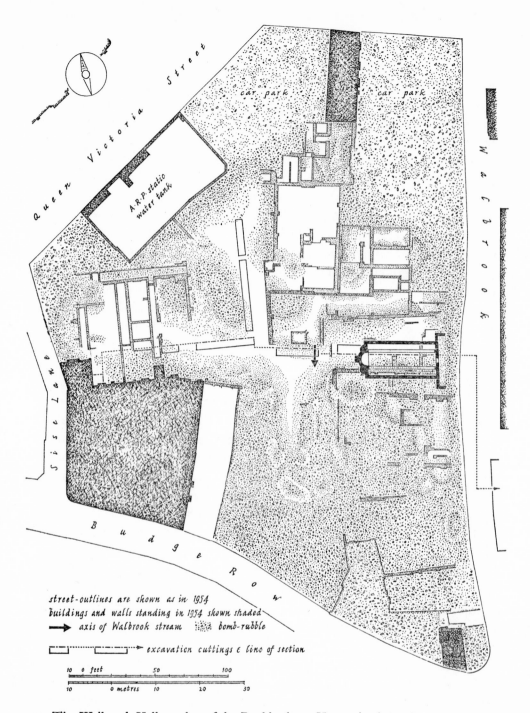

street-outlines are shown as in 1954
buildings and walls standing in 1954 shown shaded
➤ axis of Walbrook stream ░ bomb-rubble

⌐ ⌐ ⌐ ➤ excavation cuttings & line of section

10 0 feet   50   100

10   0 metres   10   20   30

22. The Walbrook Valley: plan of the Bucklersbury House site (*44, 45*), showing the temple of Mithras and cuttings in the area in relation to the distribution of bomb-rubble.

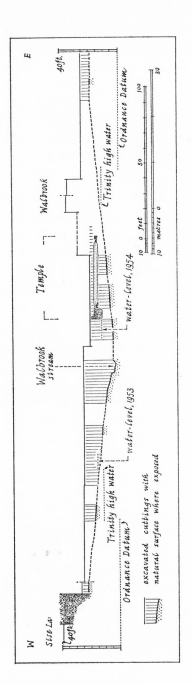

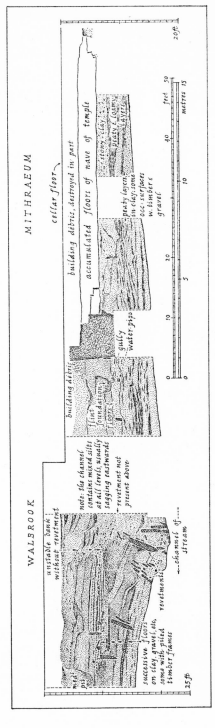

23a. Composite section across the Walbrook site (Bucklersbury House) (44, 45).

b. Detailed section, simplified, of the middle part of a.

living-surfaces. The timber structures were mainly related to the floors themselves or to the various devices used for dealing with the wet conditions on the site. These devices included a number of gutters whose construction followed a constant pattern (Plate 31). They were flat-bottomed, up to about 2 feet wide and perhaps 6–8 inches deep, plank-floored, with their vertical sides revetted with planks which were held in place by pegs driven into the ground against them on both sides. In several places were found wooden pipe-lines formed of bored lengths of timber, quadrangular in section, with iron collars.[1] One such, a few feet west of the temple, was still functioning and adding its quota to the continually accumulating water in the cuttings during the excavation.

Apart from the temple, the only stone building in the area was represented by a small scrap of mosaic on the east side of the stream and towards the north. The remaining buildings were all of timber. It was at no time possible to recover the complete plan of any one of these buildings and interest concentrates therefore on the methods employed by their builders to ensure their stability on a not very satisfactory site. On the eastern margin of the area during building operations on another site there had been an opportunity of observing the Roman use of wooden piles to under-pin a stone building, a method which has been recorded elsewhere. On this, the wetter part of the area, underpinning was extensively employed to support the wooden floors on which some of the huts appeared to have been erected (Plate 32). Short (3–4-foot) closely-set piles were driven into the ground in parallel lines to carry quite massive beams, resembling modern railway sleepers. The beams seem to have been laid at right angles, with overlapping ends to form a framework, on which was laid in turn a plank floor. Some of the planks seen were up to 15 inches wide. As has already been said, it was impossible to recover a complete plan because, as usual, more ground could not be opened up: it would appear, however, that timber buildings were erected actually upon these floors, perhaps being assembled in prefabricated parts.

Away from the stream towards the north-west, there were indications of huts of a more normal kind, in an area which was not as waterlogged either in Roman or in more recent times (44). Here was a succession of hut-floors

---

[1] For the type see *London in Roman Times* (London Mus. Catalogue: 1930), p. 39 and Plate XII.

—or working-floors—irregular in contour, at least one of which was over-laid by the remains of a collapsed thatched roof. In the cutting that produced these remains there were signs of leather-working. One surface still bore the surviving portions of a skin held down by the pegs which had been used to stretch it for cutting up; and amongst the fragments of leather were recognisable parts of shoes.

The picture of this part of the Walbrook as presented by the 1950 in-vestigations is therefore that of a shallow valley, wet in places, its surface in process of being built up artificially and carrying at times (in its earlier phases) remnants of the birch and alder thickets that would no doubt have been its natural vegetation—certainly a curious set of conditions for an area at the centre of the chief city of the Roman Province. But there was no significant change in this situation throughout the whole of the Roman period; for while the datable material has yet to be examined in detail a superficial examination shows that the sequence came down to the late fourth century at least. Surfaces of this date capped in the shallower areas about 6–8 feet of deposit, about 4 feet below the cellar floors as existing in the 1950's and 23 feet below the modern street.

The stream itself must however have been brought under control at quite an early date. Mention has already been made of the smaller rivulets of which there were indications towards the west side of the valley. These did not outlast the earliest periods and it must be assumed that at some point above Bucklersbury they were diverted into the main stream, thus no doubt simplifying communications and bringing more ground into use. However this may be, immediately west of the temple the flow of water along the stream-bed was controlled by revetments of planks held in place by fairly massive dressed uprights; and the building up of the surface as already described went on behind these constructions, which in time were often forced outwards over the stream by the growing pressure of the material behind them (Fig 23b). The period of the timber-revetted channel was succeeded by one in which the banks were less stable, though the process of raising the surface continued: this state of affairs seems to have prevailed through late Roman and early post-Roman times. For some centuries, therefore, the lower part of the Walbrook stream, judging both by this evidence and by surface indications, did not vary its course in the slightest. It must have flown pretty directly to the Thames, as can be seen by the dip in Cannon Street, which no doubt reflects the natural contours beneath the modern surface.

3. THE TEMPLE OF MITHRAS

The Temple of Mithras (45) was thus set in an area which had a character markedly different from what would have been expected so near to the known centre of Londinium. There was no concentration here of stone buildings of quality but a shallow somewhat depressing valley with a tendency to wetness, and a scatter of timber huts and a sporadic industrial activity. When the temple was built, at a date provisionally fixed towards the end of the second century A.D., deposits up to 8 feet deep had accumulated on the eastern side of the stream. Lying east-to-west the building itself projected pier-wise into this raised ground; but at its east end with its vestibule would almost certainly have confronted a street, the predecessor of the modern street, which may be guessed to have followed the lip of the basin, running more or less parallel with the stream itself.

While this is not the place in which to attempt a detailed account of the temple and its exploration, it should be said that only the generous co-operation of the site-owners, Messrs. Legenland, and the contractors, Messrs. Humphreys, made possible the extended excavation by which the ground was opened up beyond the original cutting to enable the near-complete plan of the building to be recovered. The result was to reveal the main body of the temple as a rectangular building $58\frac{1}{2}$ feet long by 26 feet wide, entered from the east end, with a semi-circular apse or sanctuary at the west (plan, Fig. 24; Plate 33). The building was remarkably free from later disturbance; and though there had been some inevitable destruction not the least surprising feature of this aspect of the site was the way in which even modern foundations had not seriously damaged it.

As already mentioned, attached to the east end was a narthex or vestibule, the ends of which projected beyond the side-walls of the main building to give it an overall width of $36\frac{1}{2}$ feet. The complete building would thus have been T-shaped in plan; but some part of the narthex lay—and still lies—under the modern street. Its full depth from front to back remains unknown.

Externally the most impressive feature of the building must have been the apse with its massive buttresses, themselves an indication of the unstable

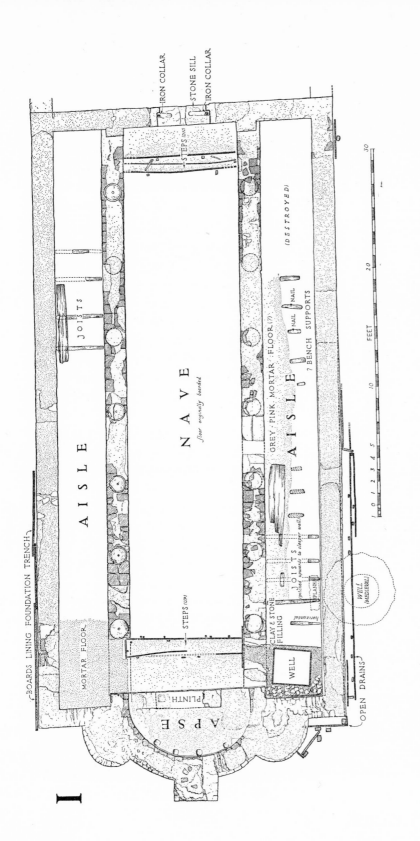

24. The Temple of Mithras: plan of the original building as revealed by excavation.

nature of the ground on which the temple had been built. The convex buttresses in the re-entrant angles of apse and west wall seen from the outside would have suggested that the temple had a triple apse; but the buttresses were solid.

Entrance to the temple by way of the narthex was through a double door-way, the original features of which were remarkably well-preserved (Plate 34). The sill was a single block of stone making a double step down, with much-worn margins on the inner side. In the door-rebates the sockets still retained the iron collars for the door-pivots. Immediately within the door, double steps downwards, their wooden risers in place, gave on to the sunk floor of the central body of the temple.

Internally the building was revealed as of basilican plan, with nave and side-aisles defined by sleeper-walls which had carried the stone-columned arcades: the positions of the columns were marked only by their settings; their number, seven aside, probably symbolised the seven grades of the cult. There were indications that the floor of the nave had originally been boarded, though the one or two boards which survived were no longer in their original positions. The aisle floors were at a higher level, and here the signs of timber fittings were more definite. On both north and south transverse joists supporting occasional planks had survived; and there were vertical earth-set uprights also which might have carried fixed benches (Plate 36). Such equipment was a normal part of the aisles of a mithraeum, since on them members of the community would have gathered to witness the ritual performed before the altars at the west end.

Along the front wall of the apse (Plate 42) two steps upwards from the nave floor corresponded with those at the entrance. The upper step was wider than the lower, no doubt to accommodate the altars which would have been ranged below the Mithras Tauroctonus, the representation of the god slaying the sacred bull, the chief image of the temple. There were indications that the opening of the apse had been divided into three parts by a pair of columns on a central raised plinth: an arrangement which would have enhanced the withdrawn mysterious quality of the image on the high floor of the apse. Finally, in the south-west corner beside the apse was the shallow timber-lined well which through the early years of the temple's history provided the water required for ritual purposes.

But the building did not retain its original basilican features: long before

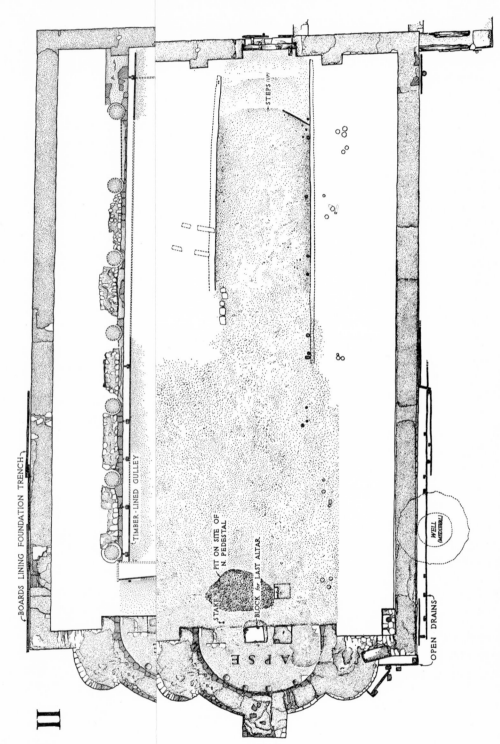

II

BOARDS LINING FOUNDATION TRENCH

'TIMBER-LINED GULLEY

STEPS (UP)

PIT ON SITE OF
N PEDESTAL

STAKE

BLOCK for LAST ALTAR

A P S E

WELL
(MEDIEVAL)

OPEN DRAINS

25. The Temple of Mithras: later phases in the building's development.

the end of its useful life it had undergone many changes which in part at least were a reflection of the local ground conditions (Fig. 25). The wet nature of the site must from the first have given trouble with standing water. The floor-level, first of the nave, then of the body of the temple as a whole, was gradually lifted through a succession of surfaces. The final result was to raise the general level to that of the apse (a matter of about 40 inches above the original surface of the nave); but the changes were not carried out at the same rate everywhere because different parts of the building had their own special functions to fulfil and were therefore treated differently. There were nine successive floors in all in the nave, and before the last had been reached the door-sill had already been covered, making necessary a different arrangement for working the doors, with a wooden frame taking the place of the original socket-and-pivot device. The waterlogged nature of the site had its problems for the modern excavator also; but one overriding advantage at least was that the wet conditions were admirable for the preservation of organic materials, so that wooden features survived, not as flimsy and elusive ghosts, but as their solid original selves.

It is impossible here to describe in detail each individual phase in the building's history. The two most important in their effect on its general character related to nave floors 3 and 7 respectively. In the former an attempt was still being made to retain the difference in level between nave- and aisle-floors or benches which is a standard feature of all mithraea. With the construction of the third floor this difference in level was no longer adequately maintained. The aisle floors were therefore raised also above the tops of the sleeper-walls which had previously contained them and short lengths of walling were now built on top of the sleeper-walls, between the columns, to provide a revetment for these additions (Plate 37). The only variation in this treatment was in the third bay from the west on the south side. Here planks on edge replaced the stone wall and the bay was defined by a timber framework—differences which suggested that this particular bay served some special function (Plate 38).

The second series of changes was more drastic and must have involved a large-scale remodelling of the upper part of the building. It may be that the primary cause of this was a structural weakness. Movement of the south wall had taken place with serious consequences for the south-western corner, where a large hole in the angle of convex buttress and wall had been packed with a large slightly-damaged column-drum. (It is not certain that the drum itself actually came from the temple.) Whether or not these events are closely related, however—and it is practically impossible to 'date' the repair just described—the columns were taken down, the holes left by them being filled with stones.

It is not easy to visualise the effect of these changes and at least two explanations of them are possible. One is that the series of quite rough (and slight) timber posts which was set up along the south side only, may have provided support for a new and lighter roof. As they were found by the excavators these posts occurred in some numbers, singly and in clusters, along the line of the sleeper-wall, sometimes over, sometimes beside it. But they were obviously not all of the same date; and some of them had been driven forcibly on to the top of the wall without actually penetrating it (Plate 43), in such a way as to suggest that the existence of the wall was not realised by those responsible for putting in those particular posts. The wall had, of course, been lost to sight for some time when many of these timbers were inserted.

There was no corresponding arrangement of posts along the north side of the temple at any time in its later history, though here too the columns had been taken away. If therefore the posts served as supports for a pitched roof the result must have been of lop-sided appearance—an odd-sounding arrangement which would have resembled that of many modern factory roofs.

The alternative interpretation, suggested by Professor Frere, would replace columns and architraves by a beam and king-post construction, the ends of the beams resting on the outer (aisle) walls, since the removal of the arcades must have meant also the dismantling of the clerestory above them. On a normal interpretation of the plan of the original building this must have meant some lowering of the overall height of the temple, since the aisles would not have been as high as the nave. The height could only have been maintained by adding to the aisle walls. The width between walls (22 feet) is not an impossible span for scarfed timbers: beams of up to 17 feet were actually used in the later stages in the temple itself (see below). Under this arrangement the posts along the south side would relate to a bench or screen; and while the difference between north and south would remain the result would have been to open up the interior of the temple and give a view of the sanctuary which would have been impossible while the columns were in place.

Whatever the truth about these arrangements—and it must be admitted that there are difficulties about both of the interpretations set out above—the structural and other evidence certainly suggests that in its later years the temple had become a somewhat ramshackle affair. Yet throughout it retained its essential division of nave and side-aisles or benches. Beams were laid lengthwise now along the body of the temple from apse to east wall. They followed approximately the line of the original sleeper-walls, running thus with the timber uprights. They supported the joists of a wooden floor, one or two of which had survived (Plates 39, 40). But the joists lay outwards from beam to main wall, across the aisles: they did not extend across the nave. The nave now appeared therefore as an earth or mortar floor only a little lower than the aisle floors on each side of it: the difference was no more than the thickness of the longitudinal beams *plus* the timbers of the floors that they supported.

But this was not the final development. The last floor of the temple at the west end was level with the floor of the apse, which hitherto had always been at a higher level than any other surface in the temple (Plate 41). This was a continuous floor, extending across the full width of the building, doing away with the nave-aisle division and masking the great beams, that on the south remaining unmoved in its place. To the east, however, the division was still maintained, the build-up of the floors being carried out separately to leave the beams exposed: the floor level was now appreciably higher even than the raised door-sill and the surface sloped upwards from the sill in a couple of irregular steps.

The dates of these major changes, with all their pronounced effects upon the appearance and character of the building, will not be exactly determined until the considerable amount of pottery from the site has been worked over: here, as elsewhere in this book, all comments on this aspect of the subject are given with the warning that some adjustment may be called for in the light of more complete evidence. The limited series of coins from different levels of the temple suggests that, as already mentioned, the building was erected towards the end of the second century A.D.; floor 3 of the nave produced a coin of Marius (A.D. 268) and was probably laid during the late third century. The latest floors (5–9), on the other hand, were put down at a time well into the fourth century. Coins of this period (Constantine I (308–20), Urbs Roma (330–7), Licinius I (307–34)) came from levels in the altar area before the apse which corresponded approximately with floors 5 and 6 in the nave. From floor 6A came a fragmentary dedicatory inscription with a reference to the four Augusti, which must have been dismantled after, perhaps some time after, A.D. 307–8 (Plate 52). The make-up of floor 8 produced a coin of Constantine II as Caesar (A.D. 330–5).

The major changes had naturally been attended by modifications in the furniture and fittings of the temple. The well in the south-west corner must have been filled in and covered over some time before the last floor was made: overlying it in the later periods was a masonry block, built into the angle and containing a post-hole 5 inches across (Plate 35). The filling of the post-hole produced a small roundel of marble decorated with cult-symbols and it is thought that the hole may have held an upright on which votive or similar objects were hung. What substitute was provided for the original well is not known. In the last phase a wooden 'box' was sunk into the floor in the north-east corner of the building—the point furthest from the apse. It was intended to take a liquid of some kind, for its pit was lined with a thick layer of impervious clay. Its filling gave no clue as to what it had contained or as to the purpose it had served: one possible explanation would regard it as a substitute for the original well.

Changes also took place in front of the apse, which was always the focal point for ritual. The steps had certainly been buried by the time that floor 3 came to be laid: the arrangement of altars that would have stood in this position originally cannot therefore be known. On floor 5, however, a few feet back from the face of the apse, a pedestal-like stone stood in a position which it continued to occupy throughout the remaining process of building up the floors, its broken top just appearing through the surface of the final floor (Plate 42).

This stone is apparently without parallel: it is not an altar in the normal sense. Its back, towards the apse, is flat; on its south and east faces it has a heavy chamfered plinth; on the north there is a low shoulder-like projection. The complete form of the top of the pillar (which as it survives is 20 inches high) is uncertain: there are the remains of a broad groove or slot directed towards the apse, but the sides were broken away. The stone was set to south of the centre line of the temple and there can be little doubt that it had been one of a pair placed symmetrically. Its companion had remained in place beside it until a late stage, to be removed some time after the last floor was laid. An irregular hole had been dug to extract it, the rough filling of which contrasted with the smooth surface of the surrounding floor.

Other features must be mentioned briefly, though they are not readily explained on present knowledge. They were a small timber-lined box sunk in the middle of floor 3 of the nave and various pieces of narrow planking set on edge obliquely towards the east end in floors 6 and 7. At the west end, in front of the apse, there were the remains of a number of small wooden stakes of varying sizes and sections which had been driven vertically into the floor from more than one level; one such was something over 10 inches long overall, its broken top just showing in the final floor. Such stakes could not have formed part of any kind of structure. A possible explanation for them is that they served to carry votive offerings: the fact that they were concentrated in the altar area supports their use for some kind of ritual purpose.

Not that all the altars had been set before the apse. Commonly altars were placed along the nave-sides and an example on the south side here was of interest both for its position and as an indication of the decline that had taken place in the temple's fortunes. For the altar was simply the top of a small column the moulded capital of which had been squared off and the shaft tapered for insertion in the soft floor, to form a makeshift which stood only a few inches above the surface. The top of the capital had been irregularly hollowed to provide the rough *focus* in which the offering would have been burnt (Plate 39).

One other structural feature calls for comment. It related to floor 3 of the nave and consisted of a gully or channel along the inner face of the north sleeper-wall. The channel was 8 inches wide and 12 deep. It was lined on the side away from the wall with thin planks supported internally by oblong-sectioned uprights. The supports were braced against external pressure by wooden distance-pieces, which were nailed horizontally to their tops and were of sufficient length to bear against the face of the sleeper wall at their inner ends. The excellent state of preservation of the timber made it possible to see exactly how the arrangement had been contrived.

Because the strictly basilican plan is not commonly used for mithraea the excavation was well advanced before it was realised that the cult concerned with the Walbrook temple was that of Mithras—and, indeed, even the first discovery of a Mithraic sculpture might have had only an accidental relationship with the building. This, a fragment of a large figure of one of the god's companions, was found with two plain altars and some building fragments in débris outside the south wall. The figure, carved in a niche, is about half life-size and only the lower part survives: sufficient remains, however, to show that the subject represented is Cautopates (Night), in his characteristic stance with legs crossed and symbolical torch turned downwards. With a companion representation of Cautes (Day), with torch turned upwards, this figure would have been set up near the east end of the temple, the two confronting one another across the nave.

Final doubts, however, were dispelled by the discovery of the head of Mithras as the first of the series of outstanding pieces of sculpture which as a whole can be claimed the equal of any so far recorded in the Western Roman Empire.[1] The sculptures were actually found in two groups, the first, made up of the Mithras and the Minerva, in a depression in the later material overlying the north sleeper wall near the first column-setting from the east; the second, consisting of the Serapis, the large hand and the Mercury, from another irregular hollow in the floor of the nave just inside the entrance, where it was accompanied by a stone water-stoup or bowl, mouth downwards, the base of which just showed in the floor-surface (Plate 47). The Mithras and the Minerva had been protected by fragments of roofing-tile laid over them: there was no indication that the second group had been protected in the same way.

The head of Mithras as found was in a delicate state. The surface of the marble was 'sugary' and heavily encrusted with iron deposits from the rather moist gravelly layer which had been in contact with it for so long. The neck was found as a separate piece: the two parts were treated and joined in the British Museum Research Laboratory under Dr. H. J. Plenderleith's direction (Plate 44).

Unlike the other images, the Mithras is not a conventional portrait. The eyes look upwards; and seen from certain angles there is a sense of tension

[1] For an authoritative detailed account of the sculptures from the temple see Jocelyn M. C. Toynbee, *Art in Roman Britain* (Phaidon, 1962), pp. 2–3 and nos. 12, 20, 24, 29, 31–2, 36–8, 61, 69, 110. Nos. 31–2 and 69 are the finds made in 1889.

about the neck which suggests that the head is intended to be turning away or slightly straining backwards. On this evidence it is justifiable to assume that the head was only part of a larger subject the remainder of which was removed, leaving no trace behind. There can indeed be no doubt that the subject would have been a Bull-slaying, in which the god is usually represented in the attitude above described.

There are of course many complete examples of the Mithras Tauroctonus from Roman Mithraea. Here it is fitting to refer to the London sculpture which, found in 1889, is now known to have come from this temple (Plate 45). On this block, 17 inches high by 20 wide, the various participants are shown in their characteristic relationships at the moment of crisis in the Mithraic legend when the bull is slain. The left hand of the god pulls back the animal's head while his right hand plunges the dagger into its shoulder: the god's head is turned away and upwards. Cautes and Cautopates, the attendants of Mithras, are set one on each side of the main group, and there are other symbolical creatures both as part of the main scene and outside it. It seems very likely that the head found in 1954 was part of the sculptured group which would have been set upon the apse, for while other fragments show that there was at least one other representation of the same subject the quality of this piece amongst Roman work is outstanding.

Something of a problem is presented by the 'sugary' condition of the surface of the Phrygian cap over the god's forehead, which in the opinion of the experts is due to the action of fire. No sign of the effects of fire was observed anywhere in the temple itself, so that the possibility of damage from a general fire must be ruled out: it may be that the damage to the head was due to contact with torches or the like in the course of ritual activities on the apse.

The head of Minerva, unlike that of Mithras, can be regarded as a portrait (Plate 46). Here the marble is undamaged though unusually dark in colour. The head has a somewhat boyish look and when found, in the dusk of a long day, was thought to be male. The treatment of the hair, however, is that of a woman; and the identity of the deity is fixed by the fact that originally the head had carried a metal helmet. This would have rested on the plain band above the forehead, and the artificial arrangement of the hair round the ears was also intended to accommodate the helmet. Finally, the top and back of the head have been left rough and towards the front there are two holes, part of the device for keeping the helmet in position.

Of the second group, the hand is roughly $1\frac{1}{2}$ times natural size (Plate 50). A somewhat mechanical rendering of the subject, it clasps the handle of a dagger which has at its base a hole for a (presumably) metal blade, now missing. Behind the wrist projects a $4\frac{1}{2}$-inch iron shank set in lead. The hand could conceivably be part of another Tauroctonus, but the mere size of a single figure on a comparable scale must rule out this interpretation of it. The hand can only be a piece of symbolism, for which there appears to be a parallel from the mithraeum of Santa Prisca in Rome.[1]

The Mercury (Hermes) stands apart from the other pieces for its worn and damaged condition (Plate 49). Not only are its surfaces blurred, and the base detached from the main body of the subject: the figure itself had been broken across in antiquity—an accident which led to the loss of the right hand—and had been repaired by a rivet through the left knee. The figure has all the attributes of the god. In the hair are two small wings; the left hand carries a bag-purse; the right foot rests on the tortoise from whose shell the first lyre was made. The ram reclines at the god's side to symbolise his function as the guardian of flocks and herds.

The outstanding piece in the second group is the head of Jupiter Serapis (Plate 48), a remarkably preserved work with an exquisitely finished creamy-patinated surface. Serapis, a divinity of mixed Greek and Egyptian origins, is god of the Nile, god of the underworld, and god of fertility. The last function is symbolised by the corn-measure (*modius*) carried on the head, with its decoration of sprays of olive and the small hole in its upper surface in which were placed ears of corn. The head had suffered slight damage in antiquity: the rim of the *modius* was chipped and two of the locks over the forehead were broken.

From what has been said it will be clear that these two groups of images had been deliberately buried. The floor containing them was in use at the end of the third and in the early part of the fourth century. The dating-evidence other than that of the pottery is as follows: from the underlying floor 4 a coin of Gallienus (A.D. 260–8) and a barbarous radiate; from

---

[1] *Illustrated London News*, 8 January 1955, p. 61. The hand, which is not illustrated, is said to be 'a large gilded right hand, which like that found in the Walbrook Mithraeum holds part of a rod, perhaps an oar or part of a cornucopia'.

floors 6–6A the 'four Augusti' slab of A.D. 307–8, which, as noted on p. 104, would presumably not have been discarded until some time after this date. It is of course a well-known fact that in the rivalry between Christianity and Mithraism at this time many Mithraic communities resorted to burying their images and dismantling their temples to prevent their desecration by the Christians. In the Walbrook Mithraeum, however, the building was not given up after the sculptures above described were buried: two floors succeeded that which contained the sculptures, and it must be assumed that the temple continued in use, apparently without a break, until at least the middle of the fourth century. As already stated (p. 104) coin and other evidence, tentative as it must be at present, indicated that the last phase of the building went on until this time.

What may be called the last structural feature in the temple was found, as might have been expected, at the west end (Plate 42). Here, on the chord of the apse a rectangular hole had been dug in the final floor. In the hole had been inserted a rough stone block, evidently a base or support for an altar—the last to be set up, though at this time one at least of its predecessors was presumably still showing above the floor surface. The block was supported on a number of pieces of timber laid in an oblong frame. From the black soil enclosed by the wood came a small votive deposit which included two coins, one of Licinius I (A.D. 307–24), the other of Constantine the Great, of the period A.D. 309–13, and from the London mint. The coins are in fairly good condition, indicating that the block must have been put in place in the early decades of the fourth century.

One other important discovery belongs to this last period. The last major piece of sculpture was found, not buried, but lying on the final floor near the north-west corner, in which at this time was the wooden container already described (p. 104). By a sad misunderstanding this piece was irretrievably damaged before it was recovered: there is reason to believe that as it lay in the ground it was more complete than it now is. The subject is the god Bacchus (Dionysus) with some of his companions (Plate 51). The god is the central figure. Behind and above him is a vine: his arms are raised into its branches, in which also is entwined a serpent. To the god's right is a growing tree-trunk probably not part of the vine: on it sat a figure of Pan of which only the left leg survives. In front of the vine the fat drunkard, Silenus, sits side-saddle on his donkey, his wine-cup clasped to his stomach. On the god's left are two more companions, a satyr and a maenad, their heads damaged, accompanied by a panther.

On the basis of the sculpture is roughly incised the inscription, HOMINIBVS BAGIS BITAM, a difficult phrase meaning apparently '(give) life to men who wander': the B's are interchangeable with the V of classical Latin. This piece is later than the other sculptures (mid-third as compared with the latter part of the second century) but while it lacks their quality it is not without a charm of its own. From the fact that it was found lying on the last floor of the building it may be assumed to have remained to the end as part of the furnishings of the temple.

The identification of the Walbrook temple has resolved the mystery of a long-standing London discovery to which reference has already been made (p. 107). The find in question consists of a group of three pieces of sculpture, the Mithraic relief already described, a head and torso of a sea- or river-god, and a small figure, the head missing, of a Bonus Eventus (Good Fortune) or perhaps a personal god or *Genius*. These pieces, from the Ransome Collection, are now in the London Museum; it is recorded of them only that they were found 'at the middle of the Walbrook at a depth of 20 feet'.[1] The Mithraic panel has of course long been recognised as a clue to the existence of a mithraeum in the area: the hint that it provided when the temple was found was not taken because, as already stated, the building was not obviously of Mithraic type and was thought in the absence of knowledge of the rest of the area to be perhaps only one of several temples in close proximity to one another. In fact, the definition of the position of the find of 1889 fits neatly the siting of the temple, and there can be no real doubt that all the earlier marbles were part of the furnishings of the building. What cannot now be known is the circumstances that attended the discovery. These marbles also may well have been deliberately buried; on the other hand like other more fragmentary pieces (below) they may have been lying sporadically in the temple or its neighbourhood. In any case, the amount of modern rebuilding that had taken place along the western side of Walbrook (the street, not the stream) was such that the sculptures may have come from any foundation-trench thereabouts which penetrated to Roman levels.

The images in the temple were not limited to those already described:

[1] *London in Roman Times* (London Museum, 1930), pp. 44–6.

there were others which, like the Cautopates, had not received such careful treatment. One fragment evidently belonged to another Tauroctonus on a much smaller scale: it was part of the draped left forearm of the god, the hand clasping the bull's muzzle. The material is oolitic limestone from the Cotswold area. Two other fragments were the torsos of small male figures, one found in the filling of the small room at the south end of the narthex, the other built into an isolated masonry base, apparently of late fourth-century date, which was revealed some distance away on the west side of the Walbrook stream while the excavation of the temple was still in its preliminary stages. It is difficult to account for this scattering of damaged statues. It might be taken to indicate that the temple had suffered some degree of damage with the dispersal of some of its possessions. In fact, however, there is no evidence that this was so. It has been seen that the condition of the building declined as time went on; and while the large-scale remodelling that took place in the early fourth century might be regarded as catastrophic it does not seem to have marked any break in occupation: the floors succeeded one another with regularity, with no intervening deposit that could be regarded as destruction-layer.

A few other features call for comment. As to the narthex, the area available for examination was so limited that not much can be said about it. It would appear, however, that the original intention had been to build a narthex the same width as the main building and the foundations of the outer walls were extended eastwards with this in view. In practice, however, this foundation was never used. It was sealed by a clay floor at the level of the door-sill which covered the whole area of the extended narthex, the walls of which, with drains passing through them at low level, were built against the corners of the temple proper in straight joints. The part of the narthex south of the temple doorway had been cut off from the rest to make a separate chamber by the building of a secondary wall eastwards from the temple wall. This wall also appeared to be a late addition: it was not bonded into the main wall and its foundation was at a comparatively high level.

Certain of the small finds from the floors are of interest for their bearing on temple practices, about which little is known. Amongst much broken pottery small cups of various forms and wares, but of a general type commonly used for votive offerings, were fairly frequent. The bones of

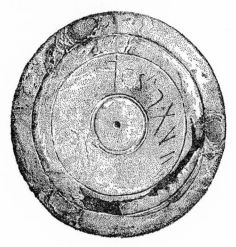

26. The Temple of Mithras: silver-gilt canister.

27. The Temple of Mithras: the extended decoration of the canister and the strainer.

chickens, the remains of ritual feasts, were found scattered over the floors at various levels, sometimes occurring in small clusters. From the first floor of the nave came a pine-cone, a common fertility symbol which has been found elsewhere. A metal dagger-blade and a dagger handle of jet were found in the upper levels of the aisle floor on the north side: neither was suitable for use and must have been intended for purely ritual purposes.

Other ritual objects were candlesticks of various metals and a pair of stone lavers, in very fragmentary condition. The more complete was a shallow bowl 23 inches in diameter, with a central raised flat-topped boss.

Finally in the matter of finds the most intriguing was made in the closing stages of the excavation (Figs. 26, 27). This was a silver-gilt canister containing a silver strainer. It was found in cleaning the top of the north outer wall of the temple, towards its west end, buried in the mortar of the wall. The strainer was perfectly preserved within the protective covering of the canister. Its wall is solid: the perforations make an attractive geometric pattern in the base. A three-limbed bar at the top was provided for lifting it in and out of the canister. The canister was much corroded; and while it was obvious that both the wall and the lid of the vessel were elaborately decorated the amount of corrosion from the copper in the silver was so great that the nature of the ornament could not be determined at the time of finding.

Laboratory cleaning showed in due course that the decoration was of a distinctive type and of the same general character on wall and lid. The subjects consist of individual groups of men and/or animals which do not appear to make up a connected story. On the side of the canister they display a tendency to be arranged in two horizontal zones broken occasionally by gnarled shrub-like trees which carry flowers with wide-spreading petals. The significance of some of the groups is not always obvious, but in general they present scenes of violence or of hunting, with men fighting animals, or animals fighting one another. On the lid of the canister the scenes have a haphazard arrangement which recalls that of late Samian ware with so-called 'free-style' ornament. Centrally here is a somewhat static elephant with what appears to be a kind of howdah strapped on its back, engaged in combat with a lioness or similar large cat. But greatest interest attaches to three scenes near the margin of the lid. In two of these, mythical creatures, griffons with eagle heads, are shown apparently examining long coffin-like boxes; while in the third a man is apparently being helped out of a similar box by a companion who is partly hidden amongst rocks or vegetation. Professor Jocelyn Toynbee, to whom the Council is indebted for an authoritative account of the temple's works of art which will appear in the final report, suggests that these scenes as a series represent attempts to capture griffons by using a man in a box or crate as a decoy, the animals presumably being captured while they are trying to open the crate. Support for this interpretation comes from the only known parallel: this is part of the famous hunting-scene mosaic in the villa of Piazza Amerino in Sicily, where a griffon is shown examining an oblong container in exactly the same manner. In the larger scale of the mosaic the box can be seen to be slatted, with a man's head visible between the slats.

The lid of the canister is hinged; it is kept closed by an ingeniously simple catch with an animal-head button, whose pointed end slides forward to engage a hole in the rim of the canister. The vessel originally stood upon three feet, as shown by the impressions left on the underside. Here too is a somewhat corroded incised graffito which so far has defied precise interpretation.

The canister is without parallel.[1] It must be assumed that it was an article of ritual use in the temple, perhaps in the preparation and reservation of one or other of the secret fluids that had a part in Mithraic ceremonies. Its hunting and fighting scenes suggest a connexion with Mithras the Hunter; an oriental link is provided by the pointed caps of some of the human beings represented. Attempts have been made to identify the distinctive-looking tree-species, but without success. Apart from the griffons, the animals—elephant, hippopotamus, lion, deer, wild boar—are all of known types. Professor Toynbee considers that the canister is probably of late third or early fourth-century date and that it had its origin possibly in an east-Mediterranean workshop.

The position in which the canister was found in the wall is consistent only with the view that like the Mithras and the other marbles, it had been deliberately concealed. For this it would have been quite easy to remove one or two stones from the wall-face, but the survival of the vessel in relatively undamaged condition apart from the effects of corrosion is a matter of great good fortune. A nineteenth-century foundation actually rested upon this

[1] For a full account of it see J. M. C. Toynbee, *A Silver Casket and Strainer from the Walbrook Mithraeum in the City of London* (Leiden, 1963).

piece of wall, the top of which had been only slightly lowered to take it. If the Roman wall had been reduced by only one more course the result must have been to disturb the canister. In its corroded condition it might well have been destroyed unrecognised, even if dug out by hand rather than by the mechanical excavator of today, which would have destroyed it unseen.

The Walbrook Mithraeum is one of several temples of the cult which have been excavated in Britain during the last ten years. At Carrawburgh and Rudchester in the north and at Caernarvon in Wales are examples of frontier temples, with all the rugged treatment of architectural detail and ritual furnishings appropriate to a military area dependent largely upon itself and remote from centres of gentler civilisation.[1] It would be mistaken to divide rigidly the different elements of the god's many-sided personality, for all must have appealed to those who followed him; but it is probably not untrue to say that it was the quality of Mithras as god of the manly virtues (sometimes finding ritual expression in barbarous practices) which constituted his greatest appeal to the soldiers who carried his cult to the remote frontier areas of the Empire.

The London temple—not, probably, the only one in the Roman city and its environs—presents Mithras in his other character, as Mithras the Law-Giver, the god whose care was for order, justice and right-dealing amongst men. Here he is the chosen deity of the business community, the traders and others whose lives depend on the observance of order and good faith in trading and commercial activity. Here therefore there is not only wealth but also contact with the Mediterranean centres of Roman civilisation: both are expressed in the quality of the original building and in the implied richness of its furnishings, with the large number of high-quality cult statues of Mediterranean origin. In so far as they were not purely structural the reasons for the drastic decline in the building's condition even while it continued in use over a considerable period of years present something of a problem. It may be wondered whether the state of the

---

[1] For Carrawburgh see I. A. Richmond and J. P. Gillam, 'The Temple of Mithras at Carrawburgh', *Archaeologia Aeliana*, 4th ser., XXIX (1951), pp. 1–92, with a note on 'The Background of Mithraism', pp. 52–61. For Rudchester, J. P. Gillam, I. MacIvor and E. Birley, 'The Temple of Mithras at Rudchester', *Arch. Aeliana*, 4th ser., XXXII (1954), pp. 176–219. And for Caernarvon, G. C. Boon, 'A Temple of Mithras at Caernarvon—Segontium', *Arch. Cambrensis*, CIX (1960), pp. 136–72.

temple in the fourth century reflected conditions in London generally at that time, though there is little real evidence from which any general conclusion might be drawn. The fall in standards is demonstrated by such things as the makeshift altar in the nave (p. 105) and the piece of marble, formerly part of a moulded piece of panelling, which had been reused for the 'four Augusti' inscription—not to mention the crude character of the inscription itself. Whatever the reasons for this decline, however, the fact that the building continued in apparently unbroken use at least to the middle fourth century is interesting as showing that Mithraists were still active long after Christianity had begun to take charge in the Empire generally.

Here it is unnecessary to embark on a detailed account of the struggle between the Mithraists and the Christians. For the Christians it was a particularly bitter one, both because Mithraic practices in some important respects seemed a blasphemous imitation of the Christian, and because Mithraism had a high ethical content which set it apart from other pagan cults, making it therefore a much more powerful rival in its appeal to the more enlightened part of the population. The failure of Mithraism had roots in such features as its all-male exclusiveness, its pronounced element of mystery with its grades and their elaborate (and sometimes exacting) graduation-rites. Its communities were numerous but in their nature small —characteristics which may well have operated in opposite directions. For while this selectiveness handicapped the Mithraists in their struggle for supremacy with a rival religion which knew no such limitations, it also must have tended to create closely-knit units which could survive actively long after the main battle had been for all practical purposes lost. In some such factor should perhaps be found the impulse which enabled the Walbrook Mithraeum to prolong an active, if reduced, existence.

V

Roman Minor Sites

---

1. INTRODUCTION

THE more important discoveries having been described in earlier chapters, it now becomes necessary to deal with the minor sites whose significance for the Roman period lies in the contribution that they make to an understanding of the kind of place that London was, as well as to its history as a human settlement. Here as in other parts of the subject the historical aspects cannot be treated fully for the reason that has already been given. The considerable quantity of datable material, and of pottery in particular, has yet to be studied in detail. In this chapter therefore a brief description of the more important sites is attempted, with a repetition of the warning that any conclusions as to dates are of a tentative nature and may well undergo modification in a future time.

2. DESCRIPTIONS OF SITES

Windsor Court–Falcon Square (5: 1947, 1956)

These sites belong to the general subject of the Cripplegate fort (pp. 17ff.); they figure here also because on both of them were found signs of occupation of earlier date than the fort's defences—that is, earlier than the end of the first century A.D. In the neighbourhood of Bastion 14 there were superficial deposits apparently spread over the original ground surface beneath the fort bank; with them were associated in one place a gravel floor and in another a small U-sectioned gully. Unfortunately datable material was entirely lacking from any of these features. Further south, between Bastion 14 and the west gate, was the grave-like pit or gully which produced the bronze coin of Vespasian (p. 38). The filling of this pit had been cut into by mortar-mixing pits contemporary with the fort wall.

Further south again, but just north-east of the northern gate-turret, was a regularly cut rectangular depression 8 feet wide by 9 feet long as surviving, which lay obliquely beneath the later gravel road of the fort; the revetment stakes of the lateral drain of the road cut directly across it. The depression remained to a depth of $3-3\frac{1}{2}$ inches, but its original depth is uncertain because a mediaeval cesspit had been dug to this level, destroying the rest of the Roman features. The depression is probably to be explained as a hut-floor, hollowed like a modern carpet-well to take planking, as seems to have been the case with a larger and better-preserved example in Cheapside (Honey Lane: *40*: below, pp. 139–40).

For what they are worth these disjointed elements imply sporadic activity, including some actual settlement, in this area, during the latter half of the first century A.D. To them should be added the enigmatic early wall beneath the north road of the fort gateway (p. 32), as well as some first-century pottery from a pit in the central area of the fort on the presumed site of the headquarters building (Wood Street–Silver Street: *19*). Even at this comparatively early date, therefore, the occupation had begun to affect these more remote areas away from the river-frontage and the twin hills, so that the building of the fort must have involved some clearance of the ground.

Gutter Lane, Cheapside (25: 1946)

This site was one of two examined in the preliminary excavations sponsored by the Society of Antiquaries. The total depth of the deposit below the cellar floor was 9 feet, so that the surface of the natural brickearth was about 18 feet below street-level (Fig. 28). The Roman levels had been much cut into by mediaeval pits, the deepest of which went up to 17–18 feet below the cellar floor. Their fillings were heavily charged with organic matter, but varied considerably in texture and consistency; they contained many cavities which grew in size as the material dried with exposure and it was impossible to preserve the section-faces.

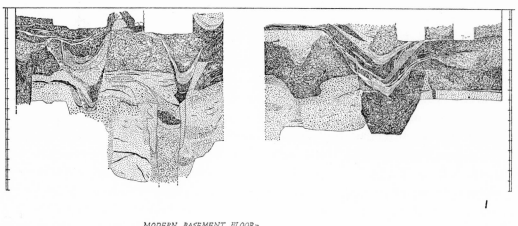

1

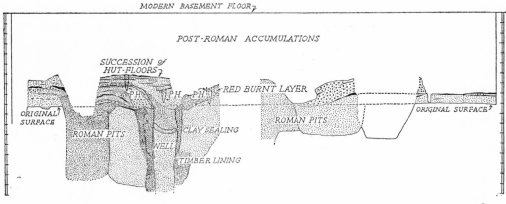

MODERN BASEMENT FLOOR

POST-ROMAN ACCUMULATIONS

SUCCESSION of HUT-FLOORS

PH PH PH RED BURNT LAYER

ORIGINAL SURFACE

ROMAN PITS

CLAY SEALING

WELL

TIMBER LINING

ROMAN PITS

ORIGINAL SURFACE

2

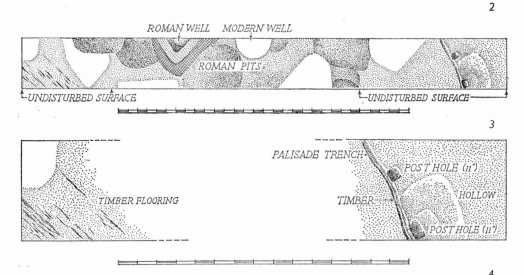

ROMAN WELL   MODERN WELL

ROMAN PITS

UNDISTURBED SURFACE

UNDISTURBED SURFACE

3

PALISADE TRENCH

POST HOLE (11")

TIMBER FLOORING

TIMBER

HOLLOW

POST HOLE (11")

4

28. Sections and plans of the Gutter Lane, Cheapside, excavation (25). (*Scales of feet.*)
1. The complete section; 2. the section with post-Roman features
omitted; 3. plan of Roman features at low level; 4. details at each end of 3.

The evidence for the Roman occupation of the site consisted of a 'build-up' of floor surfaces belonging evidently to timber-framed huts: there was no trace of a stone building. With these floors were associated a well and several pits which defied excavation in most cases because they were only partly in the cutting and their interiors were therefore inaccessible except at the impossible cost of widening the cutting. The floors were best preserved at the west end. Here on the original surface were the almost completely perished remains of a plank floor surviving as a series of irregular brown lines lying obliquely across the south-western angle of the trench (Plate 53). Above this layers of various materials—clay, gravel, *opus signinum*, 6 inches or more in thickness, alternated with streaks of black occupation-deposit, the maximum total depth of the deposit being about $4\frac{1}{2}$ feet. The higher and therefore later layers sagged over the pits dug through earlier floors, including the well, which was associated in the first place with some of the earlier floors. For the reasons already stated it was impossible to reach the bottom of the well, which was filled up and sealed before the process of building up of the floor levels was complete. There were indications that its lower part had been timber-lined; its upper 5 feet however had a lining of clay which had been added to as necessary to conform with the raising of the surface.

At various places in several of the floors sporadic post-holes were encountered. They were fairly uniform in size, being up to 6 inches across and 16–18 inches deep below their respective surfaces. Their posts had all been pointed. As always, recovery of the plan was out of the question; the posts must have supported the hut-frames and the roofs, though no trace of the latter had survived. The huts on this site appear to have been of comparatively slight construction and the absence of roofing-tiles, present occasionally elsewhere, suggests that their roofs were of thatch or other perishable material.

At the eastern end of the cutting the most interesting feature was what appeared to be the remains of a fence, or possibly of the wall of a timber building. This, at a depth of about 7 feet below the cellar floor, consisted of a vertical-sided slot 5 inches wide and 10 inches deep with square post-holes set at about 3-foot intervals, centre-to-centre, along its eastern side. The slot contained a gravelly filling evidently deliberately inserted, in which could be recognised, against its western side, a thin brown line of decayed timber. These arrangements suggest a plank wall or fence with spaced-out bracing-posts; it seems likely that it enclosed a yard rather than a building.

Though only about 150 feet north of the line of one of the few undoubted Roman streets in London, along Cheapside, the Gutter Lane site has thus produced evidence only of comparatively slight timber buildings. The beginnings of this occupation may be dated tentatively to the third quarter of the first century A.D. and the latest hut-floor in the western half of the cutting appears to carry the story down to about A.D. 180, after which neither structures nor objects were clearly defined. The hut-layers were succeeded by several feet of sterile soil through which were dug the mediaeval pits.

Billiter Square, Fenchurch Street (51: 1946)

This excavation also was undertaken in the preliminary season sponsored by the Society of Antiquaries. The site chose itself as the only group of cellars containing no bomb-rubble in the eastern half of the city: the remainder, both in Billiter Square and elsewhere in a north-to-south belt between Leadenhall Street, Fenchurch Street and Great Tower Street, were at this time encumbered with débris which remained in place almost everywhere until the new buildings came to be erected.

Though so near the administrative centre of the Roman city—the cutting was less than 200 yards to the east of the basilica—the site was remarkably featureless. The surface of the natural brickearth, which was very irregular in places, was 8–10 feet below the modern cellar floors (16–18 feet below street); and as usual this and the Roman deposits were cut through by later pits. At the north end of the cutting these intrusions had almost completely destroyed the Roman features. In the middle part of the area there was a depth of about 4 feet of horizontal deposits which appeared to be due to dumping: the materials were mixed; and while one irregular black layer suggested actual occupation there were no recognisable structural remains of dwellings. At the south end, on the other hand, at or near the base of the deposit there were two overlapping layers of occupation-soil which appeared to relate to huts, the upper one set in a shallow hollow of a type met with elsewhere. These floors were succeeded by mixed deposits up to about 4 feet thick which displayed pronounced tip-lines, suggesting also the raising of the level by dumping; and the sequence was completed with a more or less regular surface $3\frac{1}{2}$–4 feet below the cellar floor, upon which lay a featureless mediaeval deposit of dark soil. Finds were not abundant; the occupation was of the first/second century but there was no trace of Boudiccan fires.

The evidence suggests an open space which seems to have retained its character throughout the Roman period. Not far to the west of this site and between it and the basilica, was the Roman building examined by the staff of the Guildhall Museum when the cellars on the Lime Street frontage were cleared in 1951.[1]

Mark Lane (52: 1949–50)

This site took up the eastern part of a bombed area extending along the Great Tower Street frontage between Mark Lane and Mincing Lane. The cellars in their original state contained a great deal of bomb-rubble, but this material was cleared some time before rebuilding and the opportunity was taken to investigate sample portions of the area. The modern levels were not the same everywhere. Over the middle and southern parts of the site the surface exposed by clearing (which had removed the modern floors) was apparently approximately that of the original natural brickearth. To the north a limited area much cut up by modern foundations retained a varying depth of artificial accumulations on a very irregular natural surface; and against the boundary wall of the site over a distance of 28 feet there was a narrow strip with about 3 feet of material overlying natural.

In these circumstances only the lower levels and pits could survive over the greater part of the site. As to the latter, the feature of note was the contrast between the respective fillings of the Roman and the mediaeval pits, in itself a clue to different practices and modes of living. The later pits all revealed a consistently black mixed clayey content which was evidently heavily organic and made up of decayed domestic refuse. In the Roman pits the deposits were lighter in colour and consisted of sands, clays and gravels which were stained and discoloured by humic matter and often contained much charcoal in the form of tiny flecks. Sometimes also there were deposits of burnt material, bright red in colour from the particles of burnt clay which were their chief constituent. Though these pits might also

[1] *Journ. Rom. Studies*, XLII (1952), pp. 97–8.

yield black layers in which oyster-shells were prominent, most of them, on this site and elsewhere, had clearly not served as domestic-refuse containers. Their features seem best to be explained as the outcome of the dismantling of old floors and hearths whose débris was filled into pits some of which at least may have been dug to provide fresh flooring materials. In any case the Roman pits could not have been as unpleasant in their setting as their counterparts must have been in the mediaeval city.

On the better-preserved portions of the site there was no indication of stone buildings. In one section, as already stated, the top of the undisturbed brickearth was irregular, the result, presumably, of the sporadic surface digging. The irregularities, the deepest of which penetrated nearly 8 feet below the modern level, had been evened out and raised by the dumping of miscellaneous materials which included quantities of the brick-red burnt clay already mentioned in connexion with the pits. It should be added that this burnt material was not due to fire on the spot: there was no sign of burning on any of the surfaces with which it was in contact and it had clearly been re-sorted and redeposited as found. The point is not without importance, because similar accumulations or dumps occur elsewhere in the city and there is a danger that they may be interpreted as relating to one or other of the two great Roman fires for which evidence indeed exists.

On the second site, on the other hand, extensive burning had certainly discoloured the ground-surface over the available area and various gullies had been dug into this burnt layer. After this destruction, which it is tempting to relate to Boudicca's revolt of A.D. 60–1, the level continued to build up and there was a sequence of surfaces with occupation débris which incorporated many amphora-fragments as well as broken tiles and stones. Two at least of these surfaces seemed to be associated with hut-hollows, not enough of which remained for their outlines to be determined. The last structures on the site were pits only the bottoms of which had survived. Limited as the picture was, the remains were reminiscent much more of a native Iron Age occupation-site than of a Roman town-site.

Austin Friars (50: 1950–1)

The site of the church of Austin Friars was one of a limited number of small devastated areas towards the north side of the city and in its eastern half. In

1950 the area of the church was cleared in preparation for a new church for the Dutch Community to a level about 6 feet below the present street, an operation which involved the removal of the burials in the body of the building. The investigation was therefore concerned only with the deeper deposits. It seems likely that nothing important was lost in the site-clearance. The mediaeval church was of simple type and appeared to be of one date (mid-fourteenth century).[1] Apart from its outer walls its only surviving feature was the double row of detached foundations for the piers of the nave arcade. The various mediaeval pits in the area examined presumably belong to the period before the establishment of the Augustinian house on the site in 1253.

Partly because of other needs, partly because of soil-disposal difficulties on the site itself, it was not possible to explore the whole of the exposed area. The south-western quadrant was completely cleared, with parts of that to the north-west; and one longitudinal (east–west) and two partial transverse sections were obtained.

On this site also there were no stone buildings. The natural surface, partly brickearth, partly gravel, was uneven, with a tendency to dip towards the west, where it was $4\frac{1}{2}$ feet below the existing surface. Here an irregular partly vertical-sided pit, $2\frac{1}{2}$ feet deep, contained an alternating sequence of dark occupation layers with make-up of dirty buff clay. The deposits suggested a hut-site; but there were no post-holes or other features that could be associated with a structure. Other irregular hollows in the natural surface were smaller in extent and generally shallower. In addition to the mediaeval pits already mentioned there were several basin-like pits, oval in outline, the largest at least 9 feet across, which were sealed by floors of Roman date. The filling of one of these pits, on the north side of the cleared area, was cut by a U-shaped gully of which a second version existed at a higher level, when the surface in the middle part of the area had been raised almost another 2 feet. This and fragments of other gullies all appeared to be linear: they did not seem to enclose house-sites.

Over the western part of the excavated area it was not easy to distinguish a definite natural surface: the 'clean' brickearth passed upwards gradually into a discoloured layer and both produced pottery. On the stained loam, however, there was a definite clay and mortar surface with an overlying

[1] RCHM, England, *London (The City)* (1929), pp. 32–4, with plan on p. 32.

occupation deposit which in one place was 8 inches thick. A feature of this layer was the quantity of oyster-shells that it contained.

The discoloured loam was present over the whole of the western part of the site. In places on it gravel patches suggested flooring. To the east there was a more definite floor of hard-rammed gravel 6 inches or more in thickness. The only structural features otherwise were a few scattered post-holes of varying sizes, which made no ordered plan, and quantities of wall plaster, sometimes in concentrated patches, the most definite covering an area about 12 feet across. These fragments were all small and featureless in themselves; they are nevertheless the clue to the character of the buildings on the site, which were evidently of the plaster-faced clay-walled type discussed later (p. 139). The significant find at Austin Friars was a tiny portion of a plaster floor *in situ* near the southern margin of the excavated area. The floor was an inch thick; it retained along one edge a few inches of a quarter-round moulding, above which in turn projected the broken edge of a vertical surface, obviously the facing of a wall. Of the wall itself, however, there was no trace: it had no foundation-trench, so that planning of the remains was impossible. The plaster-fragments, sometimes in horizontal layers, sometimes scattered through the dirty buff loam, and the buff loam itself (as the spread material from the wall-cores) were all that survived.

The first-stage occupation represented by lower-level gravel floors and plaster débris would thus appear to have ended with the dismantling of the buildings and the spreading of their materials over the site, thus raising the level by more than a foot in places. The spread material showed little sign of stratification, but there were indications of intermediate floors and intermittent occupation layers containing charcoal, oyster- and mussel-shells, particularly towards the eastern side. The second main period of use of the site was marked by a fairly consistent but irregular surface at its maximum 2 feet above the natural level. The character of the occupation as reflected in the associated remains had undergone no change. In the eastern part of the site this level was overlaid by a deposit of bright red clayey material which appeared to have been derived from elsewhere. This material filled also several deep irregular excavations, guessed to be clay pits, on the south, but did not extend over the central part of the excavated area. This, the uppermost clearly recognisable Roman feature, gave the total Roman accumulation a maximum depth of rather less than 3 feet. The material above it was a dark fairly stiff loam, gravelly in places, but quite without stratification or other features.

Salters' Hall, St. Swithin's Lane (49: 1949)

This 40-foot cutting was made in the eastern courtyard of the old Salters' Hall while the building itself was being demolished. The level of the courtyard was that of the modern street, but the hope that in consequence something tangible would be learned of the later deposits was defeated. The top 7 feet of the section were made up of mixed unstratified soil, grey-black in colour and featureless. The base of this deposit coincided more or less with the wall-tops of two small cellars of about the same size (8 feet long by 5 feet wide internally). That to the east, entirely of brick and still retaining part of its vault, was set within two earlier walls to east and west, its floor 13 feet below the modern level. The cellar to the west had walls of stone as well as brick; its irregular slab-paved floor was 11 feet down. Both cellars contained a loose brick rubble-filling. They were of late seventeenth- or early eighteenth-century date and had continued in use into the early nineteenth century. The buildings to which they belonged must have been swept away, no doubt when the nineteenth-century hall was built.

The ground into which these small structures were sunk was of that tantalisingly featureless or indeterminate character which constitutes one of the problems of the post-Roman archaeology of London. The materials varied in consistency, becoming more clayey towards the east; but they displayed no stratification and produced no finds of significance, apart from some fragments of late baked tiles from a flat-bottomed disturbance sunk to a depth of 17 feet and penetrating the Roman deposits. This material was all of it apparently post-Roman and rested directly upon the Roman levels, into which had been cut one or two pits—but these also lacked definition, and if they were dug through the dark soil could not be recognised in it.

The older walls mentioned in connexion with the more easterly of the two small vaults were mediaeval in a broad sense, but that to the east rested upon an earlier wall which might have been Roman (see below). Both walls were of stone and seemed to enclose a deep pit or cellar, the floor of which almost coincided with the pre-Roman natural surface of the ground. The lower part of the filling ($2\frac{1}{2}$ feet) was almost entirely a stiff black clayey soil.

127

From here upwards were mixed materials containing a good deal of mediaeval tile rubble, deliberately introduced. Neither wall could be completely seen. The western wall was faced externally to a depth of 2 feet 9 inches (11 feet 9 inches below the modern surface) where an external offset coincided with the top of the recognisably Roman deposits. This would suggest that the mediaeval surface at this stage coincided with the Roman last surface; but it seems unlikely that the level could have remained unchanged for several centuries, nor was there any sign that the later deposits had been dug away.

The only other wall in the area exposed was a small piece at the full depth of the cutting, its foundation let into a shallow trench dug into 'natural'. This wall, which was aligned north–south, was probably Roman but not enough could be seen of it to make a final conclusion possible.

In the western part of the cutting the Roman elements consisted of a succession of more or less horizontal layers which reached a maximum height of 7 feet above the natural surface. The lower 3 feet of these deposits contained little in the way of actual occupation material and were made up of loam or gravel layers, some of which were stained and dirty and contained the occasional oyster-shell and potsherd. The features of these deposits, which covered in date the latter half of the first century, were a clean, hard-compacted gravel taking up the last 8 feet of the cutting and present in both faces; and a U-sectioned gully the bottom of which penetrated into 'natural', and in the top of whose dark loamy filling was a second shallower gully with a flat bottom. The compacted gravel was evidently a road. It had a horizontal upper surface the eastern margin of which had been cut away by mediaeval disturbance; but it seems likely that the upper smaller gully belonged to it. The filling of this gully produced a 'second brass' of Domitian (A.D. 81–96). Over the road to the west was a 3-foot-deep accumulation of mixed dark soil, unstratified: it was cut into by the later disturbance which had mutilated the road, so that its relationship with the more varied deposits to the east could not be determined. These deposits were more definitely due to occupation on the site: black layers alternated with layers of clay or gravel, showing a tendency to dip westwards over the gullies already described. One of these was composed of the bright red burnt material discussed under Mark Lane (above, p. 124). This also was redeposited: the material was mixed, containing some gravel, with no indication of burning on the spot. Post-holes were associated with three of the levels. They point to a succession of timber-framed buildings on the site; but, as always, there was no possibility of recovering even a partial plan.

Walbrook House, Walbrook (46: 1954)

In a brief interval which followed the clearance of this site Messrs. Rybot and Atkinson were able to undertake a short (40-foot) cutting near its northern boundary, which though not completed because of the time factor was valuable for the information that it provided on the topography of the area. Approximately 6 feet of accumulation overlay the natural surface and the deposits were entirely domestic in character, with no sign of the wet conditions which prevailed on the west side of the Walbrook Street. Here as to the north under St. Swithun's House therefore, the position was well clear of the depression of the Walbrook valley (Fig. 23).

The levels as far as they could be examined were of first/second-century date. The feature of the upper part of the cutting throughout much of its length was a layer about 12 inches in thickness of bright red burnt clay which was immediately over a 4-inch *opus signinum* floor: it was difficult to decide in this case whether the burnt material had been dumped or whether it was due to fire on the site. The *opus signinum* surface was sagging and irregular in a way which suggested that it covered pits or other disturbances, but it was not possible to explore these. Towards the eastern end of the cutting were two flat-bottomed open drains or gullies whose timber linings coincided in level with the floor, suggesting that floor and gullies were contemporary in use. The linings were recognisable but not well preserved. The gullies impinged on one another and the western one appeared to be later than that to the east. It was filled with the red burnt material. The nature of the building of which the *opus signinum* floor would have formed part was not apparent in the area uncovered. The remains of a wall of Kentish ragstone beneath the floor in the middle section of the cutting suggested that there had at some earlier stage been a more substantial building on the area. The wall was pursued to a depth of 4 feet 9 inches, but its base was not found.

The *opus signinum* floor had been cut by pits in several places: the removal of the filling of one of these established the level of the natural surface referred to above. Below the floor was a series of made-up layers of clay and other materials only a tiny part of which, to a depth of about 5 feet below the modern surface, could be examined.

St. Michael Paternoster Royal, College Hill (47: 1949)

This excavation had a limited objective: the search, undertaken at the suggestion of the late Canon J. A. Douglas, then Rector, for the tomb of the famous Richard Whittington, who died in 1423. The hope of success was not very strong, since quite apart from the reconstruction of the church after the Great Fire of 1666, in the course of which there must have been considerable disturbance, the tomb itself is said to have been disturbed at least twice in the later Middle Ages. Tradition variously ascribed the tomb to both the north-east and the south-east corners of the church, but neither area yielded any sign of it. On the north-east an eighteenth-century vault would have destroyed all trace of it.

The excavation in the south-east corner produced no sign of Whittington, but gave a complete section of the deposits in this part of the church, the cutting being carried in this place to a depth of 14 feet below the church floor. To a depth of 8 feet the ground had acquired the loose fine texture which results from the presence of much chalk and old mortar in it, combined with the frequent disturbance that was inevitable with the continual use of the site for coffined burials in the eighteenth/nineteenth century. From this limited space, about $11\frac{1}{2}$ feet by $7\frac{1}{2}$ feet, came in all 24 burials, all of them anonymous. The conditions in the ground were excessively confused, with many detached bones scattered through the soil and decaying and collapsed wooden coffins some of the earlier of which had obviously been disturbed, sometimes seemingly after quite a short interval, by the insertion of later coffins. The disorder presented a sombre contrast with the elaboration of the fragmentary coffins with their decorative patterns of dome-headed nails. The whole complex provided a graphic illustration of the problems which confronted those whose task it was to dispose of the dead in a densely populated city inadequately provided with burial grounds.

Below the eighteenth-century level was a heavier clayey soil about 5 feet deep into which had been inserted the foundations of the pre-Fire church. Unfortunately none of the lower deposits produced datable material in the limited area that was available for examination. They may well have been

Roman. In any case an *opus signinum* floor was met with 12 feet down; and below that again, to the maximum depth of 14 feet referred to above, were two further floor-levels with intermediate layers of black occupation soil. At this depth also was a 12-inch-deep wall foundation, certainly Roman and linked with one or more of the lowest floor-levels. Standing water and the restrictions of the site made it impossible to pursue these features further.

Bucklersbury, Cheapside (43: 1955)

This site stands on the western flank of the Walbrook valley to the north of the main Walbrook site (pp. 92ff.). The underlying contour is no doubt reflected in the southward fall of the modern street-surface of Bucklersbury; and apart from a deeper hollow at the north-west end of the cutting the natural floor where seen at the base of the deposits also showed a fall to the south-east. The conditions resembled those of the other site also in being remarkably wet at an unusually high level. Standing water was present from a depth of about $3\frac{1}{2}$ feet downwards—an advantage for the preservation of timber; an inconvenience in other respects. In the hollow at the north-west end the maximum depth of the deposits was just under 11 feet; over the remaining two-thirds of the area exposed the level fell from about $9\frac{1}{2}$ to 10 feet at the south-east.

Once again there were no stone buildings within the area of the cutting. The general evidence showed that the level had been built up gradually by the accumulation of materials of a very mixed character which were no doubt deliberately dumped. The succession of floors thus provided had served for hut-sites. The structural remains of these consisted of stake- and post-holes and sometimes of the posts themselves. More significant were the actual floors, which had frequently been boarded and retained the remains of their timbers in more or less recognisable form. Other floors of clay or other material were provided with a light edging of timber held in place by 'two-by-three' pegs: two such appeared at different depths at the north-east end of the site. Inevitably, no coherent plans were attainable. The 'edged' floors at least seemed to be rectilinear in outline and a foot-wide band of sandy soil against one side of one of them may have marked the site of a clay wall. But while there were one or two fairly continuous levels, particularly at 8 feet 6 inches, 6 feet and 4 feet down, the evidence suggested rather a series of small unrelated structures than a single building. Quantities of broken tiles figured frequently in the layers of make-up, but all looked as if they had simply been deposited on the area, and they were without exception quarries: there were no roofers which might have been derived from buildings on the site, though one or two large post-holes could have taken timbers strong enough to support a tiled roof.

Several floors had been fired in part at least to a bright red colour, but there was nothing to suggest that the burning was due to anything other than normal domestic activity and the remains of one or two hearths were actually exposed. A feature of the middle part of the cutting at the 6-foot level was a layer of coarse loose lumps of clay which had been burnt a bright red. This material was contained in a matrix of dark soil, and lay immediately on an uneven wood surface. It may be that it is evidence for the destruction of a building by fire; but if so the heat was not sufficient to char the underlying timber, the condition of which was due to normal processes of decay.

An interesting feature of the south-eastern end of the cutting was a wattle 'fence' or revetment which crossed the cutting obliquely (Plate 55). The bottom of this 'fence' was at 7 feet 3 inches below the cellar floor: it survived to a height of 12 inches (Plate 56); its original height is uncertain. The construction consisted of withies interlacing stakes set at 10–12-inch intervals, the 'fence' being anchored to larger posts one of which had survived in the cutting at a point where on the east the wattle turned southwards through an angle of about 140°. The wattle reappeared in the south-west corner of the cutting so that it must have turned at that end also, and appears therefore to have enclosed a space only about 9 feet in width, though its length is uncertain. Its purpose also must remain uncertain, but it is of interest as showing that Roman and mediaeval Londoners alike made use of the same devices: indeed the position here was complicated by the fact that two mediaeval pits dug to the same depth as the Roman wattle were equipped with wattle linings. That on the west side of the cutting had cut through the earlier timber work in such a way that the mediaeval pit-lining appeared to continue the line of the Roman 'fence'. The problem of the relationship of the two was solved by the stratigraphical evidence, by which it was possible to separate the wicker-work inside the pit from that outside it: the latter was set in the ground into which the pit had been dug (Fig. 29).

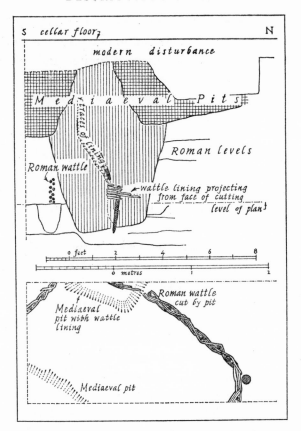

29. Bucklersbury, Cheapside (43): Roman and mediaeval wattle structures
(see also Plates 55, 56).

The later occupation of the site seems to be represented by the accumulation of a succession of floors at narrow vertical intervals, one of which, 2 feet below the cellar floor, could be correlated with a vertical-sided timber-lined pit about 7 feet 6 inches wide and just under 3 feet deep, which in general character resembled a Saxon hut-pit (p. 155). This pit was sealed by the later floor levels, the last of which immediately beneath the cellar floor sealed in its turn a big mediaeval pit.

Apart from the quantity of pottery which awaits detailed study the site produced several finds worth mentioning. Fragmentary quern-stones were found in the early levels, several at depths of up to 8 feet. A quantity of corn came from the surface at 6 feet, beneath the coarse burnt clay described above. At the 4-foot level was found a heavy yoke-like object, 68 inches long, of wood. The later deposits yielded in one place a quantity of coal and iron-slag suggesting industrial activity on a limited scale near at hand.

Cheapside, South (38: 1955)

Since Wren recorded the presence of a Roman 'causeway' on the site of the tower of St. Mary-le-Bow Church it has been an accepted axiom that Cheapside lies on or near the course of the Roman street which would have been one of the main thoroughfares of the city, linking the eastern centre on Cornhill with the important gate in the west wall at Newgate (see above, pp. 40ff., and Fig. 7).

The existence of this road was confirmed in two short cuttings which a group of volunteers led by Messrs. Rybot and Atkinson were able to make in cellars just to the west of the church and between it and Bread Street in 1955. The indications were of several surfaces, the best preserved (or more fully visible) being at a depth of just under 6 feet below the cellar floor. The natural surface of the ground was more than 2 feet lower than this at 8 feet 3 inches: between the two there were other incomplete gravel layers which may have been the remains of earlier roads; and above the main surface there was another thin layer of gravel, with an intervening deposit of clay and burnt brick, which might have marked the final Roman street level. The gravel of the 'main' road was hard-rammed, with a minimum thickness as surviving of 4–6 inches; its surface carried a number of irregular hollows, and some shell was incorporated in it. Pottery from the deposits beneath it ranged through the second century, and from the clay and burnt material above it came a coin of the house of Valentinian (A.D. 360 or later); so that this version of the road belonged to a late phase of the Roman city.

As surviving the road extended southwards about 15 feet from the modern building frontage (Plate 63), its visible width in the cutting being a little over 8 feet. It ended on a flat-bottomed trench or drain, the floor of which was 9 feet 6 inches below the cellar floor. This feature had a row of small shallow stake- or post-holes along its north side, set slightly less than 18 inches apart. It was probably the lateral drainage gully for the road. The latest pottery from it indicates that it is at least of the late fourth century.

Though traces of the road were observed in the cutting to the west of that described above their condition was not very good. Unfortunately, for a number of reasons it was not possible to complete the excavation, but both areas were in any case much disturbed by mediaeval and later pits. These cellars were almost the only ones available in this large area of bomb damage on the east side of Bread Street. The remaining cellars were either too deep or retained their bomb-rubble; they were pressed into service as car parks up to the time of rebuilding on the site.

Blossoms Inn, Lawrence Lane (41: 1955)

These cellars were the most northerly of a group on the north side of Cheapside in and about Honey Market, between Lawrence Lane on the east and Milk Street on the west. Three cuttings (A, B and C) were made in the hope of recovering more of the elements of a plan than is normally possible. In all three the amount of post-Roman disturbance was relatively limited and later levels were actually present only in Cutting A, the features elsewhere being the usual mediaeval pits. The interesting discovery here was an arrow-shaped brick structure, evidently from its filling a cesspit. The brick lining of this pit first appeared at a depth of $2\frac{1}{2}$ feet below the cellar floor; it was found to be just under 18 inches deep, but had probably lost some of its depth through later disturbance. The pit would have been of eighteenth-century date and was an unusually elaborate example of a type of construction which is only too common (from the point of view of an excavator concerned more immediately with earlier periods) in London.

In the completed cuttings the surface of the natural brickearth was encountered at a depth of about 7 feet below the cellar floors 14–16 feet below street-level. The lower deposits in Cutting B in particular were waterlogged: one deeper pit in this cutting could not in consequence be completely excavated. The surface was also very irregular and had been much disturbed and dug into, so that in the absence of weathering the true surface remained uncertain.

There were no stone buildings on the site. The deposits had been built up in a series of more or less horizontal layers which were very closely set in Cuttings B and C and only slightly less so in Cutting A. The sections displayed a succession of loams, gravels and clays, often carrying black or red-burnt occupation-material and containing post-holes and other features, as

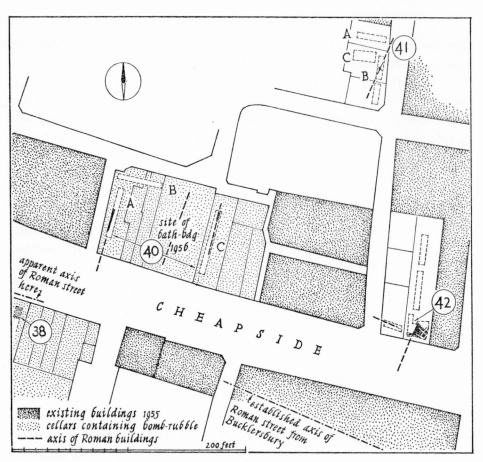

30. Sites 38, 40–42 in eastern Cheapside.

well as one or two gullies of a type met with elsewhere. It is not possible here to go in detail into the various changes, but two things are of interest.

The alignment of the various structures on this site, about 300 feet back from the nearest known Roman street in Cheapside, appears to have been approximately NNE–SSW. It is thus in broad general agreement with the other fragmentary buildings (sites *40* and *42*) which have been recorded in the neighbourhood (Fig. 30), including the bath-building in Cheapside investigated by the Guildhall Museum.[1] It is tempting to try to use the slight changes in direction that these buildings make towards the west to support the case for a change in alignment in the Cheapside Roman street

[1] *Journ. Rom. Soc.*, XLVII (1957), p. 220 (plan by I. Noel Hume).

discussed on p. 41, but as was observed there, the variations are not sufficiently constant to allow of any definite conclusion.

In all three cuttings the evidence was consistent in showing a steady building-up of the levels with make-up and hut-floors of various materials and intervening layers of occupation-soil. A feature bearing upon the character of London buildings was the presence in Cutting B of wall-slots for light partitions of timber (Plate 54). They occurred at more than one depth, but the best-preserved example was about 5 feet down and consisted of a pair of slots intersecting at right angles on a somewhat worn post-hole (Fig. 31). The slots were 4–6 inches wide where undamaged and retained

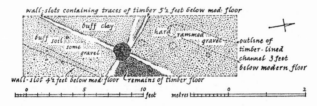

31. Blossoms Inn, Lawrence Lane (41): plan of Roman wall-slots in cutting B.

traces of timber in places in a gravelly matrix. The surface associated with them was a gravelly loam on a foundation of hard-rammed gravel; there were indications of a wooden floor in the north-east quadrant. In both Cutting A and Cutting B at a depth of about 4 feet a quantity of large amphora-fragments had been laid as make-up for a floor which was covered with black burnt material; but this had not been burnt on the spot. Other relevant structural finds were fragments of clay daub with an incised herring-bone pattern on the outer face and wattle impressions on the inside; and (in a hollow in Cutting A which may have been a continuation of a gully more clearly seen in Cutting C) fragments of timber, possibly part of a collapsed fence.

Honey Lane, Cheapside (40: 1954–5)

Three cuttings were made here, in the cellars of the one-time nos. 107, 109 and 111 Cheapside. The second of these proved to be abortive and was given up at an early stage: the ground had been disturbed to a considerable depth, and the later fillings were so unstable that it seemed unwise to continue work which in any case was likely to be unproductive. The cellar floors were 9–10 feet below the street.

In the west cutting (A: no. 111) the total depth of the artificial deposits was 11 feet at the south end: it decreased slightly towards the north. In addition to the usual mediaeval pits, one of which at the north end passed through the Roman layers to some undetermined depth in the underlying natural (Plate 57), there was a number of burials, all of which were in a very fragmentary state because of disturbance. The remains were enclosed in chalk-lined graves, traces of a coffin surviving in one case, and occurred at depths varying between 4 and $5\frac{1}{2}$ feet. All were orientated east–west, with head to west. These graves were clearly of mediaeval date and no doubt belonged to the graveyard of the church of All-Hallows, Honey Lane, which stood just to the north of this site.[1]

To depths of 5–6 feet below the cellar floor the undisturbed material consisted of loam and clayey soil, dark in colour, which had traces of thin clay-covered floors in its upper part but was otherwise featureless. The Roman deposits below the 5–6-foot level were made up of a series of more or less horizontal layers which represented floors of buildings with their associated deposits, but, as usual, not all the features seen in plan in the cutting were present in the section.

At 5 feet the top of a well-built stone wall 2 feet wide lay along the west side of the cutting. The wall, which remained to a height of a little over a foot, was partly behind the face of the trench, gradually diverging from it so that the full width was within the excavated area at a point about 22 feet from the south end. A short distance beyond this, however, it was cut by the deep mediaeval pit already referred to, and did not reappear in the disturbed ground to the north. As surviving the stonework seemed to be entirely footings, but the related surface may have been a gravelly floor which was present throughout the southern part of the cutting at a depth of about 6 feet. It occurred on both sides of the wall. This surface carried a quantity of small tile-fragments embedded in mixed pink clay and mortar, suggesting a dismantled tessellated floor.

The base of the wall rested upon a bright red layer of burnt clay with mortar and brick which was a feature of the full length of the section at a

[1] See map in Kingsford's ed. of Stow, *Survey of London*, II.

depth of about 7 feet. This was clearly due to burning *in situ*; beneath it towards the north were the remains of a timber floor with fragmentary planks set in grey sand. Here part of the overlying burning was due to a hearth.

Immediately beneath the burnt layer, its base at 7 feet 9 inches, was a fragment of a plaster-faced 'clay' wall. The back of the plaster appeared in the section: it was roughly parallel with the stone wall at a higher level but

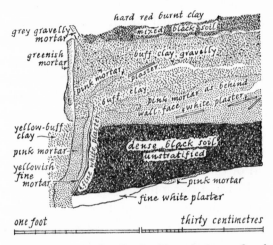

32. Honey Lane, Cheapside (*40*): detail of collapsed plaster-faced 'clay' wall.

slightly to the east of it. A short transverse cut into the section-face was all that time allowed for the examination of this feature, of which enough had survived to enable its construction to be recorded (Fig. 32). The core of the wall appeared to be made of yellow-buff clay; it was faced (on the west) with successive layers of pink and yellow-grey mortar, the final finish being a fine white plaster. The associated floor as far as it was visible was irregular and carried a thick deposit of occupation material which unfortunately yielded no datable objects in the very small part of it that could be excavated. Above this were mixed deposits made up of the products of the decay of the wall: clay and mortar with fragments of plaster; and the whole was overlaid by the bright red burnt layer described above.

In the cutting itself, at the same depth as the base of the faced wall, was a sunk rectangular hollow 2–4 inches deep, nearly 10 feet long (N–S) and

139

projecting into the cutting nearly 4 feet from the east side. It was sunk into bright red burnt material (Plate 58). The filling was a dense black and organic, possibly wood, though no timber structure was recognisable. This sunk floor and the plaster wall must have belonged to adjacent walls in the same building, though the east face of the wall was not observed during the excavation, perhaps because it had completely collapsed. The remaining deposits to the base of the cutting were made up of charcoal-covered floors on gravel or loam; one, towards the south end, consisted of fragments of roofing-tiles. There were occasional post-holes.

In the east cutting (C) the general conditions were somewhat similar. Horizontal floor surfaces at quite narrow intervals were recognisable to within 3 feet of the cellar-surface, becoming less frequent above. There was a good deal of disturbance in the middle part of the cutting, with several mediaeval pits, and a number of chalk- and brick-lined cesspits, the latter going to depths of up to 7 feet. The chalk walls were footings and were slight in character, usually less than 2 feet wide.

At the north end of the cutting a broken wall projected southwards for a distance of 8 feet, its top 4 feet 7 inches, its base 7 feet down. Its west face was rendered with whitish mortar; its east face was broken and the beginning of the eastward spread of the ruins just came into the cutting. The remaining Roman features consisted of a series of horizontal floors separated by layers of 'make-up' of various materials, usually clay or loam, but sometimes gravel, often with red or brown burnt inclusions. Several of the surfaces were a brilliant brick red in colour from burning *in situ*. The most striking of these was at about 6 feet down (the total depth of the deposit being about 10 feet); but some of the other burnt material had been dumped on the site as make-up.

Associated with these levels were a number of post-holes, some of them of large size (6–8 inches across and 2 feet deep) and sometimes still retaining their timber. There was a cluster of such post-holes across the cutting at about the middle of its length and 9 feet down; but as usual neither these nor any other of the post-holes encountered at other levels could be interpreted in terms of a plan. The occupation was domestic and associated with the black and red layers were several hearths of which the most interesting lay at a depth of about $8\frac{1}{2}$ feet and consisted of flat tiles closely set to form a rectangle 25 by $30\frac{1}{2}$ inches (Plate 59). The tiles were much cracked and discoloured by heat. Near the north-east corner of the tiled area was a small post-hole which was lined on three sides by thin tile-fragments set on edge. Part of a second tiled hearth projected from the west face of the cutting at a depth of 7 feet and was contemporary with a 4–6-inch black occupation-layer which was unbroken over a distance of 24 feet in the southern part of the trench.

Friday Street (37: 1953–4)

A series of three cuttings (1–3) north–south along the same line was made on the east side of Friday Street behind Cheapside, the overall length being rather more than 70 feet. The cellars contained much bomb-rubble and only a limited time was available for the work, so that it was not possible to dig out the deeper pits.

The depth of the artificial deposits was 7–8 feet, the natural surface being brickearth. The lower part of the cutting, up to about 5 feet from the floor, was made up of a horizontal accumulation of very mixed materials, forming a succession of surfaces with which at the different levels were associated various gullies, hollows and relatively shallow pits as well as numbers of post-holes. No coherent plan could be reconstructed of any of these features. The post-holes were frequently oblong in outline. Many were quite shallow: the deepest (20 inches) appeared in the west face of Cutting 1, to the south. One pit in this cutting was followed to a depth of 13 feet: it was vertical-sided and had been dug or redug in two stages. It was probably a well. At the base of Cutting 2 (middle) a flat-bottomed gully or water-course survived for a length of 13 feet, its ends being cut by later pits. The gully was 27 inches wide: it was sunk 6 inches into the natural surface, but had been dug from a level 9 inches above this (Plate 60). Along both its sides were post-holes, sometimes closely set in twos or threes, and of quite large size (up to 9 inches by 5 inches and 9 inches deep). These features were puzzling at the time, but subsequent work on wetter sites in the Walbrook area produced examples of similar gutters in which the timber elements had been preserved (Plate 31). Their function (i.e. whether they served as drains or as water-supply culverts) remains undecided.

Such features, combined with hearths and black occupation-layers, show once again that in this area the early occupation of the city was entirely an affair of timber buildings. At the south end of the site, however, a stone building had been erected evidently at a relatively advanced stage in the occupation. It was represented only by one wall with a stone- and tile-lined culvert on its south side. With a width of only 18 inches it is not likely to have been part of a large structure. No companion wall was found—it may have been destroyed by a more recent foundation which penetrated to about the same depth 9 feet away to the north—nor had the contemporary floor survived. The side of the wall away from the culvert was not faced and was therefore backed against solid ground. The deposits against it were all tipped, with no sign of a structural floor apart from some brick *tesserae* at a depth of about 5 feet which might have been disturbed from a higher level. The culvert was floored with tiles; it was 18 inches deep, its top being 5 feet below the modern floor. A double post-hole in the top of the main wall suggested that after the stone building was dismantled there was a reversion to timber huts.

The upper part of the deposit in the cutting was made up of dark feature-less soil of varying density. There were the usual late disturbances, including a chalk foundation which ran the full length of Cutting 2 (middle) on the east side, penetrating to within 3 feet of the natural surface. The mediaeval pits were mostly shallow but one, in Cutting 2, was given up at 12 feet 6 inches.

St. Swithun, London Stone (48: 1960–1)

The excavation of St. Swithun's Church is described in its post-Roman aspects on pp. 199ff. In contact with the mediaeval foundations, below the level of disturbance by eighteenth/nineteenth-century burials were the remains of Roman buildings and deposits. These had survived mainly in the southern half of the site: on the north mediaeval pits and foundations reached depths well below the original natural ground-surface. This, where not disturbed, was about 11 feet below the modern church floor (itself some-what higher than the external pavement surface), the depth of the Roman accumulations overlying it being 4–5 feet. (Plan, Fig. 48, p. 200.)

The most important discovery was the north edge of the Roman street, predecessor of Cannon Street, just inside the south wall of the church (Plate 61). It was seen in three places, and in so far as its direction could be determined it was approximately parallel with the existing building front-age, diverging if anything slightly to the north towards its western end. Only about 3 feet in width of the make-up of the road could be seen in section. Its maximum depth was about 4 feet and it was composed of layers of gravel of varying consistency, evidently the result of successive renewals. The road was flanked by a ditch which also showed signs of having been recut, but it was not possible to determine the sequence in the small portion of this feature that was available. The final version of the ditch contained a filling of black loamy soil which was truncated by the later burial distur-bance. It was at first thought to be mediaeval, but produced only Roman material. Along the northern margin of the ditch at the lower levels there were post- and stake-holes which made a complicated pattern and were clearly due to a series of renewals. Some of those immediately to the north of the gully were relatively large. It seems probable that they belonged to early timber buildings, but the ground above them had been cut away by the eighteenth-century vaults of the church and there was no means of relating them to any of the levels; nor were their counterparts met with in the northern part of the site. The stake-holes, on the other hand, seemed to belong to the road-ditch and probably formed part of wattle revetments such as were used in the Cripplegate fort (p. 33) and perhaps also in Cheapside (p. 134).

To the north of the road-ditch there had accumulated a succession of deposits, mainly loamy clays with some gravel and charcoal-stained occupa-tion-layers, which ranged in date through the first and into the second century A.D. With these went one or two pits, but no structural features were associated with them in the areas where they had survived and could be examined.

In any case, the timber building, if any, had been replaced by a more permanent structure, of which the walls again survived only on the southern part of the site (Plates 96–8). The walls were entirely of knapped flints and appeared to consist mainly of foundations. In plan the building as far as it could be examined within the area consisted of a passage-like compartment 11 feet wide fronting the street with suggestions of a series of smaller chambers to the north. The walls defining these rooms were not at a true right angle to the east–west walls. They were slighter and usually not as deep, so that apart from the most easterly, which passed under the church foundations, they did not survive in the disturbed ground in the central area of the church. They were not bonded into the front walls but they were so like the others that there is no reason to think that they were in fact different in date.

The level of the floor of this building was not easy to determine because of destruction. The south wall seemed to be entirely foundations as surviving with an offset just below its top, suggesting the position of a floor all remains of which had been destroyed. Certainly its external face was that of a foundation forming one side of the road-gully. Its character was confirmed by the presence in it at the extreme east end of the site, where the wall passed under and into the mediaeval church foundations, of a tile-arched culvert or drain opening into the bottom of the road-gully (Plate 62). It was impossible to examine this feature fully because it was out of reach beneath structures which could not be disturbed; but at least it confirmed the view that the deep road-gully with its black filling was of Roman date.

The north wall presented greater difficulty. It was much more regularly built and very deep, with a good face to the south (that to the north was not examined). In the disturbed deposits between the walls there was part of one surface with overlying occupation material which might have belonged to a related floor since it coincided in level with a change in the character of the wall. But it is doubtful whether this was so, since there was no corresponding change in the south wall and it seems likely therefore that (as the offset already mentioned suggested) the true floor had just not survived the post-Roman disturbance. Of the date of the building therefore it can only be said that it was probably later than the mid-second century. Though its foundations were deep the relative slightness of the walls (maximum width at the top 20 inches) may indicate that they carried a timber superstructure. Nothing can be said of the plan except that it suggests a corridor or gallery towards the street with rooms opening off it. From the evidence of undisturbed Roman deposits (which yielded no sign of a wall closing the building on the north side) within the north-eastern vault of the Wren church the north range could not have been more than 20 feet wide and may have been a good deal less.

Queen Victoria Street–Carter Lane (30–1: 1960)

In this area, immediately to the south and south-east of St. Paul's Cathedral, a number of trenches was excavated in those cellars which contained only a limited amount of bomb-rubble. Some of the cellars appeared likely in any case to be too deep. The excavations fell into two groups: a series of trenches at right angles to the street along the north side of Queen Victoria Street, with two extensions northwards on the Knightrider Street frontage (*31*); and another in the western part of the area between Carter Lane and Knightrider Street (*30*). The ground falls fairly steadily southwards from Carter Lane from about 51 feet O.D. to about 36 feet in Queen Victoria Street, steepening still more from there to Upper Thames Street.

The cuttings in Queen Victoria Street may be dismissed in a few words. None retained any of its Roman deposits, which had presumably been removed when the buildings were constructed with their basements at the time of the creation of the street in 1869. The various pits and other features revealed were mainly of eighteenth- and nineteenth-century date. On the Knightrider Street frontage a cutting at the west end of the area though much disturbed revealed a gravel layer set in a hollow in the natural surface and suggesting a hut floor. Pottery from this surface was of third-century date; but it was not sealed by a datable deposit and its association with such a stratigraphically early floor might have been accidental.

North of Knightrider Street (which has now disappeared in its original form) the slope upwards to Carter Lane is more gradual than to the south. The cellars on the Carter Lane frontage itself were mostly quite shallow (7 feet or even less); in the interior of the area they varied, with a tendency to be stepped down to the south. Some contained bomb-rubble, but they were not full. Five cuttings were made in the western part of the site. All showed a considerable amount of disturbance and nowhere did there survive a surface which could certainly be said to be that of undisturbed 'natural'. Further to the east, on the *Financial Times* site (*35*) where in general the conditions would have been very similar to those at Carter Lane, the surface of the natural gravel was consistently present at a depth of about $5\frac{1}{2}$ feet below the cellar floor, with no indication of an overlying brickearth deposit. In Carter Lane the gravel appeared at depths ranging from about 4 feet to about 13 feet, with brickearth surviving above it in one or two places to show that in parts of the area at least it had been present. The evidence suggested sporadic digging for brickearth and gravel which had resulted in the creation of a large number of irregular and sometimes extensive pits and quarries which had then gradually been filled with débris, occasionally showing signs of having carried living-floors. Conspicuous amongst the fillings were quantities of clay containing many small fragments of wall-plaster, probably the remains of dismantled plaster-faced clay or cob walls (p. 39). Fourth-century pottery was associated with two such deposits. It would suggest that in spite of what was said on p. 14 quarrying was going on at quite a late date in the western part of the city.

Many mediaeval pits, some of them containing the typical wicker lining, had been dug into and through the Roman material. A few fragmentary mediaeval foundations had also survived.

Cheapside/Lawrence Lane (42: 1961)

This site, on the east side of the junction of Lawrence Lane with Cheap-side, was examined by means of a line of north–south cuttings which were extended laterally at the south end to uncover the remains of a stone build-ing met with there.

The maximum depth of the accumulation was 8–9 feet, its base therefore being about 16 feet below street-level. The surface of the natural gravel— the brickearth was missing here—was irregular in places, and as on the other side of Lawrence Lane (41) further north, was very wet. Over most of the northern part of the area there was the normal succession of occupa-tion deposits, loam, clay, gravel and dark-stained layers, running in date at least well into the second century A.D. No post-holes were recognised. The upper part of the cutting, to a depth of about 4 feet, was made up of mediaeval and later features.

At the south end of the main series of cuttings the first clue to the presence of a building was the remains of a tile pier which projected obliquely into the trench from the east face. The pier stood 2 feet high (its base being $5\frac{1}{2}$ feet below cellar level, 12–13 feet below street); it was built mainly of roofing-tiles of poorer quality than usual, and much cracked and weathered on its visible west and north faces. Westwards the base of the pier was ex-tended by a line of stonework, possibly a foundation or the edge of a paved or cobbled area; but the line was discontinuous and there was neither room nor time to pursue it further.

On the east side the pier was linked with a somewhat irregularly planned channelled hypocaust, built mainly of Kentish ragstone incorporating some tile (Fig. 33). The foundation of the outer wall on the west of the building had survived and in level coincided at the base with the base of the pier. On the north side there had been destruction by a late pit. The channels of the

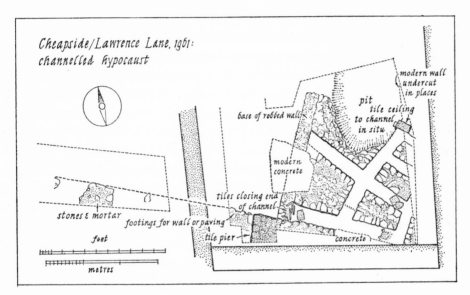

Cheapside/Lawrence Lane, 1961: channelled hypocaust

33. Cheapside, Lawrence Lane (42): part of channelled hypocaust.

hypocaust were fairly uniformly rather over a foot wide; they varied in depth up to a maximum of 18 inches and had been roofed with tiles, one or two of which were still *in situ* on the east side.

The remains would seem to be those of the rear portion of a house, the pier probably being one jamb of a furnace for the hypocaust. The condition of the pier suggests that it was not protected. Most of the building obviously passes under Cheapside; and this presumably means that the Roman street lies towards the south side of Cheapside. The building appears to be askew to the modern street, but it is difficult to say precisely what bearing, if any, this has on the course of the Roman road. Some change of direction seems to be indicated between this point and St. Mary-le-Bow where, as already noted (p. 41), the edge of the Roman road was parallel with that of Cheapside (Figs. 7 and 30). Overlying as it did more than 3 feet of accumulated deposit the building was evidently a relatively late one. Antonine pottery from levels immediately beneath the pier-base suggest at earliest a late second-century date.

Newgate Street–Paternoster Row Area (26–9: 1961–2)

The area bounded by Newgate Street on the north, Paternoster Row on the south, Warwick Lane on the west and Panyer Alley on the east had lost most of its buildings but was not available for examination because the cellars had retained their bomb-rubble and the sites around Paternoster Square had become a garage and car parks. With the agreement of the contractors it was possible to do some work on the fringes of the site during the early stages of its development. On two sites along Paternoster Row (*29* on the west (south side), *28* on the east (north side)) and one on the eastern margin (*26*) excavation on a limited scale was possible; in Newgate Street (*27*) conditions allowed only for the cleaning down of three faces and the recording of one of them which was approximately parallel with the street-frontage to the east of Ivy Lane.

Of the last it need only be said that there was a depth of about 5 feet of layered accumulation, mostly clay and gravel with black occupation intrusions, evidently building floors. Associated particularly with one intermediate level about half-way up the deposit was a series of quite massive post-holes, some of them in pairs and the biggest 9 inches across; but similar post-holes were present at higher levels (and at lower levels elsewhere) and one such, about 7 inches across, was 3 feet deep. Because of contractors' obstructions it was not possible to record the position of this section accurately. As has already been said, it was approximately parallel with the modern street-frontage and about 14 feet back from it. The lower series of post-holes made a fairly straight line, suggesting that if they belonged to buildings facing on to the street the modern street was maintaining the line of its Roman predecessor. The natural surface here was 10–12 feet below the modern street.

At the western end of Paternoster Row (*29*) the conditions appeared to be very similar to those met with in the Queen Victoria Street/Carter Lane area on the other side of St. Paul's (*30, 31*). When the surface of the brick-earth was reached at a depth of about $6\frac{1}{2}$ feet below the cellar floor it presented the appearance of one side of a ditch following the south face of the cutting, the dark filling being to the north. A trench at right angles to the first one at its western end was cut in order to test the possibility of finding the other side of the 'ditch'. But the brickearth showed no sign of rising in the distance of 6 feet covered by this extension; and it was clear that the feature was the south edge of a pit or excavated hollow of uncertain dimensions, the lower part of which—the upper had been disturbed in mediaeval times—contained a Roman filling. The floor of the hollow coincided with the surface of the natural gravel beneath the brickearth: a fact which raises once again the possibility that some of the large holes of this sort in the western part of the city may have had to do with the pottery industry.

At the east end of Paternoster Row (*28*) it was possible to cut back the face left by the preliminary excavation of the builders only a foot or two, both to obtain a straight face (on an east–west alignment) and to collect any datable material that might present itself. A limit was set on the amount of work that could be done here by the need to protect the foundations of the existing street. The deposits were preserved to a maximum height of about 4 feet above the natural surface, which apart from deeper disturbances was fairly level over a distance of something over 90 feet. There was only one pit of any size in this sector, but there were several gullies at different levels which as far as they could be seen did not follow a consistent alignment. There was no sign of stone buildings on this part of the site: only one or two post-holes also were revealed—but this may well have been a matter of accident. The build-up of layers of gravel or loam interleaved with dark occupation-deposits was characteristic and does not call for detailed description here. One floor, at relatively high level (and tipping sharply eastwards, perhaps under the influence of a pit which did not appear in the section), was of plain red-tile mosaic, showing that such floors might be provided for timber buildings. The find of outstanding interest from the site was a hoard of about 530 coins, mainly barbarous copies of coins of the Gallic Empire of the late third century A.D., the latest apparently being a copy of an *antoninianus* of Tacitus of date A.D. 275–6.[1] The hoard came from a pit

[1] Thanks are due to Mr. Ralph Merrifield, Assistant Keeper, Guildhall Museum, for a preliminary report on the contents of this hoard, which will be published in detail in a later report.

which had been cut into a 2-foot-thick layer of gravel which was possibly a road, but the actual level from which it was deposited remains uncertain because the deposits were truncated by modern disturbance. The pit lay within the western limit of the gravel, which was defined by a gully on the east; a large post-hole impinged on it on the west. The difficulty of identifying the gravel layers as a road turns on the fact that they had no gully on the west side. This is perhaps not an insurmountable obstacle; but in spite of modern disturbance such a gully should have been visible. If a road, it had evidently been encroached upon by the late third century, and the presence of a drain or gully beneath it indicates that there had been other activity on the site before it was made.

Finally, on the eastern margin of the site the work done on a very uneven face much encumbered by modern foundations revealed an accumulation of irregular occupation layers, reflecting the irregularity of the underlying surface of the natural brickearth. The total depth of the deposit from the modern surface was about 10 feet, the pottery from the lower levels being mid-late first century. A number of pits had been dug through this accumulation, some Roman, some mediaeval, and one of the former produced pottery ranging down to the early second century. No post-holes were visible here, nor were there any stone foundations.

From the above investigations and from such observations as it was possible to make while the remainder of this large area was being excavated by the contractors there would appear to be no doubt that apart from a stone building in the north-western part of the site, for which there had also been earlier evidence,[1] buildings were entirely of timber.

[1] *Roman London*, p. 135; *Journ. Rom. Soc.* III (1963), pp. 140–1.

VI

Mediaeval Sites: Part One

I. INTRODUCTION

TH E obstacles to the archaeological exploration of mediaeval sites in
London are even more daunting than those that impede a study of the
Roman remains. While over a large part of the central area of the city the
depth of the accumulations is such that the Roman levels survive to as much
as 10 feet below the cellar floors—18 feet or more below street-level—it is
only rarely that the post-Roman deposits and structures have outlived the
succession of drastic remodellings that has taken place since mediaeval
times.

During the Middle Ages, as under the Romans, the processes of accumulation were not as uniform and regular as they were once thought to be.
Mediaeval Londoners indeed were faced with problems like those of the
Romans in kind but exceeding them in degree. A more densely occupied
city, re-created on the shadow of the Roman street-plan, but lacking the
guidance of Roman urban administration and order, had to deal with
correspondingly enhanced difficulties. To generations habituated to the
public services of the twentieth century, sewage and garbage disposal and
water-supply are less than mundane matters which loom large only when
the arrangements for dealing with them develop a flaw. For mediaeval
Londoners, as well as for later generations into the nineteenth century, the
problems could be met only by the digging of cesspits, rubbish-pits, wells
and water-holes in and about their own property, with or without the
benefit of night-soil men and others whose professional task it was to be
responsible for their upkeep. The ground of the mediaeval city was therefore

honeycombed with pits of various kinds, dug from more than one level and often to considerable depths, and (as already noted) cutting through and destroying the earlier deposits. In addition, the rate of aggradation of the general surface was probably greatly increased in many areas since much material which could not otherwise be disposed of was spread over open ground in gardens and elsewhere, gradually raising the levels. Pits, therefore, and comparatively thick deposits of mixed materials often containing building débris and other rubbish, the one representing a downward movement, the other a process of building-up, are features of the mediaeval deposits of London.

The more tangible remains of buildings are scarcer. In areas which contain modern cellars it is normally found that the whole of the building itself has been swept away. All that survives in such circumstances is some part of the foundations, which are often massive and usually composed of rough chalk blocks with a lavish use of rather poor yellow mortar. These foundations can rarely be fitted into a coherent plan, if only because there is usually no opportunity of extended work covering a large area. There are frequent hints, even in these limited glimpses, that cellars or half-cellars were commonly present in many London buildings. Such features have been seen more completely on the few sites where the absence of modern cellars has preserved the earlier structures up to the level of the modern street.

But cellarless sites are rare in the bombed areas covered by this account: they can certainly be numbered by less than the fingers on two hands. In only one of these cases (below, p. 168) have the remains been sufficient to give a clear impression of the character of the building. The most rewarding mediaeval sites in the city are those which have prolonged their original use into the present day and which therefore may be expected to retain within their existing outlines some part of their mediaeval features. Apart from certain obvious exceptions, no mediaeval secular buildings in the city or its environs have survived the drastic reconstructions of the nineteenth century. It must furthermore be remembered that the Great Fire of 1666 had already cleared much of the city area and prepared it for rebuilding in eighteenth-century brick. Ecclesiastical buildings are another matter: more will be said of them below.

2. THE 'LOST' CENTURIES

Here before turning to a summary account of the more significant discoveries relating to post-Roman London something must be said on the problem of the 'lost' centuries—the period of a hundred years or so which followed the Roman withdrawal in the early fifth century A.D., and during which, according to a widely accepted view, the city was abandoned.

One of the outstanding *negative* results of the Excavation Council's work over more than sixteen years has been the absence of structural, or indeed any other, evidence for the occupation of London in the early part of the Saxon period. A feature of a number of sections has been the way in which finds other than Roman survivals have also been lacking.

Since in 1935[1] Dr. (now Sir) Mortimer Wheeler listed by their periods the chance finds of Saxon origin from the walled city and its immediate neighbourhood there have been few if any notable additions to the tally of objects falling within the period of the fifth to the eighth centuries. The number of such finds is in any case not a large one; but taken in conjunction with the distribution of churches whose dedications can be ascribed to the same period, their predominance in the area to the west of the Walbrook stream is the basis for the view that it was the western half of the city on which was centred the early Saxon recolonisation of London. Saxon London therefore developed in a direction which reversed that of the Roman occupation, spreading eastwards at a later day to the Cornhill area, which in Roman times had constituted the original bridgehead settlement. This later development, taking place over the ninth to the eleventh centuries A.D., is also illustrated in Wheeler's maps.

The absence of early Saxon discoveries referred to above is remarkable; for, as has already been noted (p. 15), the western half of the city as the area in which the incidence of bomb-damage was much heavier than anywhere else, has also been the area in which most of the Council's investigations have taken place. The first clearly defined chronological evidence, such as it is, in this region is consistently of *later* Saxon date. But again this

[1] Wheeler, *London and the Saxons* (London Museum, 1935), pp. 185–94. *Ibid.* generally for discussion of the Saxon colonisations of the London area (cf. *Antiquity*, VIII (1934), pp. 290–302, with rejoinder by J. N. L. Myres, *ibid.*, pp. 437–42, and further comment *ibid.*, pp. 433–7); and criticism by J. N. L. Myres in *Journ. Rom. Soc.*, XXVI (1936), pp. 87–92.

evidence is not associated with structural remains and is made up almost entirely of scattered sherds of painted ware of the type named after the kilns at Pingsdorf (near Cologne in the Rhineland), though it was not necessarily all produced there.[1] This ware ranges in date from the mid-ninth to the late twelfth century.

The evidence from the ground seems to indicate that the absence of early Saxon remains is not due to the later destruction of the levels in which they would have occurred. Continued absence of early Saxon relics seems to corroborate the view that London was indeed largely unoccupied for some time after the collapse of the Roman power in the fifth century. The puzzling feature about this gap in the archaeological evidence is the contradiction that it embodies with the situation in London in the late sixth and early seventh centuries as implied by the records. The ordination of Mellitus as bishop of London in 604 and the building of the church of St. Paul by King Ethelbert must be taken to mark the renewal on some scale of the occupation of London by about A.D. 600.[2] This would seem to be true even if this first attempt to establish Christianity in post-Roman London must be accepted as having failed. Yet the archaeological evidence seems to be consistent in showing no sign of life until more than 150 years later. The explanation of this apparent contradiction may be that the area of early Saxon occupation was much less extensive than has been thought. Is it possible that it was indeed limited to the immediate area of the western hill on which King Ethelbert built the first cathedral; and that even the limited expansion which would have carried traces of it to the margins of the hill did not take place until the ninth or tenth century? The hope was entertained that some part of the answer to these questions might be found in the large bombed area of Paternoster Row (26–9) immediately north of St. Paul's Cathedral; but nothing bearing on the problem was found.

In the meantime, it is in keeping with the evidence of the scattered finds that the first structural remains of buildings should be relatively late in the period covered by the 'Pingsdorf' ware already mentioned.

[1] For a general study see G. C. Dunning, 'Pottery of the Late Anglo-Saxon Period in England' *Medieval Archaeology*, III (1959), pp. 31–78 (for Pingsdorf ware, pp. 55–7 and Figs. 28–30).

[2] F. M. Stenton, *Anglo-Saxon England* (Oxford, 1947), pp. 55–7.

3. HUT-PITS IN CANNON STREET AND ELSEWHERE

The evidence in question was uncovered on the *Financial Times* site in Cannon Street, about 200 yards south-east of St. Paul's, in 1955 (35). The fringes of this site to north and south were comparatively unproductive. For some distance back from Cannon Street disturbance of all periods left little Roman material untouched: here a single mediaeval pit was interesting for its well-preserved wicker-work lining (Plate 71: p. 161 below). To the south (Knightrider Street–Queen Victoria Street) the early features had vanished for a different reason. Knightrider Street, now in part eliminated by 're-development', lay near the edge of the 50-foot terrace, which here falls fairly sharply to the river-frontage level in Thames Street. The natural contours of the area were drastically modified by the construction of Queen Victoria Street in 1869. Cellars, built no doubt as part of this construction, had been terraced into the slope above the street, with the result that only the natural gravel had survived beneath their floors (p. 145).

In the central part of the site a greater depth of artificial deposits remained. There was no brickearth, possibly because it had been removed in antiquity. The surface of the natural gravel lay 5–6 feet below the cellar floor and was much cut into by pits of various kinds, but the biggest disturbance was an irregular excavation, over 40 feet long as revealed in the cutting, and from 3–5 feet deep below the existing gravel surface. This hollow was filled with mixed deposits deliberately introduced and containing dark occupation material in irregular layers. It is most probably to be explained as a Roman gravel-pit, dug, no doubt, while this area was still outside the built-up extent of London.

More important than this, however, were two later cavities, both dug partly into the quarry-filling (Plate 67). As they presented themselves in the section it was thought that they might be hut-pits and this interpretation was in due course confirmed when the ground on each side of the original cutting was opened up. Of the two pits, that to the north was the smaller (11½ feet long), its main axis roughly north-and-south (Plate 68). By an unfortunate accident its western half was destroyed unrecorded apart from one post-hole, but it must have been about 9 feet wide. The sides of the pit, recognisable to a height of just over 3 feet above its level floor, were practically vertical (section: Fig. 34). The lower part certainly had been boarded,

155

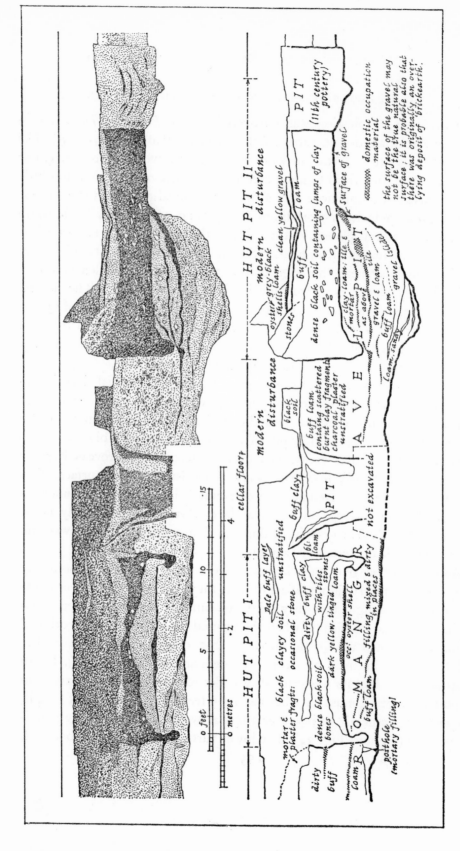

34. Cannon Street (*Financial Times* site: *35*): section across hut-pits.

HUT PIT I

mortar & black clayey soil : unstratified
plaster fragts. occasional stone
pale buff layer
dirty buff clay
dark yellow-tinged loam
occ: oyster shell
filling, mixed & dirty in places
posthole :
mortary filling?

R O M A N G R
dirty
buff
buff loam
loam

HUT PIT II

modern disturbance
clean yellow gravel
oyster: grey-black shells loam
stones
buff
loam
dense black soil containing lumps of clay
(11th century pottery)
PIT
clay: loam: tile &
mortar
as above
tile
gravel & loam
gravel (slide)
buff loam
loam, sandy
surface of gravel
domestic occupation material

the surface of the gravel may not be the true natural surface; it is probable also that there was originally an over-lying deposit of brickearth.

modern disturbance
black soil
buff loam containing scattered burnt clay fragments: charcoal plaster unstratified
buff clay
P I T

G R
not excavated

A V E - L O - P I T

the timber surviving as a sharp dense black line. There was an indication on the east side that the pit had been heightened by the addition of a bank of which a small portion remained. In the angles of the pit and at intervals along the sides were massive post-holes which looked as if they had been intended for tree-trunks split in half. Those on the sides in particular were D-shaped in plan, with their straight faces against the wall of the pit, where they had helped to keep the timber lining in place. These post-holes were normally more than a foot across and 15 inches or so deep. There was an uneven layer of unproductive occupation-soil over the hut-floor. Provision for an entrance must have been made on the west side of the pit.

The second pit ($32\frac{1}{2}$ by 17 feet: Plate 69) to the south was more complicated in its features, having existed apparently in at least two versions. It had also been much cut up by later pits and by recent cesspits and other structures. Its floor was about 6 feet below the cellar surface and the wall stood to a maximum height of 4 feet above that. Here the arrangement seems to have been that of a gully (or more probably a sleeper-trench) with very large post-holes at 3–4-foot intervals along it (Fig. 35). As with the first pit, the post-holes were often semi-circular, though less sharply cut, and rather more than a foot in depth. The site was somewhat damp, so that remains of timber had survived in a number of places. There were indications of at least two planked floors, as well as of wall-linings on the west and north sides. The entrance to the hut had clearly been through the middle of the south side. In spite of much destruction by later pits there were indications of a wooden sill or doorway and possibly also of a porch, only the eastern half of which had survived.

In this summary account many details have been omitted, but enough has been said to make clear the general character of the structures represented by these remains. They were rectangular huts sunk perhaps to at least half their total height into the ground, their roofs, presumably pitched, supported by remarkably large timber uprights. The immediate and obvious parallel for this combination of elements is provided by the Saxon huts which have become increasingly well known in this country since E. T. Leeds and G. C. Dunning published their discoveries at Sutton Courtenay and Bourton-on-the-Water in 1921–6 and 1931 respectively.[1] But while

[1] E. T. Leeds, 'A Saxon Village at Sutton Courtenay, Berkshire (Second Report)', *Archaeologia*, 76 (1926–7), pp. 59–80. (First report in *Arch.* 73, 1922–33.) G. C. Dunning, 'Bronze Age

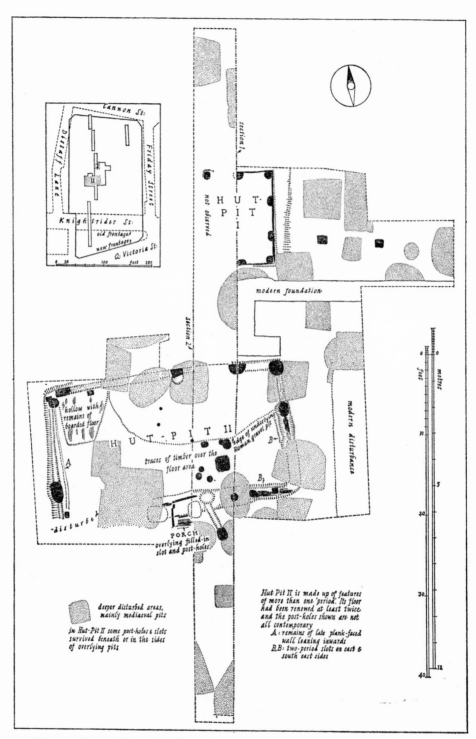

35. Cannon Street (*Financial Times* site: *35*): plan of hut-pits.

the relationships of the London hut-hollows appear to be clear enough their actual date is less easy to decide, at any rate until the evidence from the site can be subjected to a more detailed examination than it has yet received. From at least one pit which was later than the second hut came pottery which, being of eleventh-century date, shows that the huts had been given up and were at least partly filled by early Norman times. The *Financial Times* huts must therefore be regarded as of at least late Saxon date, even if at the extreme end of the Saxon period. As such they constitute the earliest structural evidence for Saxon London on the secular side; though fairly certainly they must be the successors of earlier huts of similar type which have yet to be found.

Suggestions of other such huts have been observed elsewhere. At Bucklersbury, just off Cheapside (43: p. 133), on a much restricted site, a flat-bottomed hollow which merely projected into the cutting from the east may have been a small hut-pit. It was a little under 8 feet wide, 3 feet deep, and retained traces of two plank floors, one above the other—features which entirely differentiated this pit from others on the same site. At Addle Street (Wood Street) (21) amongst a confusion of mediaeval pits and other disturbances were found the south-western angle and part of two sides of a larger hut-hollow on the Cannon Street model. The corner post-hole and two lateral post-holes had survived. The pit was deeper than elsewhere (5 feet), but there could be no mistaking its distinctive character (Plate 70).

A second pit about 10 feet square by rather over $5\frac{1}{2}$ feet deep in the same area was of the type of those that at Oxford and elsewhere have been interpreted as Saxon cellars.[1] In the filling, which had been largely destroyed by a modern foundation, was a fragment of heavy floor-boarding. These disjointed fragments may be the last tangible signs of an occupation which was associated with the traditional site of the palace of the Saxon king Ethelbert in neighbouring Aldermanbury.[2] Whatever the actual date of the huts, they make their contribution to a visual impression of London as it

[1] E. M. Jope, 'The Clarendon Hotel, Oxford. Part 1. The Site', *Oxoniensia*, XXIII (1958), pp. 1–83, and particularly for this subject pp. 5–10 and 19–20. In the latter Dr. B. Hope-Taylor argues that the pits were not cellars but latrine-pits.

[2] *Roy. Commission on Hist. MSS., 9th Report*, p. 44a.

Settlements and a Saxon Hut near Bourton-on-the Water, Gloucestershire', *Antiq. Journ.* XII (1932), pp. 279–93.

must have appeared in late Saxon—or early mediaeval—times. They suggest scattered groups of hovels laid out to no ordered plan, though they may have been associated with, or centred upon, larger houses of the aisled- or longhouse type.[1] Such hut-groups may have been distributed beyond the limits of the western hill. Recent observations have shown that stone buildings were much less abundant in Roman London than was once thought and it may be conjectured that their ruins would have presented fewer obstacles to the first Saxon settlers. Of more pretentious Saxon buildings there is at present no sign, though they must have existed. They too would have been timber structures whose isolated post-holes defy identification in areas of excavation which are not only limited but also much disturbed.

4. MINOR MEDIAEVAL STRUCTURES

Before turning to mediaeval buildings something further should be said of the pits and other features to which reference has already been made. They shed light on mediaeval habits of life but introduce practical complications into the archaeological investigation of London's past.

The structures here grouped together fulfilled a number of contemporary purposes. They were rubbish-pits, cesspits, wells and water-holes. The most striking of these remains are the rubbish-pits, which are normally present in numbers in any area within the walled city that has supported domestic occupation. On occasion the concentration of pits may have been such that they cut into one another, new pits having been dug on the site of old ones which had been filled in and therefore forgotten. The pits were usually funnel-shaped in section, with widely-splayed mouths, often of rectilinear outline. They were of considerable size: frequently 8 feet and sometimes even more across and up to 14 feet deep (and again a few even deeper) below the cellar-surface (which was sometimes lower than the surface from which the pit was originally dug).

The interesting feature of the rubbish-pits as a class was the provision that was made for revetting their sides. Normally they penetrated the natural brickearth and sometimes were sunk into the gravel below it: in this material

---

[1] C. A. R. Radford in *Medieval Archaeology*, I (1957), pp. 27–38; cf. also Rosemary Cramp, *ibid.*, pp. 68–77.

the outline of the hole was generally a regular square or rectangle, sharply cut and smoothly finished. Above this level the pits were often dug through comparatively loose ground which was made up of accumulated occupation-deposits as well as the varied fillings of earlier pits. Here the sides of the pits required support and this was usually provided in one of two ways. Stakes or poles up to about 3 inches in diameter were driven obliquely downwards against the side of the pit at horizontal intervals of 9–12 inches. These stakes then served to support an interlaced wicker-work lining of rods up to about an inch in diameter. More rarely a revetment of light planks was provided.

In the first of these pits to be excavated at Gutter Lane and elsewhere the decayed state of the remains and the partial view that was obtained of them presented many puzzles. As time went on, however, other examples were seen more completely and in damp conditions which encouraged preservation of the timber elements. In the pit already mentioned in an otherwise unrewarding cutting on the *Financial Times* site (35) the wicker-work was well-preserved and its relationship to the stakes could be well seen, though only casts of the latter had been preserved (Plate 71). Other pits in a similar condition were examined at Bucklersbury and Addle Street: previously the casts of the stakes, with the merest traces of wicker-work, were observed in the large pit on the site of the south-eastern angle of the Roman fort at Aldermanbury (14: Plate 6). Remains of a plank-lining were found in one of the deeper pits at Gutter Lane. The linings were sometimes simple, extending apparently the full depth of the pit, but often were either arranged in tiers or had been renewed, so that there was a succession of stakes, providing for two or three linings at different levels in the pit.

The fillings were of very mixed character. The materials varied so widely in consistency and moisture-holding capacity that they often presented a serious problem in the deeper trenches because of their tendency to collapse into the cutting. Differential shrinking as the side of a cutting dried out often led to large cavities, which in turn might mean loss of support for some feet of material above them. The soil fillings were usually a dense black, clayey in consistency, and evidently contained a good deal of organic matter. These might take up most of the pit; but there were usually other materials as well, including small quantities of clean gravel and clay. Sometimes, indeed, the fillings exhibited a repetition which suggested that individual pits may have served some more specialised purpose at present unknown. Sagging layers of fibrous material, usually light brown in colour, were also common. They were almost certainly decayed wood, but were quite amorphous and did not yield anything distinctive. Meat bones were abundant at times; oyster-shells were scattered through the soil and both mussel- and cockle-shells occurred in quantity. Other objects, on the other hand, were rare: quite large pits have been known to produce only a sherd or two of pottery and one very deep pit in Gresham Street (*24*), though undoubtedly of mediaeval date, gave only a fragment of Roman ware. From a pit in Silver Street (north side: *19*) came a bone chessman.

The varied nature of the fillings of these pits reflects the use to which they were put as repositories for rubbish and waste materials resulting from the general day-to-day life of the community. As has already been said, they were a feature of every excavated area within the walled city—so much so that their absence from the ground within the Walbrook temple (though pits were found outside it) was worthy of comment. The archaeologist's interest in other men's middens here as elsewhere looks beyond their contents to their wider implications. Whether or not the pits were emptied or reused, the biggest of them at least must have remained open for some time: as a malodorous source of disease and pestilence they are one of the realities behind the picturesque aldermanic posies provided to protect their bearers from the more obvious unpleasantnesses.

The use of timber for rubbish-pit linings is paralleled by its use for wells or water-holes. At Aldermanbury (*14*), sunk into the filling of the Roman fort ditch a circular shaft 42 inches across had a coopered lining of which only a small fragment remained. The rope binding the timber had left remarkably sharp impressions in the stiff clayey lining of the pit (Plate 72). Apart from the character of its construction the surprising feature of this well was its depth—or rather, its lack of depth. At its full depth of just over 3 feet it was still in artificial soil accumulations so that water reaching it through the ground would have lacked the benefit of filtering through the clean gravel substratum. Other wells of this and similar type were also relatively shallow and often passed through, and even ended in, soil which must have been heavily charged with organic matter. If their contents were used for domestic purposes to any extent such wells must have constituted a serious risk to health, the more serious perhaps because less obvious than the more spectacular effects of the rubbish-pits. Though by the seventeenth century the water-supply position in London had been very much improved with the construction of an increasing number of conduits, pumps and the like, many establishments evidently had their private wells; and the practice was continued far into the nineteenth century. Occasionally, indeed, the early wells themselves seem to have continued in prolonged use. The well which cut into the south wall of the Mithraeum in Walbrook (Plate 33) appeared to be of mediaeval construction: its contents showed that it had been open until quite recent times and probably into the twentieth century; but whether or not water was still drawn from it at this late date is not known.

The comparative shallowness of the wells (including one or two stone-lined examples) seen in the north-western area of the city would suggest that in this district at least the water-table has fallen since the Middle Ages. None of the wells so far examined was found still to contain water, and their fillings showed no signs of waterlogging. The change is no doubt to be accounted for largely by changed surface-conditions in the city itself, rather than by fluctuations in rainfall. The creation of impervious surfaces for roads, pavements and the like, the reduction of garden areas and the total provision of modern surface drainage have diverted from the city most of the water that would have found its way in 'natural' conditions into the soil.

5. SECULAR BUILDINGS

Much material exists, in pictures, maps and records, to give a vivid impression of London's buildings, at any rate in the latter part of the Middle Ages. Of these buildings very few survive today. Those that escaped the Great Fire have become the victims of later rebuilding, particularly in the nineteenth century, when widespread office-building reflected the industrial and commercial prosperity of Britain at large. As has already been said (p. 152), with obvious exceptions the mediaeval buildings of London survive only below street-level and in the areas of modern cellars are represented (if they are present at all) only by their foundations. Archaeological excavation therefore cannot be expected to augment or extend modern knowledge of the mediaeval houses and other buildings of the city on any considerable scale. Its value lies in the fact that on a strictly limited number of sites it may produce some information about details of construction and the like which other sources may not reveal and perhaps in this way may bring the living conditions of mediaeval Londoners more vividly forward than would otherwise be possible.

(a) Neville's Inn (1947: 3, 5)

One such site has clearly-attested historical associations. John Stow records that the Nevells or Nevilles of Raby in Westmorland rented a walled garden along the west side of Noble Street and between that street and the city wall.[1] The lease had been granted to Neville in 48 Edw. III by the Corporation. The garden was 95 ells (about 356 feet) long by $9\frac{1}{2}$ ells ($35\frac{1}{2}$ feet) wide: it must have extended rather more than the full length of the city wall behind Noble Street and had therefore contained beneath its surface the significant elements in the Cripplegate fort which were described in Chapter II. At the north end of this garden plot (5) was 'one great house builded of stone and timber', in Stow's time called the Lord Windsor's house, but previously belonging to the Nevilles and known as Neville's Inn. The Nevilles held the Inn in the fourteenth–fifteenth centuries, when by the marriage of an heiress the house passed to the Windsor family. The association was preserved in the name of Windsor Court, levelled by the bombing of 1941 and in 1959 eliminated by the construction of the new London Wall (Route 11).

As the Neville garden overlay the remains of the fort to the south, so Neville's Inn or Windsor House, with its frontage on Silver Street and Monkwell Street, overlay the fort gateway and the associated features to the north. Here, almost as far as Bastion 14, the comparatively high level of the modern cellar floors had preserved not only the Roman remains, but also the foundations and part of the cellars, of the mediaeval house (Fig. 36).

The outstanding feature of Neville's Inn on the north side of the site away from the street frontage, was the lavish use which had been made of chalk for foundations and for the core of walls (Plate 73). It would seem that before the house was built the area had been an open space immediately behind the city wall. As such, it contained a number of rubbish-pits, two

[1] J. Stow, *Survey of London* (ed. Kingsford, 1908), I, pp. 312, 315; II, p. 344.

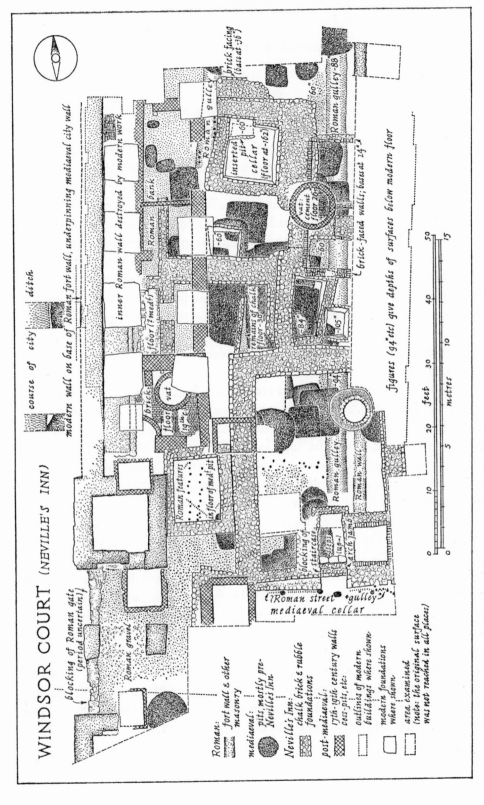

WINDSOR COURT (NEVILLE'S INN)

blocking of Roman gate
(period uncertain?)

course of city ditch

modern wall on base of Roman fort wall, underpinning mediaeval city wall

inner Roman wall destroyed by modern work

brick facing
(base at 36')

Roman gulley

Roman gulley 88

inserted
pit
cellar
(floor at 162')

-60'

-60'

vat: cement
floor 20'

brick-faced walls; base at 24'J

-60'

-60'

-84'

-05"

remains of chalk
floor 30'

Roman bank

floor (?medil)

brick
vat

floor
(19th c.)

Roman features

(in floor of medl pit

-94'

Roman gulley

Roman wall

blocking of
staircase

(up-)

arch jamb

figures (94' etc) give depths of surfaces below modern floor

Roman gravel

0   10   20   feet   30   40   50

0   5   10   metres   15

"Roman street" "gulley"
mediaeval cellar

Roman: fort wall & other
masonry

mediaeval:
pits, mostly pre-
Neville's Inn

Neville's Inn:
chalk brick & rubble
foundations

post-mediaeval:
17th-19th century walls
cess-pits, etc:

outlines of modern
buildings where shown

modern foundations
where shown

area examined
(note: the original surface
was not reached in all places)

36. Windsor Court (3): plan of remains of Neville's Inn.

of which in particular were of very large size, being more than 12 feet deep.

In putting in their chalk foundations the mediaeval builders took full account of the variations in the ground which resulted from these disturbances. They were not content to let their structures rest upon the soft dark pit-fillings but penetrated everywhere to the light-coloured gravel or clay-loam; and the depths of their foundations varied accordingly. Thus in the deep pits already mentioned a massive chalk foundation over 3 feet wide was carried to the full depth of at least 11 feet to the floor within the pits, but rose sharply to the surface of the natural ground beyond their edges. The contrast was even more strongly marked on the western side of the area. Here the clean loam or brickearth bank behind the Roman wall must have had every appearance of being natural to the mediaeval builders, though its surface was 4 feet or more higher than that of the natural ground on the eastern side of the site. In contrast therefore to the extreme depth of the foundations over part of the eastern side, those on the west barely penetrated the surface of the Roman bank.

Since the area available for excavation was limited by the depth of the cellars on the east side of the site there could be little hope of recovering more than a small part of the plan of Neville's Inn and still less hope that the part recovered would be intelligible. All original floors had vanished and the mediaeval faced walls had also gone. Apart from the foundations which have already been described the recognisable remains (Plate 74) consisted of chalk-lined pits of which one, towards the north, was faced with good dressed blocks, while a second, on the east, more roughly constructed, produced a quantity of pottery associated with a silver penny of Edward III (1327–77). On the Silver Street (southern) frontage the Inn had had a cellar, part of which was lost when the modern street-line was set back behind that of the mediaeval street. The floor of this cellar had been excavated into the natural surface, but not so deeply that all the Roman features had been destroyed. The cellar was on the line of the road from the west gate of the fort, and the bottom of the north-flanking gully of the Roman road, running with the base of the mediaeval wall, was just recognisable. The cellar had undergone reconstruction, in the course of which a stone staircase giving access to it from a higher level on the north side had been blocked up. Buried in the wall that had been carried across its opening were the battered remains of Reigate-stone jambs (Plates 75, 76). It seems likely that the doorway was arched.

It must be assumed that the mediaeval building, taken to be Neville's Inn, represented by these remains was destroyed when the Great Fire swept over this area in 1666. Overlying the chalk foundations, and much damaged by modern concrete pier-bases and rafts, were brick walls, never more than a course or two in height, which appeared to be of seventeenth–eighteenth-century date. On the eastern side of the site the chalk walls had evidently been incorporated in this later building, for they had been partly refaced with brick. Associated with this period was a series of square stone- and brick-lined cesspits, up to 6 feet across, of the type common during this period. Several of these pits had been built within the earlier structures, using the mediaeval foundations, and even the walls of the Roman guard turret, to form one or more of their sides.

Whatever the original purpose of this post-Fire building, at a later stage, probably in the early nineteenth century, some kind of industrial activity seems to have been pursued on the site. It was represented by a number of well-built circular vats whose brick linings had a nineteenth-century appearance. One such, $7\frac{1}{2}$ feet across, had a cement floor above a rubble filling at a depth of only 2 feet below the modern surface; its brick wall also was rendered with cement and it had been sunk into the earlier chalk and brick-faced walls. A second, at the south-west corner of the site, was slightly smaller but of similar depth; it retained traces of a lid which was in part supported on a beam across its centre. It was overlaid by a brick floor; and a similar floor in the north-west corner extended sufficiently far westwards to show that by this time the inner 'half' of the Roman wall (p. 48) had been reduced here and could have survived only below the contemporary floor level. What the condition of the wall was before this time it was impossible to say: it may be that from a quite early date it had been incorporated in Neville's Inn as the west wall of the building; but the modern concrete foundations had destroyed all the points of contact between the Roman and the later work. The later nineteenth-century treatment of the surviving mediaeval city wall as a division between properties in this neighbourhood has already been described (p. 90).

(b) Cheapside, South (39)

What was left of Neville's Inn does not suggest that it was a building of much architectural pretension. A fragment of a stone-built undercroft immediately to the west of the tower of St. Mary-le-Bow Church in Cheapside (39), gives some indication of the kind of building that occupied the frontage of an important thoroughfare in the city's centre, near a spot which was a focal point for public occasions in mediaeval times. That so much was preserved here was due to the fact that the building underlay a street on the west side of the church which had not been seriously disturbed since the seventeenth century. The area must at that time have been relevelled with the rebuilding of the church by Wren. The indications are that in this neighbourhood the pre-Fire surface was about $2\frac{1}{2}$ feet below the surface of today: the difference was very largely made up with building-débris, derived, no doubt, from post-Fire building activity.

The building itself was filled with mixed material which contained a good deal of similar rubbish. This filling was entirely featureless and without stratification, its disposition suggesting that the vaulted chamber had been dismantled and put out of use in a single action. The discovery of the building was due in the first place to the digging of a trial-pit to examine the foundations of the tower of St. Mary-le-Bow Church. The foundations, in the form of a series of massive offsets, had been sunk through the eastern part of the chamber so that its full east–west width could not be determined. From north to south the internal length of the building was 19 feet; on the evidence of the surviving vaulting the width of the bay, of which rather more than half had survived, would have been about 10 feet. It is impossible, however, to say how many bays may have made up the complete width.

The walls were well-built of Kentish ragstone and 4 feet 3–9 inches wide. On the north the frontage was extended westwards on the same line, with a straight joint at the angle; but not enough of the adjoining building was visible for anything to be made of it. The chamber had had a groined vault; the springers of the ribs were supported on moulded corbels which had survived in both western angles. On all three walls, as far as visible, simple flat-pointed arch-mouldings defined the outline of the vault; but the vault itself had gone and the walls were everywhere irregularly cut down below the crown of the arch. In the centre of the west wall there was a straight-

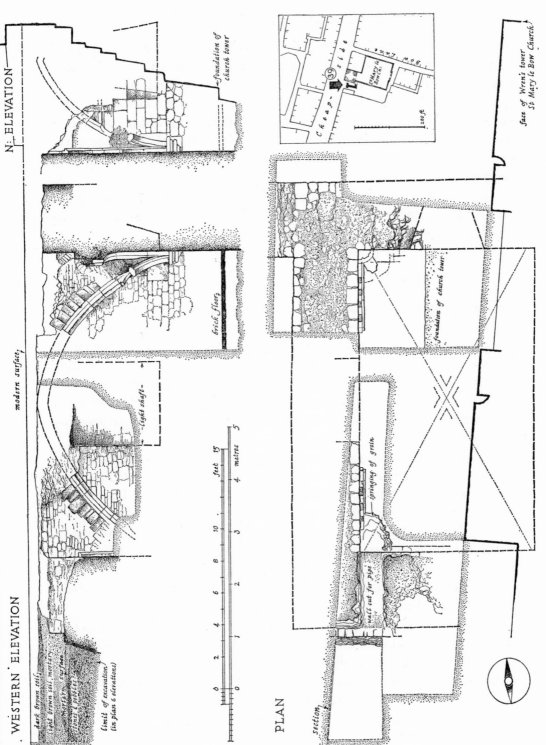

N·. ELEVATION

WÈSTERN·ELEVATION

foundation of church tower

brick floor

light shaft

modern surface

dark brown soil

light brown soil (mortar)

mottar
surface

rammed rubble

limit of excavation
(in plan & elevations)

0   2   4   6   8   10   15 feet
0   1   2   3   4   metres 5

PLAN

springing of groin

foundation of church tower

section

channel cut for pipe

face of Wren's tower
St Mary le Bow Church

Cheap-side

St Mary le Bow Church

200 ft.

39

37. Cheapside, South (39): undercroft to west of St. Mary-le-Bow Church: plan and
elevations. (*Based on a survey prepared by the Ministry of Public Building and Works.*)

sided opening 5 feet 2 inches wide immediately below the wall-arch. It had been filled in with rubble and its purpose as door or window could not therefore be determined. In the north wall, on the other hand, one jamb of a splayed recess had a sloping back rising from a sill 8 feet 8 inches below the modern road-level. Its upper part had been destroyed, but it presumably opened to a ventilator above the then external street-level. The floor of the chamber was of brick; it was just over 12 feet 6 inches below the modern surface.

The character of this interesting little structure is well shown by the accompanying illustration (Fig. 37), which is based on a measured drawing supplied by the Ministry of Works.

(c) Brewers' Hall (15)

This was a site of a different kind. The hall stood in the rounded angle of Addle Street and Aldermanbury within the area of the Cripplegate fort, the east rampart of which would have been just outside the limits of the building and its gardens. There was therefore a twofold reason for excavation here: the possibility that since the deposits appeared to be undisturbed to modern street-level evidence might survive bearing on the later history of the fort; and the likelihood that further information might be forthcoming about the hall itself.

It has already been observed (p. 35) that the first aim was frustrated because later disturbance in all the areas examined had penetrated to below the original natural surface of the ground. This was the position even on that part of the site which apparently from time immemorial had been a garden. The post-Roman elements, explored particularly in a north-to-south trench across the eastern side, which was unencumbered by modern cellars, fell into two parts: the mediaeval structures; and the later walls, mostly brickwork of good quality, which must have been part of the hall as rebuilt after the Great Fire.

The only authoritative plan of the Brewers' Hall, destroyed in 1941, is that in the City of London volume of the Historic Monuments Commission.[1] It shows that the main body of the hall was laid out on a regular rectilinear plan with an extension for domestic offices (at ground level) to

[1] In London (The City) (1929), p. 94.

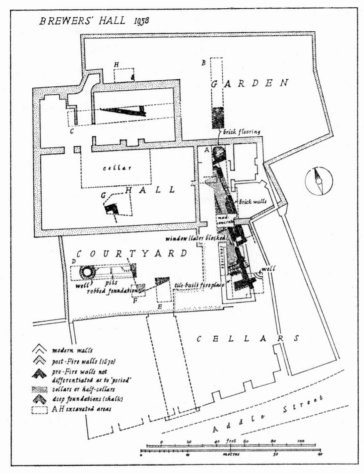

BREWERS' HALL 1958

38. Brewers' Hall (15): plan as excavated.

the north. There had been a garden of irregular outline beyond and to the
north-east, and a courtyard to the south with a staircase along its eastern
side. To the east of the eighteenth-century complex the buildings retained
the irregular outlines which linked them with the layout of the surrounding
cellars. In due time it became obvious that in rebuilding their hall after the
Great Fire the Company had pursued a policy of economy by following the
original lines and no doubt utilising as far as possible the existing structures,
on the east side of the site.

The plan (Fig. 38) shows how the Brewers' Hall thus combined mediaeval

171

and later features in its pre-1941 layout. The remains below ground were complicated and some of them are in any case not easy to explain because of the incomplete nature of much of the evidence. Broadly speaking, it is clear that the original complex had a typically mediaeval layout on which the eighteenth-century building was imposed and which had itself undergone changes which affected not only the plan, but also the levels on the site. A feature of the cutting already mentioned was a succession of walls running obliquely across it at at least three levels. These walls were faced to their full depth on the west side while on the east they were frequently rough, at any rate in their lower parts, which had clearly been built against solid ground. They were also of very mixed construction, with some brick and stone, but with chalk predominating in the earlier versions. The building-up of the external surface of the ground was well seen on the eastern side of the site. The surface that accompanied the first version was 7 feet below the modern surface: this cellar contained a splayed window-opening, subsequently blocked, near its north-eastern corner, the sill of which was 6 feet 4 inches down. Above this level was a horizontal accumulation of mixed materials the final surface of which was 3 feet 9 inches down: from this point upwards the deposits were confused and contained much modern material. The last significant alteration appears to have been the addition of a tile-floored and lined fireplace, and this also was lower than the external contemporary surface. The floor of the hearth was at a depth of 5 feet 9 inches; the external brick facing to the chalk wall coincided with a floor just over 3 feet down.

It should be added that in the course of this work few certain traces were observed of the Great Fire. Overlying the probable outer north wall of the mediaeval building, with a brick floor that evidently accompanied it, there was a thick deposit of burnt brick in a weathered state, together with a quantity of ash. This appeared to have been introduced as a filling, partly at least in order to raise the floor level. With what John Stow called the 'fayre house' of the Brewers, as with Neville's Inn, this investigation cannot be said to have added impressively to knowledge of the architectural refinements of mediaeval London; but it performs a slighter service in demonstrating some of the minor contradictions that make up the Middle Ages, as a result of which splendour and squalor could exist side by side in the buildings of important corporate bodies.

VII

Mediaeval Sites: Part Two

I. INTRODUCTION

IN this chapter are described briefly the ecclesiastical sites which have been explored by the Council down to the time of the writing of this account. Seven in all, they were very different in character, at any rate in the condition in which they presented themselves to the excavators.

Charterhouse, on the north-western post-Roman boundary of the city, ceased to be an ecclesiastical site when the monastery was suppressed in 1537. Its conversion to secular use, first as a nobleman's mansion, then as the seat of a famous charity, brought about fundamental changes in its buildings, while retaining sufficient of its monastic features to provoke discussion of their relationship to the original monastic plan.

At St. Bartholomew the Great the suppression of the Augustinian priory led to the gradual loss of the conventual buildings on the south side of the church, with the destruction of the nave itself. Drastic remodelling of much of this area had ensured the loss of most of the monastic remains, though some at least had been recorded in the more recent past. The levelling of modern buildings in the neighbourhood of the cloister opened up the possibility that some slight addition to the plan might be made on the south and south-west sides.

St. Bride's Church, Fleet Street, had been a parish church of importance throughout the Middle Ages, its unusual dedication to an early Celtic saint suggesting that its origins were to be sought some centuries before the Norman Conquest. The mediaeval church was destroyed in the Great Fire; it was rebuilt by Wren from 1671 on, and Wren's church in its turn was gutted in 1940. Here the hope was that beneath the seventeenth-century building enough might have survived to throw light upon the earlier periods of the history of the church.

The position with regard to another city church, St. Swithun London Stone, in Cannon Street, was somewhat similar to that of St. Bride. Here too the dedication suggested an early foundation. Stow had recorded a rebuilding and enlargement in the early fifteenth century; and this church, destroyed in the Great Fire, was rebuilt by Wren. Wren's church, burnt out in 1940, was not restored: a block of offices now stands on its site.

St. Alban Wood Street was a third church with an early dedication which was not to be restored, though its tower is to be retained and will provide a valuable foil to the modern buildings that surround it. The church is said to have been rebuilt by Inigo Jones in 1633–4, and after partial destruction in the Great Fire, by Wren in 1682–7. The stripping of the walls of their rendering, however, showed that they were mainly of late mediaeval date. It would seem that Jones' rebuilding was confined to work on the south side; and while Wren built the present tower and remodelled the west end of the church, he too inherited a mediaeval shell, the excavation of which revealed the structural sequence on the site fairly completely.

A site of yet another kind was the Jews' Garden, an extensive area in Cripplegate Without on the west side of Red Cross Street, which until 1177 was in the words of John Stow 'the only place appoynted them in England wherein to bury their deade . . .' An attempt was made to establish the extent of the graveyard in the parts of the site that were available in 1949.

Finally, beyond the city and across the Thames the Cluniac house of Bermondsey Abbey was represented above ground only by a wall of ancient appearance in an area which was almost completely levelled. With the help of H.M. Ministry of Works and of the Bermondsey Borough Council something was learned of the character of the monastic church, though in general only its foundations had survived.

2. THE CHARTERHOUSE

A detailed account of the Charterhouse has already been published.[1] Only a brief summary of the main results is therefore necessary here, together with a note on one or two new facts which have come to light since 1954.

In their twentieth-century form the historic Charterhouse buildings are made up of three courts from west to east, Washhouse Court, Master's Court and Chapel Court respectively (Fig. 39). To the north lies the large green, originally square but now much reduced by the buildings of St. Bartholomew's Hospital Medical College, the descendant of the garth of the Great Cloister of the monastery. The main conventual buildings were sited in the area of the courts. Washhouse Court is essentially unchanged from the time of its construction in the early sixteenth century: its monastic use as domestic offices was prolonged into the period of the mansion. Master's Court and Chapel Court, on the other hand, were the outcome of drastic remodelling to produce the house built by Lord North and the Duke of Norfolk from the mid-sixteenth century onwards. It used to be assumed that the 'chapel' at the eastern end of this complex, with the tower next to it, was part of the monastic church; and this assumption carried with it various inconsistencies both in the interpretation of the existing remains and in their correlation with the records. Outstanding amongst the latter is the famous waterworks plan which, in recording meticulously according to the standards of the time the arrangements for the water-supply, presents also by a combination of plan and elevation a remarkably complete picture of the monastery as a whole (Fig. 40) and forms part of the basis for the reconstruction attempted in Fig. 41.

For the details of the discoveries which overthrew the earlier views and of the conclusions based on them the reader must be referred to the published account. The net result was that the architects having previously established the position of the Founder's Tomb and other highly relevant facts, the outline of the church and other features was to a large extent recovered. The church actually lay to the south of the position previously accepted for it, spanning the whole of the Chapel Court and a considerable part of Master's Court to the west. In addition a number of the chapels and other buildings of the monastery were located; and the plan which

[1] M. D. Knowles and W. F. Grimes, *Charterhouse* (London, 1954).

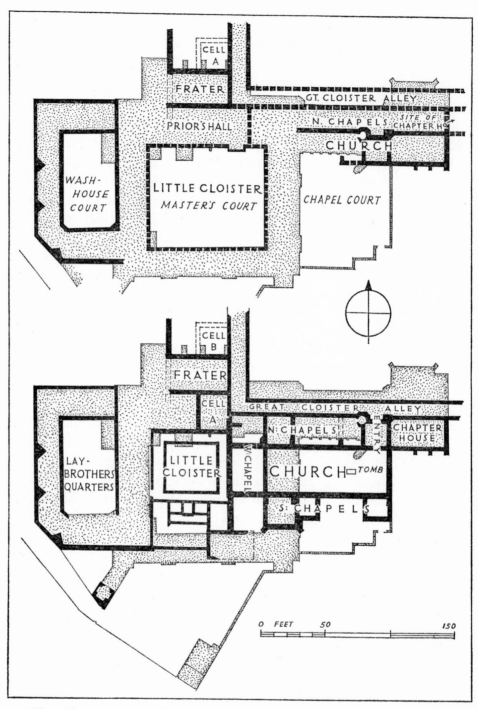

39. Charterhouse: *above:* suggested reconstruction of plan before excavation; *below:* reconstruction based on excavation.

finally resulted for the first time accorded closely with the contemporary records.

The investigations which produced these remains were concentrated mainly in the area of the present Charterhouse buildings, but opportunity was also afforded by the Medical College for the examination of the area of the Great Cloister when in 1949 a new building was erected on the eastern side of the green. The new facts here discovered have been recorded: the most valuable of them was the exact position of the north-eastern angle of the Great Cloister, together with the width of the cloister alley on the east side. But although much of the length of the main wall of the cloister was exposed no further information about the monks' cells was obtained than was already available. One much battered doorway already known to exist was seen complete for the first time in living memory, but for the rest the wall had been so extensively patched and rebuilt that no certainly recognisable traces of doorways remained. On the west side of the Great Cloister the situation was very similar. Here in the brick-faced reconstruction of the southern part of the cloister which was carried out by the Duke of Norfolk and bears on its western face the date 1571 were three blocked openings said to mark cell doorways; but excavation of the garden behind them failed because of universal disturbance to produce any traces of the accompanying cells.

Since that time progress has been made in two directions. In the first place, in pursuance of their enlightened policy of conserving all the significant features of the Charterhouse the Governors and their architects have caused the blockings above referred to to be removed, with the result that two of the cell doorways have been found to survive, with many of their attendant features in remarkable condition (Plates 77, 79). Secondly, on the other side of the cloister, work in connexion with a new building in 1959 exposed the eastern face of the cloister wall and with it the back of the doorway of Cell S, part of that of Cell R, and other features relating to the layout of these cells.

Comparison of the west with the east aisle shows that the spacing of the cell doorways was uniform on both sides: they are 48 feet apart, centre to centre. The evidence from the east side, however, for the first time enables the unit-sizes of the actual cells and their gardens to be determined. Though the ground was much disturbed the course of the foundation of the wall separating the gardens of Cells R and S could be traced for a distance of

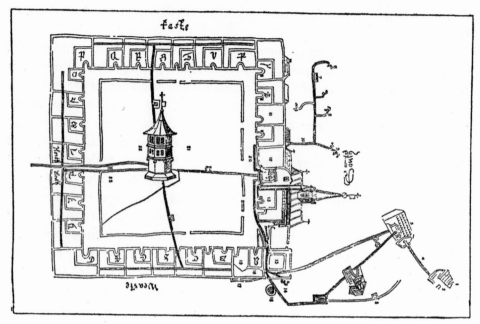

40. Charterhouse: the waterworks drawing.

about 28 feet eastwards at right angles to the cloister wall. It was 2 feet wide, 10 feet 8½ inches south of Doorway R, 32 feet 6 inches north of Doorway S —figures which, with the width of the doorway itself, give the gardens an overall internal length of just over 46 feet. In Cell S a rebated door jamb of Reigate stone still survived to a height of something over 3 feet in the cloister wall, about 7 feet 6 inches north of the cell doorway: in Cell R a depression in the wall in a corresponding position was evidence for a similar doorway there. These jambs would have formed one side of the doorways giving access from the cell to the garden. They were in the normal position for such doorways, from which would have led a covered way (pentice) along the garden side of the cloister wall (Fig. 41). The important point about these discoveries, however, is that they fix the dimension of the cell as about 21 feet internally—again, a normal size for a Carthusian monk's cell. They also confirm the accuracy of the plan arrived at by the 1948–9 investigations though some variation in the details of measurement has become necessary. And since that arrangement was based upon the waterworks drawing there is now further vindication of that work as against the

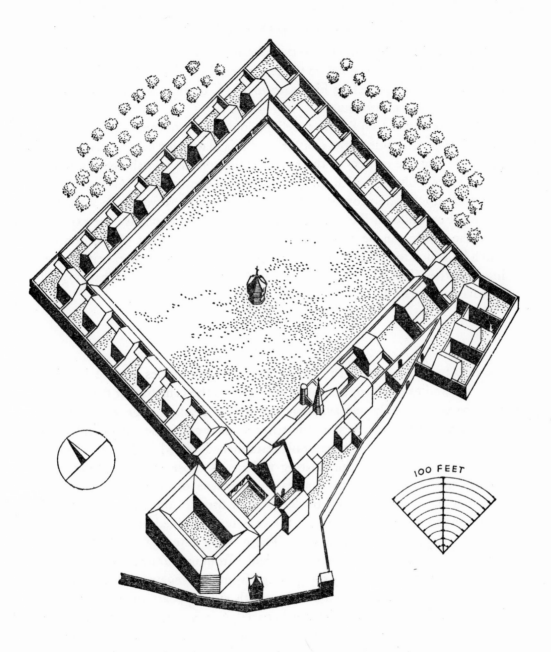

100 FEET

41. A reconstruction of the Charterhouse at its fullest monastic
development, as seen from the southwest.

variants produced by students of the Charterhouse in recent times. Cells R and S incidentally were given to the monastery by Thomas Hatfield, Bishop of Durham, perhaps before his death in 1381, though they may also have been the subject of a bequest.

The doorway of Cell S is an excellent counterpart of those of Cells B and C on the opposite side of the cloister, and it is matter for congratulation and gratitude that the owners of the new building on the Glasshouse Yard site have, in consultation with the Medical College and the Governors of Charterhouse, made provision for its permanent preservation in a worthy setting. For while on the west the outer sides of the doorways are exposed here the inside can be seen, and with it the arrangement of the service-hatch by which food was passed to the monk by the lay-brother, neither seeing the other (Plates 78, 80). It is unlikely now that further archaeological discoveries remain to be made at Charterhouse.

3. THE JEWS' GARDEN

As already noted, until 1177 (when Jewish communities outside London were allowed to establish their own cemeteries) the cemetery of the Jews in London was the only one available for Jewish dead. The general position of the cemetery was to west and north-west of the Cripplegate salient. The boundaries have been conjecturally established by Miss M. B. Honeybourne on the basis of the existing records as those of an irregular area almost entirely enclosed by houses and gardens to north-east, west and north in the block bounded by Red Cross Street, Aldersgate Street and Barbican: to south-east and south the cemetery adjoined St. Giles Cripplegate churchyard and the city ditch. There was a gate in Red Cross Street, where for a short distance the Garden had a frontage to the street and there was a short approach by way of a passage from Aldersgate on the west. The main portion of the Garden on the north side appears to have been an irregular oblong in shape, its northern edge represented by the modern Jewin Crescent. From this extended obliquely southwards a long tapering strip whose margin presumably coincided with the lip of the city ditch.[1]

[1] A full account of the site with a plan has been published by Miss M. B. Honeybourne. See 'The Pre-Expulsion Cemetery of the Jews in London', *Trans. Jewish Hist. Soc. of England*, XX (1959–61), pp. 145–59.

With the help of funds provided by the Jewish Historical Society extensive excavations were conducted in those parts of this area which were free from encumbrances. They were chiefly on the margins of the site, the centre of which retained its cover of bomb-rubble until it was removed with the undisturbed floor-deposits in 1961.

The results can be briefly told. It was found everywhere that the cellar floors rested immediately upon undisturbed natural brickearth or gravel, the upper parts of which had already been removed. In the northern part of the site, around Jewin Street, the effect of this was to destroy all traces of graves or of any structure earlier than the eighteenth century. In the narrower strip on the south side, between Well Street and St. Giles churchyard, the results were more rewarding. Here was found a series of seven graves in all. They were closely set, in an irregular line, orientated east–west and rather larger than most graves. A modern pipe-line cut transversely through the main group.

Excavation revealed that these graves had a depth of about 18 inches below the existing general surface, which was roughly 9 feet below the modern street. They must however have been a good deal deeper before the cellars were made. The surprising feature of the graves was that they contained no human remains apart from a rare metatarsal. There could be no doubt that the graves had been deliberately and carefully emptied and backfilled with made or garden soil. In one of the graves, above the floor, was the skeleton of a small dog. The significance of these facts is not very clear. The dog might be due to desecration by Gentiles, but there was in fact no clue as to its date. Whether the human remains were removed by the Jewish community when in 1290 the Jews were expelled from England or whether they were lifted by Gentiles cannot be said. Further traces of burials were found in the open cellars on the south side of Jewin Street near the middle of the area. Broken human bones came from immediately under the cellar floors in 'natural', but nothing could be made of them. There were no traces of burials north of Jewin Street.

4. THE CHURCH OF ST. BRIDE, FLEET STREET

The mediaeval church of St. Bride, destroyed in the Great Fire, was rebuilt by Wren in the years 1671–1703. Wren's church, in its turn, was gutted in 1940.[1] A drawing by the Reverend John Pridden, curate of St. Bride from 1783 to 1803, had preserved the record of a mediaeval vault which had been retained by Wren and incorporated in his new building; and when in 1952 the church authorities were preparing to rebuild the church the Excavation Council was invited to look for the vault, which was no longer visible but could be assumed to be still in existence below the present-day floor.

The Council readily accepted this invitation; but because the presumed early foundation of the church carried with it the possibility that other pre-Wren features might have survived, asked to be allowed to extend the operations beyond those necessary to uncover the vault. With the approval of the authorities (who generously defrayed the major part of the cost of the work) the whole of the area of the church was examined; and the result was to reveal in remarkable completeness most of the phases in the growth of the church of St. Bride down to its destruction in 1666. The vault was found at an early stage in the north-eastern corner of the eighteenth-century church, whose walls had been carried over the mediaeval structure on massive relieving arches. But this was not the only part of the older church to be incorporated in Wren's work. A feature of the site was the way in which Wren imposed his regular Renaissance building upon the remains of a developed mediaeval church which the excavations showed to have embodied a succession of changes covering the whole of the Middle Ages. The following account outlines the main sequence (Figs. 42, 44–7).

The history of the site begins in the Roman period, when at the eastern end, under Wren's sanctuary and extending beyond it, was a stone building with a plain floor of red and some yellow tesserae. Only a very small part of this structure was available for examination and it was in any case so damaged that very little of it survived beyond the east wall of the church. Apart from a scrap of wall on this side, two walls on the west were imperfectly seen, the

[1] What was known of the church down to the time of the excavation is set out in W. H. Godfrey, *The Church of St. Bride, Fleet Street* (monograph no. 15 of the London Survey Committee), 1944.

later, of tile, overlying the tessellated floor at about the middle of its length. The wall contemporary with the floor was on the northern edge of the exposed area. In front of it and lying on the floor were many fragments of plaster, evidently fallen from its face. No evidence was forthcoming to date this building and so little could be seen of it that its purpose must remain quite uncertain. It appears however to enjoy the distinction of being the only Roman building yet to have been recorded between the River Fleet and Westminster.

The pavement of the building was 10 feet below the 1952 floor-level of the church and there were indications that it lay in part on the natural gravel. Westwards, within the body of the church, the surface of the gravel (in this area containing a good deal of sand) was several feet higher. The difference in level indicates that the Roman building must have been erected on some kind of shelf in the gravel surface, the level of which would not have been very different from that of the surface of the neighbouring street (Bride Lane) at the present day. The destruction of the Roman levels by the various church-foundations between the Roman building and the gravel-surface to the west makes it impossible to say whether the 'shelf' was natural or due to artificial levelling: on the analogy of similar features in Thames Street (p. 58) the latter is at least possible. On this surface small patches of Roman deposit had survived the destructive effects of the later grave-digging, particularly at the east end, amongst the foundations of the early sanctuary. The deposits consisted mainly of gravel, with which were intermixed quantities of stone and tile. Much of this material was in weathered condition, suggesting that it was building débris which had been dumped on the site. It produced several fourth-century Roman coins.

An unexpected feature at the west end of the church was a Roman ditch, enough of which had survived to show it to be the south-eastern angle of an enclosure far the greater part of which must have lain beyond the church to the north-west. The northern lip of the ditch could not be found because of overlying later features, but the ditch cannot have been less than 15–16 feet wide, and it was rather more than 7 feet deep from the surface of the natural gravel as surviving nearby, with a broad irregular-U profile. On this scale the ditch is larger than that of the Roman city itself and the possibility was considered that it might be part of a military enclosure of early date; but although the angle is about 90 degrees the curve would appear to be too 'tight' for a normal fort. At the same time, the possibility remains; and since the area enclosed must have been fairly large, building excavations in the neighbourhood ought to be closely watched for any further signs of it. The angle is only about 150 feet south of the central line of Fleet Street, and if this was indeed the course of a Roman road westwards from the city the enclosure must surely have straddled it.

It must be admitted that in spite of the early date implied by the dedication already referred to there is no archaeological evidence from which the date of the first church of St. Bride can be firmly determined. It will be seen that the oldest part of the first church as it survived in the ground was the south wall of the nave. Possibly preceding this, possibly contemporary with it, were a number of burials which displayed features suggesting an early Christian date, though they also were not directly dated. Two of these burials were completely cleared (others had survived only in a partial state). They lay just beyond the limits of the first nave and consisted of extended skeletons, with head to west. The sides of one grave were defined with irregularly-set stones and tile-fragments; the second was less well provided for, though the head was enclosed by tile-fragments and a large piece of tile lay on the chest under the chin, keeping the lower jaw in place (Plate 82).

From the grave-filling of the second burial came some late Roman material; but its presence may be accidental and it cannot be said to date the burial except in so far as it provides a *terminus post quem*. A late Roman date cannot indeed be ruled out, but the general character of the burial suggests an Early Christian origin; and with its fellows it could be explained as belonging to the cemetery which would have accompanied the early church. The question is not without importance since, as will be seen below, the date of the earliest burials on the site has a bearing on the whole problem of the continuity of use of the area as a cemetery since Roman times. Of a more definitely mediaeval or at least Christian character were other graves, many at about the same level as those just described and usually much disturbed by later building and grave-digging activities. They were more regularly and completely chalk-lined: one infant's grave had a recessed block for the head which had been carved from a single piece of chalk.

It has already been hinted that the first church of St. Bride was a composite structure: its visible part surviving in Stow's time was called by him

'of olde time a small thing, which now remaineth to be the quire'[1] (Plate 81).
It consisted of a nave with western porch, a presbytery with a transept
or porticus to the south—there was no indication of a corresponding feature
to the north—and a semi-circular (or perhaps polygonal) apse. Of all these
elements the oldest, already mentioned, was the south wall of the nave,
which had survived for about half its length from the east (Fig. 42). This
wall was slighter in character than the rest, with a comparatively shallow
foundation about 2 feet deep, made up of alternating layers of gravel and
stone, in which were incorporated pieces of Roman masonry. The wall was

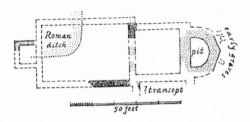

42. St. Bride Fleet Street: the first church.

$2\frac{1}{2}$ feet wide; its foundation was offset about a foot on the inside where well
preserved: the arrangement on the outside was masked by later additions as
described below. Since the ground along its full length had been disturbed
by later burials right up to its face there was no clue as to its date, but it
can hardly be later than late Saxon and its pieces of Roman masonry may
well have been derived from the ruined building at the east end of the site.

The actual junction of the nave wall with the presbytery to the east had
been destroyed on the south side. Differences in construction and to some
extent also in levels were sufficient to show however that from the opening
of the presbytery eastwards (including the stump of the north wall of the
nave) there had been drastic rebuilding which in the presbytery had involved the continued use of the distinctive gravel and mortar foundations of
the first church.

From the constructional point of view perhaps the most interesting
feature of this early church was the apse. As will be seen below, it was replaced in due course by a square east end and none of its superstructure had
survived. Its foundation consisted of a trench 6 feet deep which was filled

[1] *Survey of London*, II, p. 45.

with clean brown gravel. The upper part of the trench was lined with large undressed boulders set in white mortar to a depth of three courses (2 feet 4 inches) which where exposed by the removal of the material in front of them looked like a rough facing. They were never intended to be seen, however, and must have carried the faced wall at a higher level, no doubt with some kind of offset. These stones were laid internally on a semi-circle, externally in straight lines giving the foundation a polygonal outline. The foundation was carried across the opening of the apse and though disturbed by later burials in the centre, sufficient of it remained to show that its construction was the same throughout.

These, then, were the three main divisions of the first complete church of St. Bride. The evidence for the transept or porticus is less certain. Almost opposite the junction of nave and presbytery a short length of wall survives which is earlier than the twelfth-century tower (see below) and was part of a chamber lying to the east. Nothing more remains unless the stump of a wall which projects into the sleeper wall of Wren's south arcade about 21 feet to the east belongs to it in some way (below, p. 188). This stump is probably of the twelfth century since it appears to be of one build with the square end. The western wall is later than the original presbytery wall, against which it rested in a straight joint. But it is also earlier than the twelfth-century tower. The difficulty in all this is that not enough survives. The total length of the early church remained uncertain until the final clearing of Wren's nave, when the foundations of the north and west walls of its porch were found partly overlying the filling of the Roman ditch already described. These foundations were slight (25 inches wide), only their lower part surviving; they consisted of small stones and tile-fragments set in mortar and gravel. The church thus had an overall length of about 93 feet; its nave was about 30 feet wide.

The 'Anglo-Norman' plan of the building suggests an eleventh-century date for it in this form. The only other evidence bearing on this is provided by a potsherd from a curious oval pit at the east end. This pit had been dug to a depth of about 11 feet from the surviving surface of the natural sandy gravel. It took up much of the internal area of the apse and the gravel foundation of the chord wall had been sunk into it; so that without question the pit preceded the building of this part of the church. The filling of the pit, a dense black humified soil without stratification, suggested an ordinary rubbish-pit, but it also produced some human bones. Scattered through it were a few skulls, and towards the bottom (which was reached but not fully exposed) were bones in some quantity. The bones are best explained on the assumption that the diggers of the pit disturbed some of the early burials on the site and it must be assumed that there was ordinary domestic activity somewhere near at hand. The solitary sherd (Fig. 43) from deep in the filling is part of a pitcher of Late Saxon (ninth–eleventh century) type, of hard dark grey ware, its surviving handle, probably one of three originally,

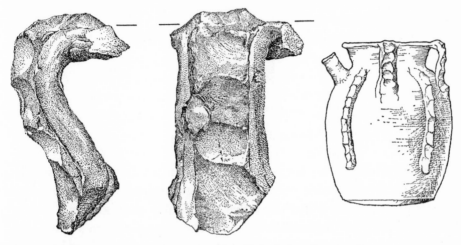

43. St. Bride's Fleet Street: fragment of handled pitcher from a pit antedating the apse of the first church (⅔) with a reconstruction of the form of the pot.

decorated with transverse thumb- or finger-tip impressions. Apart therefore from narrowing the period for the building of the first surviving complete church to about the period of the Norman Conquest or a little before, the pit provides confirmatory evidence for the existence of a cemetery in the neighbourhood in late Saxon times: it seems unlikely that human bones would otherwise have been present in such quantity.

No difficulty of dating is presented by the second stage in the development of the church. The apse was dismantled and replaced by a square end with flat angle-buttresses (Fig. 44) and a deep foundation which cut through a row of chalk- and tile-lined graves behind the apse (Plate 83). The junctions of the new with the old work at foundation-level were clearly seen on both sides but it seems probable that on the north the reconstruction extended beyond the jamb of the chancel arch. The north wall of the presbytery in its present state has an external plain chamfered plinth which is lacking on the south side, where the wall has a simple foundation offset at a lower level.

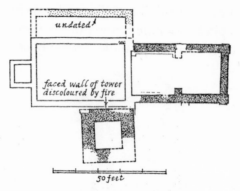

44. St. Bride's Fleet Street: the twelfth-century church

More surprising than this normal twelfth-century development was the discovery on the south side of the nave of a detached tower. This tower was 23 feet square overall, of such size that it straddled the eighteenth-century vault on this side of the church and extended beyond Wren's south wall. (Plate 84). The clues to the existence of this feature were provided by the fact that Wren retained the broad well-built north wall of the tower as a foundation for the middle pair of piers of his south arcade. This fortunate chance was instrumental in preserving the early nave wall, which would almost certainly have been destroyed if a new sleeper wall on the scale of others on the site had been provided for the new south arcade. The tower had been built against the early nave wall with a wide offset, above which its faced wall, showing slight traces of scorching by fire, still survived to a height of just over 2 feet. At its north-west corner part of the moulded plinth had been preserved and projected beyond Wren's pier (Plate 87); at the north-east, on the other hand, the corner was a plain one, and the wall appeared to have been carried up to and over the stump of the earlier wall already mentioned as part of a possible porticus or transept. These features apart, the elements that survive are those of the basement stage of the tower, as is shown by the fact that the external plinth on the west side is only about 4 feet below the Wren floor, as compared with about 11 feet for the floor of the tower itself. Internally the tower is 12 feet square. It was originally vaulted: the bases of angle-shafts of twelfth-century type survive in the three corners that are exposed in the floor of the existing vaults (Plates 85–6). The original floor had been made up at least once, the final version as surviving having been laid with reused encaustic tiles. When finally the crown of the eighteenth-century long vault was removed as a necessary preliminary to the modern reconstruction of the church the vault of the original staircase could be seen rising in the face of the wall. It is visible at the present time, underpinned by a massive brick-faced eighteenth-century filling (Plate 84). The entrance to the tower may therefore have been in its western face, with the stair to its upper stages incorporated in its 6-foot wall.

Only the east end and the tower can be conclusively recognised as twelfth-century additions to the church. A number of fragments of carved stone of this period found incorporated in the later work suggest however that the remodelling involved enrichment in which a good deal of Caen stone was used.

But something more should be said about the tower, because it appears to contradict what is known of the church as it was before the Great Fire of 1666. The various panoramas and pictorial maps of London show the church with an upstanding tower of late mediaeval type with crocketed pinnacles and it has been assumed that this tower was at the western end of the church.[1] But apart from the uncertain evidence of the drawings there is no definite statement that the mediaeval tower was indeed in the position now occupied by Wren's tower; and the apparent difference in date between the excavated remains and the tower shown in the drawings might well be accounted for by the addition of later stages to an already existing base. Only these upper stages would be visible in the drawings above the surrounding buildings.[2] It could alternatively be argued that the early tower

[1] Walter Godfrey, *The Church of St. Bride, Fleet Street*, pp. 9, 11. In the contemporary documents as there set out it does not appear that there is a categorical statement on the subject.

[2] The etching which occupies the reverse side of one of the pewter plates of the 'Agas' map in the possession of the Society of Antiquaries of London gives a complete view of the church which has a more convincing look than the other versions. The building is presented in a rough perspective and projecting behind the tower on the west is a gable-end which might be interpreted as that of the nave. The tower has three stages. It would be unwise to press the matter too far until more is known of this engraving, but this version of the church certainly suggests a southern tower

may have been dismantled and replaced by a western tower in the fifteenth century. But not only has the early tower been very deliberately incorporated in the post-Fire reconstruction: its various features have played a controlling part in the planning of the later vaults and the access to them. These facts would seem to imply its continuing existence into the seventeenth century. It seems impossible now to suggest reasons for the building of the tower in this not very common position, unless the presence of the western porch was a governing factor. In the fourteenth century, St. Bride's is mentioned as one of the four churches in the city from which the curfew was rung. If the practice was of earlier origin here the tower may have been built specifically with this purpose in mind. It may therefore have been built separately both as a matter of convenience and to carry a bell or bells which would have imposed too great a strain on the comparatively slight structure of much of the rest of the church.

The succeeding changes had the effect of extending and elaborating the body of the church by the addition of side-aisles and chapels, the latter to both north and south of the original chancel, Stow's 'small thing, which now remaineth to be the quire'. Not all these features can be closely dated, for they survive as foundations or as featureless walls (Plate 89).

On the north side the first addition was a narrow aisle which extended only the length of the nave (Fig. 44). Its construction must have involved the piercing of the original nave wall, but the exact nature of the alteration here cannot now be known since only the stump of the nave wall remains. To the east of this aisle was added an extension the full length of the chancel and presbytery but somewhat wider than the aisle, so that its west wall turned back through a right angle to rest against the outer face of the aisle. At the eastern end of this addition (Fig. 45) was the three-bay crypt recorded by Pridden. The crypt seems to be contemporary with the rest of the work, and has a narrow doorway in its north side and a low window to the east, both subsequently blocked and the blocking of the window rendered with plaster. The masonry of this eastward extension is of distinctive character when compared with that of the rest of the church: squared rubble blocks, some of them of chalk, give it a chequered appearance. The wide vertical

towards the west end of the nave. (For the etching see *Proc. Soc. Antiq. Lond.*, 2nd ser. XXII (1909), pp. 535–9; *Trans. London and M'sex. Arch. Soc.* NS, III (1916), p. 270, and S. P. Marks, *The Map of Sixteenth Century London* (London Top. Soc.), 1964, pp. 20, 25.)

joints are packed with stone chips and the horizontal courses are defined frequently by shallower bands of small stones. The addition as a whole is of the fourteenth century and is pretty certainly the Lady Chapel, built by the Brotherhood or Guild of St. Mary, which is known to have been on the north side of the chancel. References to the Guild go back at least to the early fourteenth century.[1]

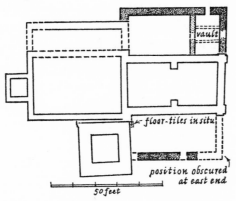

45. St. Bride's Fleet Street: the fourteenth-century church.

The third major development on the north side took the form of a further enlargement of the aisle, together with the remodelling of the arcade and the extension of the nave itself (Fig. 46). The new outer north wall prolonged westwards the line of the Guild Chapel. The intervention of a small brick vault and the more massive character of Wren's foundations at the west end of his church made it impossible to follow the mediaeval foundation throughout its course, but there can be no doubt that it was one with a wide chalk foundation (Plate 90) which would have closed the west end of the nave only 8½ feet short of Wren's west wall. For various reasons the series of square piers that replaced the original north wall of the nave must be regarded as belonging to this reconstruction. Four piers survive: the addition of a fifth at the west end, where it would have been destroyed by Wren's tower foundations, fits admirably the interpretation of the chalk foundation as that for the mediaeval west wall. Though once again no datable features are associated with all this work all the evidence points to its having been carried out during the fifteenth century. Stow's brief description of St.

[1] Godfrey, *op. cit.*, p. 182, footnote above, pp. 16–18 and 116–19.

Bride's as it was in his day goes on to say that the early church was 'encreased with a large bodie and side Iles towards the West at the charges of *William Vinor* [Vyner], Esquire, Warden of the Fleete, about the yeare 1480, all of which he caused to be wrought about in the stone in the figure of a vine with grapes and leaves, etc.'; and fragments of such carvings were found during the excavations. But in fact the records show a succession of legacies 'to the fabric' or 'to the fabric of the nave' throughout the fifteenth century; so that Vyner (whose benefaction is not otherwise recorded) was not solely responsible for this reconstruction.

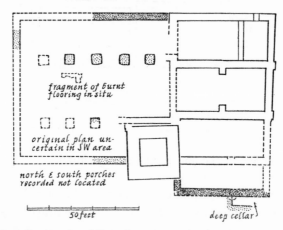

46. St. Bride's Fleet Street: the fifteenth-century church.

The succession on the south side of the church is more difficult, for there the complicated post-mediaeval situation has left a less complete picture of the earlier remains. Apart from the way in which later walls generally mask what is left of these features the greatest problems lie at the east end. Whereas to the north the relationship of the fourteenth-century undercroft to the twelfth-century chancel can be clearly seen, to the south the passage-like eighteenth-century vaults break through the mediaeval walls at quite low levels and in places have completely replaced them. Detailed discussion of the evidence is not possible here. It must suffice to say that while fragmentary foundations suggest the existence of a small chapel at the southeast angle, perhaps contemporary with the twelfth-century square chancel, the undoubted later features are two additions: an inner aisle or chapel which abutted on the tower at its western end while extending eastwards the full length of the presbytery and chancel of the main church; and out-side this on the south another chapel, the outer wall of which lay outside the line of the south wall of the tower and was turned inwards through a right angle to rest on the tower's south-eastern angle (Fig. 46).

The south wall of the inner chapel (or aisle) was utilised by Wren as the foundation for his own south wall. There was a suggestion of this in the external long vault, but the position only became clear when the removal of the crown of the internal vault exposed its full length where it survived. Its last few feet to the west had been replaced by Wren; but there can be little doubt that it abutted against the east face of the tower. It was rendered with a rather poor plaster and below the level of Wren's rebuilding part of a blocked south doorway still survives. With an internal width of about 16½ feet the south-eastern chapel should have balanced the guild chapel on the north side of the chancel (Fig. 46).

As already observed, the south wall of the outer chapel turned inwards at the west end to rest upon the south wall of the tower. The outer face of this return can be seen in a recess evidently deliberately left for it, in the east wall of the small vault (the so-called 'charnel-house': Fig. 47); and the junction of the tower and chapel foundations is visible in the external long vault. It is not possible to say how this wall was joined to that of the earlier inner chapel at the east end because of destruction, though the south wall itself had survived to its full length. The only feature of the building, apart from its good ashlar, is its hollow-chamfered plinth, dating it to the fifteenth century.

Other features on the south-east side defy explanation at present. Beneath the west wall of the fifteenth-century chapel is what appears to be an earlier chalk foundation, visible only in this one place. And outside it at the east end is a chalk-walled pit or cellar whose floor is 17 feet below the churchyard surface and 11 feet below the base of the faced wall of the chapel. This structure is 4 feet wide; it could have been as much as 14 feet long if it extended as far as the east end of the church. But it did not pass northwards under the chapel, for immediately beyond the chapel-wall, in the vault, there is solid natural ground.

It remains to consider the south-western side of the church. Here again there is some doubt. Beneath Wren's main wall, from the tower westwards, is a rough foundation which might mark the extension of the south aisle.

But there is no way of being certain in the matter and it can only be said that the workmanship differs somewhat from that of Wren's foundations, particularly in the character of the mortar used. Incorporated in the sleeper wall of the seventeenth-century south arcade is a roughly square base which, though it partly carries Wren's column, has a mediaeval look. This may be part of the south mediaeval arcade: with some variation in the span the space between the Norman tower and the late mediaeval west wall would have allowed for four bays. But this is perhaps to read too much into the very limited evidence.

The church of St. Bride that was destroyed in 1666 was thus a fully developed mediaeval church of some elaboration of plan, in which was incorporated work of several styles and periods, with a good deal of decoration hinted at in the chance finds of carved fragments. The number of side-chapels revealed by the excavations is in keeping with the six altars referred to in contemporary wills. It has been necessary to cast doubt on the existence of a western tower, but there is documentary evidence for north and south porches, the former at least with an upper storey.[1] All trace of the south porch will have vanished in the post-Fire changes; something of the north porch may well survive below ground.

Of the Great Fire itself there was little sign. The intensive use of the body of the church for burials during the eighteenth and early nineteenth centuries had caused the almost complete destruction of the earlier levels. At the west end of the nave there was a small fragment of flooring consisting of bricks and tiles which had been crazed, warped and blackened by intense heat (Plate 91); there was a 6-inch deposit of burnt material outside the mediaeval wall in the north-west corner; and the surviving face of the Norman tower was reddened by fire as were some of the decorated fragments recovered during the excavation.

In his reconstruction of the church Wren was materially assisted by the fact that in spite of its mixture of periods the mediaeval building had been essentially symmetrical in its final form, with flanking chapels and aisles of equal width on each side of the original chancel and nave (Fig. 47). In laying out his new church, therefore, he ignored the irregular elements: the tower and the outer chapel on the south-east. The walls to be reused were reduced to a fairly uniform height of about 4 feet above their foundation offsets and

[1] Godfrey, *op. cit.* above, pp. 11–12.

the new walls were built directly on to their levelled-off tops, with no intervening levelling course. The new walls also were of much the same width as their mediaeval predecessors wherever they were tested: they sometimes overhung, sometimes were set back on, the earlier line. The variation is particularly noticeable at the east end. Here Wren's projecting chancel rests obliquely on the twelfth-century chancel wall, which is askew; his aisles end inside the ends of the mediaeval aisles and the east wall of the north aisle is carried over the lightly-built vault of the mediaeval crypt on a massive

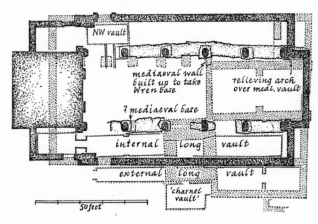

47. St. Bride's Fleet Street: Wren's post-Fire church (heavy stipple) in relation to the mediaeval church (light stipple).

relieving arch (p. 190). The retention of this small crypt was no doubt partly for utilitarian purposes, but it also reflects Wren's antiquarian feeling. The sleeper wall of his north arcade was carried over the crypt in the same way.

At the west end the aisle walls were extended beyond the limits of the mediaeval church. The foundations of the great steeple had inevitably cut through all pre-existing features. Within the church as excavated the dominant seventeenth-century elements were the sleeper walls which carried the paired columns of the arcades. That on the north side ran the full length of the church. It is built entirely of stones from the mediaeval building, many of which can be seen to be dressed and some carved; and though irregularly laid it is of very solid construction because of the hard grey mortar used in it. The mortar extrudes from the joints in characteristic fashion: all the rough foundation work here exhibits this feature and it was

195

observed also in the vast foundation, over 20 feet deep, of the seventeenth-century nave of St. Mary-le-Bow Church in Cheapside. Wren's north sleeper wall respects the remains of the older church: it lies along the north side of the chancel and bends outwards to allow for the slightly greater width of the bases of the mediaeval arcade, which it partially clasps (Plate 88). This arrangement presented its own problems when Wren came to erect his own bases upon it. The first and second bases from the east overhang the sleeper wall on the south side, the latter by 18 inches; and there the builders were constrained to add to the height of the neighbouring mediaeval wall to give the edge of the base extra support.

On the south side the presence of the solid basement of the Norman tower with the earlier nave wall to the north of it as already described produced a more complicated solution. Wren supported his middle pair of bases on these walls. To the east the respond on the south side of his sanctuary and the first base were carried on a sleeper which lay closely along the outer face of the twelfth-century chancel. This sleeper ended 10 feet to the east of the tower. The position to the west of the tower seemed much less ordered. The masonry, though continuous, consisted of a number of irregular units, all except one carrying the obvious signs of seventeenth-century workmanship already mentioned in connexion with the north sleeper wall. The exception is the roughly square base (about 4 feet each way) on which stands Wren's fourth column; but it has already been suggested that this base originally belonged to the south arcade of the mediaeval church (p. 193) which by a fortunate chance was in a position where it could be reused.

Finally, there is the treatment accorded to the tower and the external chapel at the south-east, both of which were incorporated in the brick-lined vaults that extend the full length of the church, one inside, the other outside, its south wall, Only the north wall of the tower was retained to carry part of Wren's arcade, as already described: the other three were cut down, though part of the west wall was kept as one side of the single original entrance to the vault. The plan of the vault very much reflects the presence of the tower, whose north wall, with its original plaster and perhaps one side of an oblique entrance to the chapel on the east, remains untouched. The external long vault and passage must have been formed by lowering the surface inside the chapel and along Wren's south wall, exposing the mediaeval foundations, which it was not thought necessary to encase in brick. This vault had an additional entrance at its eastern end, from Bride Lane.

Wren's church of St. Bride therefore demonstrates archaeologically the economy and ingenuity of a great architect in moulding an existing situation to his own very different purposes. In so doing he wasted nothing, even using his unwanted materials to raise his floor-level to the bases of his new walls. Modern techniques of floor construction employed in the twentieth-century remodelling make it possible to study the methods of Wren and his predecessors on this site as perhaps nowhere else in Britain at the present time. The continuity of use and purpose enshrined in these remains extends backwards over a period of ten centuries or more; but if the caution of the excavator shrinks from guesswork in the absence of evidence either in the ground or in recorded history, speculation as to earlier origins persists. These excavations have produced no result which can be said to comment on the early association of the Celtic St. Bride or Bridget with this site. There is no evidence that can be used to link the Roman building beneath the east end of the church with the church itself, except that which says that the church-builders used the Roman building as a quarry. Yet a continuity there may have been; and it comes from the use to which this part of the city outside the walls was put in Roman times. The evidence of burials found in the angle of Shoe Lane and Fleet Street in 1927 shows that here was a cemetery which was in use at least well into the third century A.D.[1] The burials in question were by cremation in urns and the cremation rite gave way gradually to the burial of the body during the second and third centuries. It cannot be claimed for any of the simple inhumation burials recorded at St. Bride's that they are certainly of Roman date; they nevertheless display features which would be considered 'early Christian' rather than mediaeval, and they are supported by the finds of human bones in the pit at the east end of the early church (p. 187) which show that there must have been many inhumation burials in and about the area in pre-Norman times. The gap between these burials and those of the earlier Roman period may well be filled in due course by some lucky chance. In the meantime the theory that the presence of an early church here with a Celtic dedication owes something to the use of the area as a burial ground since Roman times has much in it that is attractive.

[1] *Roman London*, p. 165; *London in Roman Times* (London Museum Cat.: 1930), pp. 42–3.

5. THE CLOISTER OF THE PRIORY CHURCH
OF ST. BARTHOLOMEW THE GREAT, WEST SMITHFIELD

The sequence of events by which the conventual buildings on the south side of the church of St. Bartholomew the Great changed hands after the dissolution of the monasteries was treated at length by A. E. Webb in 1921 when he published his two-volume *Records of St. Bartholomew's, Smithfield*. The process was one in which the buildings were first of all adapted as town-houses by members of the nobility, to whom they were granted by the King, gradually undergoing modification as time passed and the quality of the occupiers declined. By the late eighteenth century, when Thomas Hardwick made the plan which is now in the collections of the Society of Antiquaries, some of the mediaeval buildings had vanished completely; and destruction was carried very much further during the nineteenth century, with the building of warehouses and new offices in the area.

During the prolonged period of restoration work in the late nineteenth–early twentieth century the plan of the eastern side of the site was recovered with fair completeness, though not all the remains found could be preserved. Of the western part of the area to the south of the nave very little was known, apart from the east walk of the cloister, which was finally restored in the 1920's. Here successive alterations had destroyed the monastic buildings unrecorded, apart from the Hardwick drawings already mentioned. This, however, was also the part of the monastic area which had suffered most severely from bombing: the buildings, all apparently of nineteenth-century date, fronting the north side of Bartholomew Close had been destroyed, together with most of those which lay between the north-westward extension of the Close and Little Britain; and advantage was therefore taken of the opportunity to explore the area before a new building for St. Bartholomew's Hospital was erected on the site.

Hardwick had shown in his plan the remains of an 'ancient brick house' near the site of the south-western corner of the cloister and it was found that some part of this still survived in the ruined shells that were at that time (1955) about to be demolished. The features of this building were a doorway with four-centred head opening eastwards and a two-light cellar window, also with four-centred heads, in brick. The date is sixteenth century. In the spandrels of the doorway, below the square moulded frame were conventionalised stiff vine-sprays with shields bearing the letters W and A respectively, presumably the initials of the builder; but so far WA remains unidentified. The building must therefore be a relic of some re-building activity in the period immediately following the suppression. It could not have been of the monastic period, for as Hardwick's plan shows, it lay athwart the angle of the cloister and may well have incorporated in its structure the inner wall of the south walk.

For the rest, in spite of much disturbance, sufficient remained of founda-tions and of robber trenches to establish the position of the cloister walk on both the south and the west sides and to determine at least the extent of the south range, that of the frater, as a building 96 feet long overall by 26 feet wide. It seems likely also that, as Webb suggested, the kitchen extended southwards from the western end of this building; for here the bases of ancient walls also were found in part to underlie the outlines of the more recent cellars. On the west the evidence was less complete because of the existence of the north-western limb of Bartholomew Close. The north-western angle of the cloister-garth was found, together with part of the inner wall of the west range; but nothing otherwise had survived and the layout of the guest-house block therefore remains uncertain. The result of this investigation has been to define the area of the cloister (which was not in fact quite the rectilinear figure that Hardwick's plan suggests). Nothing more can now be learned from the ground about this part of the Priory.[1]

6. THE CHURCH OF ST. SWITHUN LONDON STONE (42)

Though the dedication of St. Swithun's Church is thought to be an early one the position here is not the same as for St. Bride's. The Saint died in A.D. 862; the dedication could not therefore in any case be earlier than the late ninth century. The association with London Stone is of course simply one of proximity, for in a well-known passage Stow describes the stone as standing on the south side of the street (that is, Candlewick Street, the modern Cannon Street) 'neere unto the channell'.[2] The incorporation of the

[1] Thanks are due to Dr. Gweneth Whitteridge, F.S.A., and Miss Veronica Stokes for much help and information relating to the records of the site.

[2] Stow, *Survey of London*, I, p. 224.

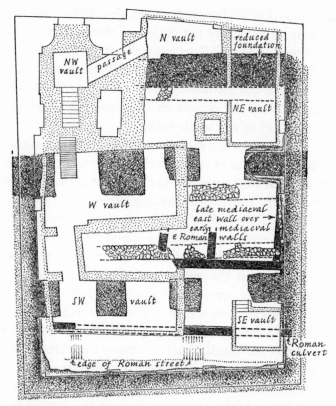

Roman █ 'early mediaeval' ▨ early 15th. centy.
Wren's church (1677+) in outline; 17th century vaults etc stippled
30 feet

48. St. Swithun London Stone: plan of church as excavated.

stone as a sadly reduced fragment in the south wall of the church was an event of much later date, so that there could be no hope of learning more about it when it was removed in 1961, to be replaced later.

The church which was burnt out in 1940 was built by Wren in the 1670's to replace that destroyed in the Great Fire of 1666. It was a small building on a restricted site, with its long axis north-to-south and a tower at the north-west corner. The interior was much taken up with vaults, all post-Fire, except for one on the north-east which was outside the mediaeval church and was probably of mediaeval date. The areas available for excavation were therefore limited (Fig. 48).

The Roman features have already been described (pp. 142ff.). The general result of the excavation was to show that disturbance by late burials had penetrated to a fairly uniform depth of about 6 feet below the existing floor of the church, the original natural surface being about 5 feet below that. As elsewhere, pre-existing stone foundations were left largely undisturbed by the eighteenth/nineteenth-century grave-diggers; and since in addition the early foundations were also preserved in the floors of the vaults more information was forthcoming than seemed likely from a first inspection of the site.

Two churches in succession had preceded Wren's church. Of the first of these, except in one place, only the base of the foundations had survived, incomplete and much broken up, as a single layer of chalk blocks (Plate 98). Within the area of the church there were three walls lying east-to-west at uniform depths of 6–7 feet below the modern surface. Of the north and middle wall only scraps remained. They were 16 feet apart. The wall to the south lay between the later vaults and was therefore better preserved. It was 8 feet from the middle wall. The arrangement suggests a relatively simple church of nave and single aisle having an overall width of 32 feet. The foundations were only 30–4 inches wide, so that the building could not have been of massive construction. Its internal length was presumably that of the later building (about 45 feet); but only on the east was there any indication of the end wall. There the original east wall could be seen to have been preserved between the later arcade-bases, the enlargement having been built up to it on each side (below and Fig. 49). One of the north-to-south Roman walls was incorporated in its foundation (Plate 96). Here also the chalk foundation of the south wall runs parallel with, and where best preserved touches, the east-to-west Roman wall. At its eastern end it rests directly upon the north-to-south wall already mentioned, but is cut by the foundation of the later mediaeval church (Plates 96, 98).

The date of the first church is uncertain, except in so far as it can be said to be post-eleventh century, for pits producing pottery of this date were found within its area and had preceded its construction. This result would seem to contradict the view that the dedication was an early one, though the possibility cannot be ruled out that a timber church may have occupied the site in the beginning. The traces left by a timber church would have been slight, but some part of it would no doubt have survived in the area available, had it existed.

Stow says that 'Licence was procured to new build and encrease the said Church and steeple in the year 1420.'[1] This may or may not imply that the early church already had a tower of some sort. The fifteenth-century church followed more or less the outline preserved by Wren's church on the south, east and west sides, but was narrower in its north-to-south dimension, so that its north wall lay within that of the post-Fire building. The late mediaeval church had internal dimensions of about 46 (east–west) by 52 feet and was probably a fairly regular rectangle, though its west wall was largely masked by later additions. Beyond the north wall was an irregular open space beneath which was the mediaeval north vault previously mentioned.

Internally the church was an affair of three bays, with nave and north and south aisles. The piers on the east side were particularly massive, no doubt because there was no room for external buttresses (Plate 99). Those at the west end also were large, but had been cut down to make way for the later vaults. Of the other bases the second along on the north-west was larger than the others, probably because it had played a part in supporting the mediaeval tower, which must have stood on the site occupied by Wren's. No trace of the mediaeval tower had survived the construction of Wren's characteristically massive and deep foundation.

Once again no contemporary deposits remained in association with the building. The only finds, all from disturbed ground, were a few casting-counters.[2] At the south-east corner the mediaeval wall made contact with the south wall of the Roman building, which had not been removed; its foundation over the lateral ditch of the Roman street was curiously constructed of alternating layers of large stones, water-worn pebbles and gravelly clay. The structural sequence in the east wall was interesting as showing how the enlarged fifteenth-century church had been built outside the early church to north and south. The new walls had been carried up to the remains of the early wall from both sides, the junctions with the old wall being at its inner angles with the east–west walls (Plate 97; Fig. 49).

[1] *Survey of London*, I, p. 223.

[2] During the demolition of Wren's church subsequently an inscribed slab which had covered the heart-burial of Johanna, second of the three wives of Sir Fulke de St. Edmund, of early fourteenth-century date, was found incorporated in the south wall near the south-east corner. The slab is now in the Guildhall Museum.

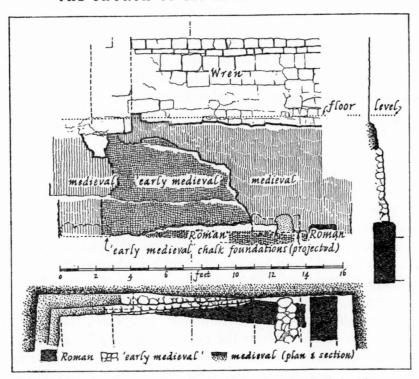

49. St. Swithun London Stone: plan and elevation of east wall of church, showing relationship of walls and foundations of successive periods.

Wren's walls, as already observed, followed the fifteenth-century outline except on the north, where the irregular open space was taken into the building: their bases rested directly on the mediaeval work. His single isolated pier on the north side penetrated to an undetermined depth (more than 15 feet) into the disturbed ground on the north side of the church. But he retained much the same floor-level as had existed before and may even have lowered it slightly. There was no sign at St. Swithun's of the drastic raising of the floor which was a feature of St. Bride's.

7. THE CHURCH OF ST. ALBAN WOOD STREET (22: 1961–2)

John Stow has little to say about this church: his brief references to it lack the valuable hints that are contained in his account of St. Bride's. The dedication to the British saint and martyr is one of the 'early' group. It is said by Matthew Paris to have been a chapel of King Offa in the eighth century; and it belonged therefore to the traditional area of early Saxon activity which was centred upon the palace of King Ethelbert.[1]

According to the Royal Commission on Historical Monuments the church was rebuilt in 1633–4 by Inigo Jones and restored or rebuilt by Sir Christopher Wren in 1682–7 after partial destruction in the Great Fire of 1666.[2] As already stated (p. 174), the building was gutted during the war and it has now been completely removed except for the tower, the restoration of which was completed in 1966.[3]

The excavation of the church in 1961–2 was carried out in circumstances which were not entirely satisfactory. In particular the removal of the burials proved to be a very lengthy process, reducing the time that was available for the archaeological investigation; secondly, while the men engaged in the preliminary work did their best to be helpful it was not possible to pay close attention to details, some of which went unrecorded. The church contained no large vaults, but there were many brick-built tombs in its eastern parts and earlier walls had suffered accordingly. In general, the result of the excavation was to demonstrate the existence of a building of successive phases some of which were incorporated in the surviving structure. From this it would appear that the reconstructions of the seventeenth century (apart from the final version of the south aisle) were concerned not with the shell of the building, but with its arcades, vaulting and other internal details.

[1] It is worth noting, at a more speculative level, the possibility that what can now be recognised as part of the forward area (*praetentura*) of the Roman fort seems to have been a site of some importance in the Anglo-Saxon period. The matter is incapable of proof, but it may be just possible that the continuing primacy of the district in Saxon times descended from its proximity to the central area of the fort. There are parallels elsewhere in the siting of churches or other important buildings on or near the centre of earlier Roman settlement, whether military or civil—and indeed, this kind of continuity has been traditionally claimed for the Church of St. Peter, Cornhill, as the successor of a Roman church on the site of the London basilica (see, for a convenient summary (Sir) Mortimer Wheeler, *London and the Saxons* (London Museum, 1935), pp. 102–3). The dangers of dabbling in such traditions, legends or ideas are sufficiently obvious, but sometimes it has been found that there lurks in them at least a grain of truth.

[2] *London, IV: The City*, p. 89.

[3] It should perhaps be added that Professor Pevsner (*Buildings of England: London*, I (1962), p. 687) refers to the restoration of the church as 'complete'. But this is a slip: elsewhere (e.g., p. 64) St. Alban is correctly grouped with the churches which under the re-organisation scheme for the City were not to be retained.

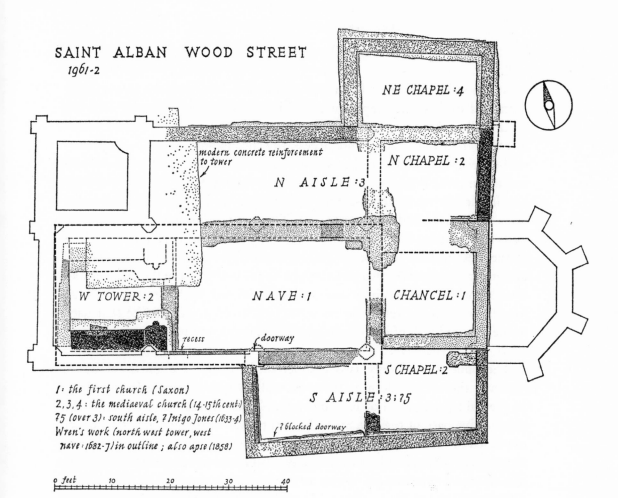

NE CHAPEL :4

modern concrete reinforcement
to tower

N CHAPEL :2

N AISLE :3

W TOWER :2

NAVE :1

CHANCEL :1

recess

doorway

S CHAPEL :2

S AISLE :3 :?5

?blocked doorway

1: the first church (Saxon)
2,3,4: the mediaeval church (14-15th cent.)
?5 (over 3): south aisle, ?Inigo Jones (1633-4)
Wren's work (north west tower, west
nave: 1682-7) in outline; also apse (1858)

0 feet   10   20   30   40

50. St. Alban Wood Street: plan of church as excavated.

The first recognisable church on the site may already have been a composite structure (Fig. 50, 1a, b). It consisted of a simple nave about $51\frac{1}{2}$ by 19 feet internally, the western part of which was cut off by an inserted cross-wall, and a chancel about 16 by 14 feet, the whole having an overall internal length of about 70 feet. The chancel wall on the south side made a straight joint with that of the nave, but there was no means of knowing whether this feature indicated a difference in date. There was nothing to suggest that the square chancel had replaced an apse. The north wall of the chancel presented problems for which in its ruined condition no answers could be found. The surviving fragment was unusually thick

205

but appeared to be of one build, both in itself and in relation to the east wall.

At the west end the walls of this first church were largely concealed or destroyed by later developments. The junction of the cross-wall with the south wall of the nave could be clearly seen and left no doubt that the former was structurally though not necessarily chronologically, later. The interval between this and the remains of a wall surviving at a relatively low level and taken to be the west wall of the church was 16 feet. The west wall lay just inside the seventeenth-century west wall. Its junctions with the side walls of the nave had been destroyed. The justification for regarding these walls as belonging lay in the close similarity of the masonry. The full width of the west wall could not be determined. The remaining walls were all uniformly slightly over two feet thick (with the exception in the chancel wall already mentioned) and built mainly of Kentish rag, with some chalk in the foundations. Stones retaining traces of pink Roman mortar like that used in the repaired wall of one of the fort buildings (p. 37) were common in the south wall of the nave.

The building had only two distinctive features. One of these was a recess in the south side near the cross-wall described above. It was about $4\frac{1}{2}$ feet wide, with a sill of Reigate stone blocks. It was heavily overlaid by the massive base of the seventeenth-century wall and could not be further examined in the time, but it is likely to have been a late insertion, whatever its purpose. The second was a doorway, also in the south wall, 20 feet west of the angle. The overall width of the opening was just under 3 feet, including raised slabs on either side of the main sill (Plate 92). Its western jamb survived to a height of about $3\frac{1}{2}$ feet. It was heavily rendered with plaster but quite plain and without a door-rebate.

The door sill, whose much damaged edge projected beyond the wall-face, was 2 feet 8 inches below the floor of the mediaeval tower. It was about 4 feet above the top of the Roman deposit. This does not of course give its true relationship to the underlying Roman levels, part of which had certainly been removed; but it indicates that the early church floor must have been laid down when the artificial deposits on the site were relatively shallow.

All the indications are therefore that the first church of St. Alban was indeed Saxon and at least of eighth–ninth century date. Its proportions resemble those of the slightly larger Saxon church of All Hallows Barking;[1] its simple relatively elongated plan and slight walls (apart from the problematical north-eastern corner), the frequent use of Roman building material, and the plain door-opening are also consistent with such a period. Presumably then this was the chapel of King Offa. The fact that none of its possible architectural embellishments has survived is easily explained by the low remaining height of the walls, but very little would in any case have been left above ground after the various later additions had been made.

It is not possible to date those additions beyond saying that in the mediaeval period they seem to have been mainly of the fourteenth and fifteenth centuries. There was no evidence of Norman work. Blocks of what appeared to be Caen stone were incorporated in the polygonal apse, built, according to Professor Pevsner, by Gilbert Scott in 1858.[2] But they may well have been derived from elsewhere.

The mediaeval developments fall into three phases. They are recognisable as a structural succession, but the parts of each phase are not of necessity strictly contemporary. In the first phase (Fig. 50, 2) almost square chapels were added on the north and south sides of the early chancel. Both chapels made straight joints with the chancel at the east end; on the west the junctions had not survived. The south chapel was better preserved than its counterpart. The return of the east wall remained for a foot or two. The foundation incorporated two well-built arches (Plate 95) of a type met with elsewhere.[3] At this stage, therefore, the church would seem to have consisted of the original nave with chapels added, the chancel walls being pierced to provide access on each side.

In the second phase (Fig. 50, 3) of the mediaeval sequence the chapels were extended westwards to form north and south aisles. Again the structural evidence on the south was the clearer: the foundation of the extension lay against that of the chapel in a straight joint, and turned through a right

---

[1] For the account of the post-bombing discoveries at All Hallows, Barking, see T. D. Kendrick and C. A. Ralegh Radford in *Antiq. Journ.* XXIII (1943), pp. 14–18. Dr. Radford has very kindly supplied the figures for the dimensions of the Saxon church, which are based upon later discoveries.

[2] *Buildings of England: London, I* (2nd edn., 1962), p. 133.

[3] The best example is of course that of the brick arches behind London Wall (*23*: p. 83); arches of the same kind also occurred at St. Swithun and St. Bride's.

angle to block the early doorway in the Saxon nave. In the course of its destruction the north aisle wall was seen to be of mediaeval type beneath its heavy renderings of plaster: chalk rubble in the core; ashlar clunch with successive coatings of plaster on the inner face; mainly, but by no means entirely, knapped flints externally. Near the tower there were indications of a blocked window-opening so mutilated that a date other than late mediaeval could not be suggested for it.

Leaving for the moment the complications of the west end, the third phase (Fig. 50, 4) on the north side was represented by the north-east chapel. Its wall abutted on the north wall of the aisle of phase 2. While however it looked like late mediaeval work the change at the corresponding place (Fig. 50, 5) in the sequence on the south side might well have been the work of Inigo Jones in 1633–4. This took the form of a re-building of the south aisle almost on the same line as the old but slightly extended westward. The west wall as surviving was built entirely of brick; brick was also the dominant material in the south wall. At the eastern end of this latest version of the south aisle part of the arcade uniting the aisle with the body of the church survived in the form of a respond (in Reigate stone) which though not bonded into the east wall may have been contemporary with it.

The eastern part of the church, then, at the end of the mediaeval development consisted of nave and chancel with asymmetrical side aisles and a north-east chapel. It is unlikely that by this time any of the Saxon church would have survived above floor-level, except for the east wall of the chancel. The east wall no doubt was re-furbished with a window appropriate to the time; the remains of the nave walls probably helped to support the arcades between nave and aisles, though no clearly recognisable traces of additional supports for the piers could be seen.

This relative clarity stands in contrast to the situation on the west, in the area south of Wren's tower. The most important junctions here were either masked or destroyed by the Wren alterations or by modern concrete insertions the purpose of which was to protect the tower.

The outstanding feature of the later mediaeval church at the west end was a massive well-built wall, carried on a correspondingly large foundation which ended on the east in the jamb of what must have been a big arch opening into the church (Plate 94). The wall was at least 3 feet 6 inches wide. The corresponding wall and jamb on the north side had been destroyed by the modern concrete referred to above, but at the west end in a gap between the church wall and the concrete the lower part of the foundation had survived to show that the structure was symmetrically placed about the long axis of the Saxon church. The remains must surely be those of a western tower.

It would have been impossible to resolve all the problems posed by this complex without more time and facilities for excavation which would have added to the problems of traffic-movement in Wood Street. On the east side the wall of the Saxon church could be seen to pass behind the mediaeval tower wall (Plate 93). At the west end Wren's foundations had destroyed the upper parts of the early work, but here too at the lower level the mediaeval tower wall was found to make a straight joint with the west wall of the Saxon church. Whatever happened then above the mediaeval floor-level it would seem that the foundations of the tower were set inside the walls of the Saxon church.

The western tower completed the mediaeval church which underwent the rebuildings and restorations referred to by the Royal Commission. This investigation has shown that as the Commission suggested the outer walls of the building were retained, but apart possibly from the final version of the south aisle these were the walls of a mediaeval, not an early seventeenth-century church. The tower is Wren's and it replaced the mediaeval tower to the south of it; so also was the south-western part of the nave as far as its junction with the south aisle. How much otherwise was to be ascribed to Wren, how much to Inigo Jones it now seems impossible to say. The windows were evidently all renewed and the church was provided with plaster vaults throughout. The piers and responds of the arcades were carried on brick foundations which could not in themselves be closely dated, though the eastern respond of the south arcade overlay the respond that was associated (above, p. 208) with the final reconstruction of the south aisle. In any case, Wren's problems here were not on the same scale as those of the larger church of St. Bride. In terms of cost he had much less to do: £3,165. 0s. 8d. at St. Alban; £11,430. 5s. 11d. at St. Bride.[1] In their respective development the two churches somewhat resemble one another. The significance of these investigations in another context is further discussed below (pp. 239ff.).

[1] RCHM, *London IV (The City)*, p. 199.

8. THE CLUNIAC ABBEY OF ST. SAVIOUR, BERMONDSEY
(1956, 1962–3)

The account of the work at Bermondsey[1] is much facilitated by the existence of papers on the abbey by Dr. Rose Graham and Mr. A. R. Martin,[2] the former dealing with the history, the latter setting out what is known from the records of the topography and of the architectural development of the buildings.

As to the first, Dr. Graham gave good reason for viewing with distrust the monastic *Annals*, which, compiled as she thought about 1433, purport to give the history of the monastery from its foundation in the late eleventh century. It seems probable that a London citizen, one Alwyn Child, was the first benefactor when he gave rents in the City of London to the monks of La Charité-sur-Loire, the great Cluniac foundation which was the mother-house of several other houses in England besides Bermondsey. This, according to the *Annals*, took place in 1082. On the other hand, the actual site for the monastery did not become available until in 1089 William Rufus gave to La Charité the Manor of Bermondsey; and here the monks took possession of the 'nova et pulchra ecclesia', the new and handsome church which is referred to in the Domesday Survey.

Once established the monastery enjoyed much favour. It had wealthy benefactors and was a place of resort both for pilgrims and for important travellers, ecclesiastical and lay alike. There is evidence also from material remains, where records fail, of building activity at various times in the twelfth and thirteenth centuries.

The main and almost the only source of information on the structural features and layout of the abbey is a group of three manuscript volumes in

[1] The 1956 season's work was under the immediate supervision of Mr. Dennis Corbett. It was concerned with the larger, eastern portion of the site, and was financed by the Ministry of Public Building and Works and by the Corporation of Bermondsey jointly. The excavation of the western end in 1962 was also financed by the Ministry and the Corporation and was completed at the Excavation Council's charge in 1963.

[2] R. Graham, 'The Priory of La Charité-sur-Loire and the Monastery of Bermondsey', *Journ. Brit. Arch. Soc.* 2nd ser., XXXII (1926), pp. 157–91. A. R. Martin, 'On the Topography of the Cluniac Abbey of Saint Saviour at Bermondsey', *ibid.*, pp. 192–228. Also R. Graham, 'The Church of the Cluniac Monastery of St. Saviour at Bermondsey', *ibid.*, 3rd ser., II (1937), pp. 146–9.

the British Museum, compiled by John Chessil Buckler between 1808 and 1820. As Mr. Martin records, the most important of these for topographical purposes is the volume of plans and drawings, which not only constitute a painstaking pictorial record of the site made only a few years before it was submerged in modern development but also incorporate many measurements which have the appearance of being quite precise.

As Mr. Martin rightly says, without Buckler's records it would be impossible to establish even the site of the church. With them the outlines of the monastic property can be fixed: the main west gate was at the junction of Abbey Street with Bermondsey Street; the church itself straddled the intersection of what are now Tower Bridge Road and Abbey Street, with the claustral and other buildings to the south. When Buckler made his record the main buildings on the site (apart from the original west gate-house) were those of the mansion built in the 1540's by Sir Thomas Pope. Pope used the south wall of the church as the basis for the north walls of his main buildings, the area of the church itself remaining as open gardens. On the north the gardens were delimited by a brick wall, evidently on the site of the north wall of the church, a feature of which was a rectangular bay projecting 15 feet northwards from the main line, its western return about 340 feet in from the outer gate. The siting of this wall is of crucial importance for the determination of the site: it is the one wall which Buckler accurately records with stated measurements on his tracing of the 25-inch plan and to it many of his other measurements are ultimately related.

As a result of the bombing the buildings on the north side of Abbey Street between Tower Bridge Road on the west and Riley Street on the east had been almost completely destroyed: all that remained was a small group of buildings on the north-west corner of the site. Incorporated in these buildings and forming part of the south wall of the block was a wall of very mixed masonry of 'early' appearance which extended a little way eastwards from the buildings. Excavation subsequently showed that this wall, which elsewhere consisted largely of brick, was in fact relatively late, but was built on top of an older wall which had originally been equipped with buttresses on its north side (Plate 102). The buttresses had been removed, only their foundations remaining. When Buckler's wall came to be plotted according to his measurements it was found to coincide exactly with the line of the

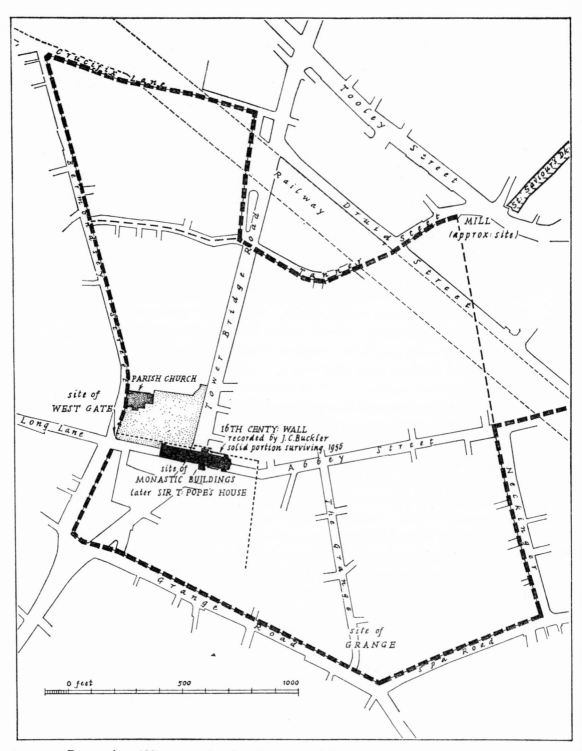

51. Bermondsey Abbey: map showing the extent of the monastic precinct and the position of the church.

old wall just described; and there can be no doubt that they are one and the same (Fig. 51).

The excavation of the bombed area was handicapped as always by modern obstructions and disturbance, the chief being a series of bomb-shelters along the Abbey Street frontage. The deposits were everywhere mixed to depths of 6 feet and more below the surface and nowhere had original floor-levels survived. The undisturbed natural ground consisted of a loamy sand, usually of a brownish colour, overlying gravel; the surface of the sand was at about 6 feet, that of the gravel at about 9 feet. Very little of the faced stonework of the walls had survived. Chalk foundations remained in some places, their bases resting on the gravel (Plate 101): elsewhere walls could be followed by their robber trenches, which normally contained a filling of loose mortar with small chalk rubble.

Apart from the usual post-mediaeval features, cesspits, wells and the like, five structural elements were recognisable. First towards the north-eastern part of the area explored there was a series of foundations and robber trenches, very incompletely seen, which were so incorporated with the other remains as to leave no doubt that they were earlier than anything else on the site. The meaning of these features is not at all clear. They do not fit into the plan of the church. They are not recognisable as part of the pre-monastic church whose existence seems to be implied in the Domesday statement (above, p. 210). Nor, on the authority of Mr. H. M. Colvin, is there any reason for thinking that there would have been buildings of importance in the manor when the royal gift was made to La Charité in 1098.

The second group of structures related to the first, Norman, phase of the church. The area involved extended eastwards from the new (1963) frontage of Tower Bridge Road for about 110 feet, northwards for a maximum of 40 feet (except for an extension at the western end). On the basis of the measurements recorded by Buckler this would have represented rather less than half, the northern half, of the full width of the church. The excavation revealed that the area encompassed lengthwise the eastern part of the church from the eastern chapels to the main transept; but some part of the transept lies under Tower Bridge Street.

It is not possible here to discuss at length every feature revealed by this excavation and a number of problems remain—and will remain—unsolved.

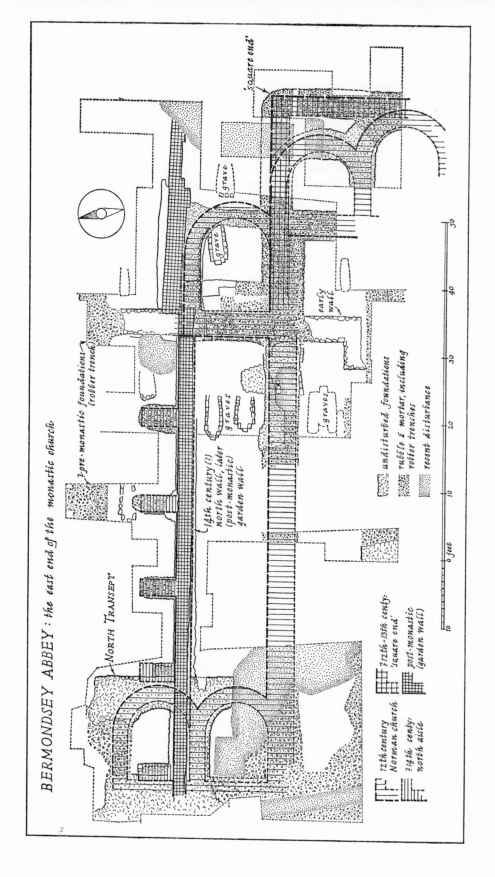

BERMONDSEY ABBEY : *the east end of the monastic church*

NORTH TRANSEPT

'square end'

?pre-monastic foundations (robber trench)

grave

grave

graves

early wall

graves

graves

?12th century (?) north wall, later (post-monastic) garden wall

0 feet 10 20 30 40 50

?16th century Norman church

?12th century north aisle

?12th–13th cent. 'square end'

post-monastic (garden wall)

undisturbed foundations

rubble & mortar, including robber trenches

recent disturbance

52. Bermondsey Abbey: plan of the east end of the church as excavated.

The early monastic church (which must surely have replaced the Domesday church) was evidently in the tradition of the mother-church of La Charité[1] and of its sister foundation at Lewes,[2] though smaller than both (Fig. 52). It had parallel apses at the east end, the central feature of which probably consisted of three apsidioles with outer apses forming projecting wings or transepts some distance westwards on each side. The main transept, 50 feet to the west, contained two apsidal chapels represented by solid chalk foundations the full extent of which to the west could not be seen. The north wall of the presbytery, linking both transepts, survived mainly as a robber trench. When this church was built the area had already been used for burials: a grave built of chalk blocks partly underlay the foundation of the eastern transept; but apart from one or two carved stones similar to some already recorded by Buckler no significant evidence of date was recovered. In the complete absence of floors this was almost inevitable.

Buckler located the west end of the church, but did not determine its eastern limit. With the new information relating to this the church can now be seen to have had an overall length of about 310 feet, as compared with 440 feet for the Cluniac Priory of St. Pancras at Lewes.

It is impossible on the existing evidence to arrange the next two phases chronologically. One of these involved the replacement of the apses by a 'square end' which had the same width and length as the original central feature. It survived as a foundation trench (Plate 100), but could be seen to cut through the foundation of the central apse. The result was a Lady Chapel relatively squat in outline: there is nothing to indicate its internal arrangement.

More drastic was the modification to the north side of the presbytery which completely remodelled it, and no doubt the whole of the north side of the church. This is represented by a wall, parallel with and about 25 feet north of the original presbytery wall. At the east it abutted the north–south wall which defined the eastern transept: this evidently became the new north-eastern angle of the presbytery. Westwards it crossed the foundation of the main transept, which it undoubtedly replaced. This wall was equipped

[1] For the plan of this part of the church of La Charité see Plate II, facing p. 158, in R. Graham, *op. cit.*, p. 210, footnote above.

[2] W. H. St. J. Hope, 'The Cluniac Priory of St. Pancras at Lewes', *Sussex Arch. Collections*, XLIX (1906), pp. 66–88; cf. W. H. Godfrey, *Arch. Journ.* CXVI (1959), pp. 258–9.

with external buttresses at intervals of 12–14 feet (centres): the most westerly were built against the foundations of the early transept which must have carried some part of the superstructure of the buttress itself.

It seems likely that this change involved the construction of a new transept somewhat to the west of the original, for Buckler records foundations on the south side which suggest a transept with an east wall about 22 feet west of that of the Norman version. Such replanning must have led to some remodelling of the conventual buildings on the west side of the cloister to the south. How it affected the rest of the church can only now be guessed at. If the Norman date ascribed to a two-light window at the west end of the nave which figures in Buckler's drawings is right the south side of the nave remained untouched. With the presbytery, on the other hand, a similar piece of evidence suggests that the south side was remodelled also, for here Buckler shows incorporated in one of Sir Thomas Pope's buildings a doorway which has a fourteenth-century look.

The final phase relates to the post-dissolution activity of Pope, who used the church as a quarry for his buildings, leaving its area to be gardens as already observed. It was the wall just described which in modified form became the garden wall to which importance was attached as a datum for measurements at the beginning of this account. Its buttresses were removed and as a mere garden wall it was rebuilt in mixed materials incorporating a good deal of brick. In keeping with its late date, the level of this wall, built on the base of the mediaeval wall, was higher than anything else on the site; and it had survived at least in part to be incorporated in the nineteenth-century buildings.

This investigation has thus drastically modified the interpretation proposed by Mr. A. R. Martin but was carried out in advantageous circumstances which were not available to him in 1926. It must be emphasised, even so, that while the broad lines of this development seem to fit the accumulated facts a number of features revealed by the excavation remain unexplained. It should be borne in mind for the future that while most of the site of the church is out of reach beneath Abbey Street a considerable part of the northern half of the nave lies within the former churchyard of St. Mary Magdalene. Investigation here might well resolve some of the difficulties.

The question remains of whether the building sequence outlined above can be fitted into the historical framework provided by Dr. Graham and Mr. Martin. It has added nothing positive about the Domesday church apart from the possible implication that the early building had been replaced, or was sited elsewhere. The possibility that the two churches existed as it were side by side seems to be suggested by an early fourteenth-century reference to 'the greater church of St. Saviour'; and in its excavated form the Norman church has a monastic rather than a parochial look. But this leaves unaccounted for the early walls which are incorporated in the eastern end. The Norman church must surely be of the twelfth century, with the completion of the presbytery in 1206, in spite of the absence of reference to building activity at this time which Mr. Martin notes. Mr. Martin records that the Lady Chapel was already in existence by 1310, but it cannot certainly be said that this was the 'square end' described above. The remodelling of the presbytery, however, was almost certainly carried out in the fourteenth century, which was a period of great activity, culminating in the dedication of the 'greater church' in 1338, according to the *Annals*. While the actual year is wrong Mr. Martin's view is that the church could have been substantially completed by this time.

VIII

Epilogue

IN this, the last chapter of this book, I propose to write in more personal terms about the fifteen years of work whose results have been summarised in what has gone before. Any opinions that emerge from this vaguely auto-biographical effort will be my own and some if not all are likely to be dis-claimed by perhaps a majority of my colleagues on the Excavation Council. They will not in any case have much value for future archaeological work in the City of London. This will presumably continue along the traditional lines of rescue-operations undertaken incidentally to the redevelopment of individual sites, with little opportunity of control by archaeologists for archaeological ends.

Such rescue-work apart, it must be recognised that not merely the end of a phase, but the end of all hope of further information on the early past of the City within the walls has now arrived. The effect of rebuilding in the post-1945 era is to destroy once and for all the evidence from which such information may be obtained. The excavations for new buildings nowadays are total: they cover the complete area of the site; they penetrate to depths well below those reached by the deepest human deposits; and they leave behind therefore nothing for the successors of our post-war generations to do. This is a fact that is still imperfectly appreciated and it is only slightly mitigated by the survival undisturbed of a few open spaces, old churchyards and the like, which may perhaps receive more generous treatment in the distant future.[1]

---

[1] These words, re-read in proof, now seem perhaps unduly pessimistic. There are signs of a change of heart in authority. The fact that in 1966 funds were allocated specifically for the

There have of course been those who without necessarily realising the full seriousness of the situation have publicly and elsewhere criticised the efforts that have been made to deal with it, saying, in effect, 'too little and too late'. For my own part, when I look at the map which is Fig. 2 here and contemplate for each of the areas that are numbered on it what has actually been done I wonder what we have to show for the £40,000 that all this has cost.

But the outcome could only have been different if the controlling factors themselves could have been changed. The problems of facilities to work and of money to finance work are closely related when they reflect the attitudes of those in whose hands lies the power to be helpful. The first requirement would have been a change in the traditional policies of the Corporation of London, for the situation in 1945 was one for which the established procedures were not adequate. Down to the inter-war period care for the archaeological finds from building-sites had rested on a very uncertain basis. The Corporation's officers found themselves in competition with private collectors and dealers, including the redoubtable G. F. Lawrence, whose name was known to all building-labourers and site-workers in the London of the time. Charles Roach Smith had earlier attacked vigorously the indifference of various authorities to Roman London; but the enthusiasm and self-sacrifice of Roach Smith and of many others since his time cannot be regarded as absolving the City authority from the need to devise an ordered policy for dealing with discoveries as the counterpart of the creation of the Guildhall Museum in 1876. This is not to demand of one age that it should operate out of the hindsight of the next. The complaint is that having accepted that the safeguarding of London's antiquities should be on a commercial basis the City did not itself set the pace, but allowed the initiative largely to pass into the dealers' hands.[1]

[1] The point is illustrated by a wartime experience that came to me in 1942–3, when I had no idea that I would ever be concerned with Roman London. I was at that time seconded to the

archaeological exploration of a city site (albeit a somewhat special one) encourages the hope that for areas yet to be re-developed a new policy may be forthcoming. The change, if there is to be one, comes too late to affect the bombed areas, of which there are very few left. It is to be welcomed none the less for other sites of potential importance which will otherwise be a heavy burden for those who have been unfairly charged with the problems that this work presents when facilities in time and labour are left to chance.

Thus in 1946 the task of recovering and recording antiquities was evidently to be left to officials, no doubt with such volunteer and free-lance help as they could get, who would have been obliged to treat each investigation as a rescue-operation governed by the building requirements of the site. The magnificent archaeological collections of the Guildhall Museum owe their range and quality mainly to the courageous and self-sacrificing efforts down the years of officials who have had to do all their own labouring in uncompromising conditions which have become more difficult in recent times. This work has of course continued throughout the period with which this book is concerned; but valuable as its results have been and are, it could not in itself have been enough. What was wanted was a readiness to recognise the special nature and the urgency of the problem; and this the Corporation showed itself unwilling to do either by giving more than token help to the Excavation Council or by providing its own museum officials with facilities that more closely measured up to the tasks that they had to perform.

The creation of the Excavation Council at the instigation of the Society of Antiquaries of London was mentioned earlier (p. 1). Deputations to the

---

Ministry of Works to investigate antiquities that were being destroyed in the making of aerodromes and other war-works. The labourers on these sites were of course drawn from widely-varying sources and many were old hands who had worked on London buildings. On several occasions, learning what I was there to do, men asked me whether I knew, or had heard of, 'Old Tup'ny'. It would then emerge that 'Old Tup'ny' was one of two characters who used to tour the building-sites to buy antiquities from the workmen. From internal evidence I was able to establish his identity as that of a well-respected officer of the Guildhall Museum. His rival was 'a man named Lawrence'; the Lawrence referred to above. My informants would explain that whenever possible they preferred to hoard their finds until Lawrence arrived: for any given object they might receive a shilling from him, while from Old Tup'ny they could hope only for—tuppence. Lawrence (whom I never met) does not appear to have been actuated by the regard for accuracy of record and other detail that concerned Old Tup'ny and the study of the past of London is hampered accordingly. Gratitude is nevertheless due to him for the quantity of material from the London area generally that found a permanent home in the collections of the London Museum (for which he had the title of 'Inspector of Excavations') and no doubt elsewhere. That apart, much that would have been significant and that might have reached the City museum if the Corporation had been more actively concerned, must have escaped, being now lost in private collections, where it presumably remains, largely unidentified and unprovenanced. It is incidentally worth noting that this traffic was entirely illegal, since antiquities, then as now, are the property of the owner on whose land they are found.

appropriate committees of the Corporation failed to obtain direct representation of that body on the new organisation, apart from the association of the Guildhall Museum with it; but the then Lord Mayor, Sir Charles Davis, consented to become its President, acting in his personal capacity. His successors followed his example and have regularly allowed the Council the use of the Mansion House for the customary annual meetings. So, too, the City's officers interpreted generously and patiently the consent that they were given to their helping us on an unofficial basis. We have every reason to feel obliged to them.

A factor in the Corporation's attitude was undoubtedly an anxiety, expressed more than once, to get new buildings erected with as little delay as possible. The archaeologists, if unduly encouraged, would get in the way. In fact, whatever may have been going on behind the scenes in those years immediately after the war nothing to speak of was happening in the bombed cellars themselves: then and later much more might have been done without in any way impeding the rebuilding. But action from the Corporation would have been essential. To one who has experienced many expressions of sympathy and is grateful for many acts of kindness from individuals the indifference of the Corporation *as a body* has been a disappointment, to say the least of it.

Undoubtedly our most valuable links in the City generally in those early days were Lord Balfour of Burleigh, the late Sir Frederick Tidbury-Beer and Colonel Sir (as he later became) Cuthbert Whitaker, who spared no effort on our behalf. It was Sir Cuthbert who urged that the 'Mediaeval' in the Council's rather cumbersome title should be spelt '-ae-'. This, he thought, might operate to prevent the word being pronounced 'medeevial' in some quarters. The logic behind the idea is perhaps not immediately apparent, whatever the justification for it. The form was in any case adopted out of a general preference for it; and the long title was chosen rather than shorter alternatives to avow an interest in all aspects of the City's past. One or two people had suggested that with so much to do we should concentrate on the Roman deposits; but apart altogether from the principle involved, as a matter of practical necessity it would have been impossible to do this because of the way in which the various elements interlocked (pp. 4ff.). Understanding of one part demanded understanding of all, whatever their periods.

When the problems of the ancient bombed cities, and of London in particular, were first discussed, the original idea, as I understood it, was that the Ministry of Works should accept responsibility for them. This presumably would have meant that the Ministry would have provided full-time paid supervision, as well as meeting the cost of labour. To what extent this arrangement was actually considered by the policy-makers I have no means of knowing; for by the time that I appeared on the scene, in 1946, it had been accepted that Local Enterprise was to be the driving-force, with grants-in-aid from the government through the Ministry to augment funds from private sources. This, in modified form, is the familiar pattern of organisation which archaeological societies and others have followed in the past, though not necessarily with subventions from the state. The money question apart, it relies, as the London Council has relied, on public-spirited individuals who have been able and willing to shoulder the administrative and other burdens. The outstanding examples of this arrangement in the immediately post-war situation were Canterbury and Exeter. At the former in particular far the greater part of the work was done in vacation-time by volunteers, some local, some university undergraduates and others from further afield; the organisation itself was given continuity by a group of citizens who accepted responsibility for all administration, including the general welfare of the volunteers. The conditions in London did not encourage this.

I shall have more to say later about the use of volunteer workers in London, where from the beginning it was decided that the special conditions would necessitate the use mainly of paid labour. We made two elaborate and widespread appeals both within and beyond the City, but support from the City generally was very much less than might have been expected from a community that tends to be self-congratulatory about its history and traditions. (I believe that I am right in thinking that the pre-war scheme for financing a succession of archaeological observers under the aegis of the Society of Antiquaries met similar difficulties.) Archaeologists, like others, will always complain about lack of the means to pursue their pet projects, but large as the sum actually spent may appear to be it ought to have been very much larger.

£40,000 over fifteen years represents on the average only £2,660 a year; it is easy to calculate what this represents in terms of man-weeks. (In fact the amount available was not as much as this, for part of the money was set on one side with an eye to the cost of future publication of results.) One factor here has of course been the steady rise in men's wages, which is a serious problem for an organisation operating on a more or less fixed income. In 1949 I was paying labourers about £6 for a week's work. In 1954 it was £8; in 1960, £12. The obvious effect of this process was of course to reduce our capacity to employ labour, since our annual expenditure had to be kept at a fairly constant rate. The list of subscribers to our funds is printed elsewhere in this volume as an expression of our abiding gratitude to our benefactors, great and small alike.

In all discussion of costs an important question is the cost of supervision. The Council was saved the necessity of finding a director's stipend—some hundreds of pounds a year, at least—because the Trustees of the London Museum acquiesced in my appointment as honorary director of the excavations. The Trustees took the enlightened view that while the museum collections themselves would not benefit directly from any of the discoveries made, new knowledge of London's past would be forthcoming in which all would share. Though a saving in one way this arrangement was disadvantageous in others. I could not allow this extra responsibility to interfere seriously with the job that I was paid to do and could not therefore put in all my time in the City, particularly when from the late 1940's onwards preparations for the removal of the museum and its rehabilitation at Kensington Palace had to occupy my attention. It was fortunate for the excavations that during the first years the situation of the museum at Lancaster House was such that only a limited amount of work could be done on the reorganisation of the collections. Over this time we employed more labour than later; and in particular it was possible to train my new foreman Mr. A. J. Haydon and give Fred (Pop) Beasley the experience that qualified him to take over as leading hand when Haydon died.

There is in any case a limit to the amount of work that can be directed by one person which is quite quickly reached with deposits as complicated as those in the City. Any increase above about four or five in the unskilled labour-force carries with it the need for more archaeologically skilled supervision which would require to be salaried and would place a disproportionate strain on a limited income. It was only when my wife joined me in 1953 that I enjoyed the benefit of experienced help, though I would not want to be thought to be decrying the part played by Haydon and later by Beasley.

The proportions of 'unskilled' labour to supervision and of both to the money available are thus governing factors in any excavation programme. This is particularly the case with professional labourers, who for all their apparent slowness move soil much more quickly than their amateur counterparts and at times may require very close watching indeed because of the speed at which they may go through complicated deposits. The point is obvious enough, but in this age of amateur excavators it seems often to be overlooked. It was one of the considerations that influenced the policy of excavation in several of its aspects. Both because of my own circumstances and because of the need for close supervision it was easier to work all the year round with a small body of men than to have a summer season, even a long one, with a larger labour-force working more intensively and demanding therefore full-time supervision from the director. Under the first arrangement it was usually possible to have alternative tasks for men to do when difficulty arose. It was in addition the only way of keeping experienced workmen whom it would have been impossible to bring together again once they had been dispensed with at the end of a season. Building-work labourers in London are the most casual that there are—casual in the sense of tending to be highly mobile, and therefore elusive, between jobs. The problems of a small organisation with limited resources in a world of high-powered building-contractors and property-developers can be sufficiently acute in any case. We could not compete with the builders by offering such incentives as long hours of overtime for the men who worked for us and concessions had to take other forms, including settled conditions of work over a period, for those who were prepared to stay. The tendency was to retain a man's services as long as possible once he showed himself reasonably competent; but there were times also when the difficulties of the labour situation forced one to keep even unsuitable men as the only way of making progress. The uneconomic effects of this had to be lightened by putting the unteachable to assist the experienced men in such harmless but useful work as barrow-pushing.

Partings in these circumstances were inevitable and at times frequent; and on occasion irritation and amusement were more or less equally mixed. Two I remember in particular. One involved a man whose behaviour had been on various occasions puzzling, to say the least of it. Our final exchange of views took place in Ironmonger Lane as he was returning from an unduly prolonged and mildly alcoholic dinner-break. The discussion followed rather inconsequential lines. It ended by his taking me firmly by the top button of my waistcoat and maintaining that whatever claims I might make for myself he at any rate had left hospital with a certificate to show that he was sane. This, he insisted, was more than I could say. It was difficult to think up a suitable reply on the spur of the moment.

The other incident, a good deal earlier than this, when much work was being done in and about Cripplegate, concerned one Tom, of whom it was credibly reported that he was selling potsherds as souvenirs to visitors. Taxed with this offence, Tom assumed an attitude of injured innocence, took off his cap to reveal an unexpectedly bald head and swore a mighty oath beginning 'May my grandmother never rest in her grave if I ever ...' His grandmother, I suppose, because his mother was still in the land of the living; but I didn't think to clear up this point until it was too late. Tom's departure was inevitable, but took place without ill feelings on either side. Some months after this he called on us at the Charterhouse. He had exchanged the cap for one of those black Anthony Eden hats, with which went a smart dark overcoat; and I wondered, but felt that I couldn't ask, on what this apparent prosperity was founded—not, I felt sure, the flogging of trifles excavated from Roman London.

Nevertheless, for all the coming and going and the problems that it raised, over the years we had a number of workmen who stayed with us for quite long periods. Far and away the best of them was Pop Beasley. He came to me with my first gang in 1947 and stayed until he died in 1957, becoming after the loss of my first foreman, Haydon, a most valued and understanding assistant. Pop could at no time have been described as a cheerful companion; domestic tragedy had left him unable to look kindly on the world in general, and to the end he remained wary, to put it mildly, of the motives and intentions of others. At the same time, he was one of the three men whom in a fairly long and varied career as an excavator I have found with an instinctive understanding of what excavation was about. He showed himself also very good at bringing other men along once he could be persuaded to accept responsibility for them.

I have already mentioned in passing the decision to rely on professional labour in London, taken in spite of the fact that amateurs had worked and were working so successfully elsewhere. The scale of the London problem and the pressure of the time-table were taken to require this course. It would not have been possible to rely on the week-end and vacation-work which is all that volunteers can be expected to manage. The use of volunteers in excavations in Britain has now become widespread. It reflects difficulty in obtaining paid labour and its very high cost as well as a very widespread enthusiasm for this kind of field-work amongst young (and sometimes not-so-young) people. In London there are now several very active groups operating under leaders who amongst other things provide the essential direction and continuity.

At various times I have had a succession of individual helpers whose contributions were of great value, one or two of whom have gone on to take up archaeological careers. In general professional labourers in London do not seem to like the prospect of working with amateurs. This attitude seems in part to reflect a deep-seated anxiety over diluted labour which derives from more distant past conditions. Sometimes it was based on the more personal dislike of the professional of finding himself expected to move other people's spoil-heaps as well as his own. The professional is only happy with the amateur if the amateur shows a readiness to shoulder his responsibility on more or less equal terms.

In answer to many inquiries and offers of help an excavation exclusively for volunteers was begun in 1949, its aim the examination of the ditch outside the city wall on the north side near Aldermanbury Postern (*16*: p. 86). The work was to take place at week-ends and Haydon and I undertook to be present alternately.

The first meeting of the volunteers was an impressive spectacle. It was also a rather worrying one, for the number present was more than the site could carry or the available supervision control when once the preliminary clearing of the cellars had been accomplished. But though the digging itself was not arduous numbers soon began to fall away as the less hardy individuals came to realise what was involved. The work went on over a long period of week-ends during which people came and went and I was under the necessity time after time of explaining the whole project from the beginning to successive newcomers. Towards the end a small core of tough workers remained with whom I would have been prepared to continue indefinitely. But when one of their number, stopped on a lonely Sunday afternoon by a policeman and asked to account for the lead in the parcel that he carried on his bike, unwarrantably used my name to extricate himself from the threat of a charge of having stolen it from a bombed site this seemed the moment to close the operation down. Subsequently two labourers finished the cutting in two or three days.

This is not to be read as a criticism of amateur diggers generally: the contribution that they make and have made to practical archaeology is well known. It is rather a comment on the conditions under which work on many London sites has had to be done. The digging takes a long time, it is often unproductive of finds, and dust and dirt from long-neglected cellars are all-pervading. Somewhere one of my contemporaries called the City cellars 'gloomy': the adjective was fully justified even where ragwort or rose-bay willow-herb in season took command. They have none of the appeal of the chalk downs of Wessex or the gravels of the Thames valley as settings for a working holiday; and people sacrificing their week-ends to them might reasonably feel that the objectives were too remote to seem realistic, with too much dead ground to be shifted in reaching them. In such circumstances the fun may go out of it, but the objectives must be reached all the same and the professionals must go on.

Much later a useful group formed around the volunteers who helped over the investigation of the Walbrook temple. It owed its vigour and sense of discipline to the leadership and control exercised by my friend George Rybot, F.S.A., and its proceedings succeeded in being at once hilarious and purposeful. Rybot's Volunteers did valuable work in unravelling the details of the defences of the Cripplegate fort in the Noble Street section (6–9: p. 33). One of their discoveries was Rybot's Turret, the small internal turret between the south-west corner and the west gate. The work carried so far is gradually being completed by volunteer groups from the University of London Archaeological Society. It will form an important part of the final treatment of London Wall in the area of Cripplegate.

It was perhaps partly out of a wish for light relief, partly as yet another essay in the good old British sport of deluding the 'expert' that one member of the Aldermanbury Postern party (whose identity I suspected, but never put to the test) 'salted' the site with a succession of fake antiquities. The first of these was found within half an hour of work starting on a hot Saturday afternoon in July, during which I had taken off my jacket and for my pains had its pockets ransacked by two small boys who then had to be pursued across the bombed cellars of Cripplegate Without. So while the date now eludes me the day was a memorable one.

The object in question was a leg-bone of sheep (or goat) correctly patinated to suit the ground from which it was supposed to have come, one end of it either broken or cut off as if it had been intended to do duty as the handle of a knife. One of the flattened surfaces of the bone carried length-wise a skilfully-executed Latin inscription which was immediately re-cognisable as combining the obverse and reverse legends of a coin of the emperor Commodus. My pronouncement that the 'knife-handle' was a fake was not readily accepted by those present, even when it was pointed out to them that it had come from a few inches below the surface of a deposit which was demonstrably post-Roman, where it could easily have been planted for quick finding. In following week-ends further 'knife-handles' appeared, with inscriptions which vary their wording only in the names and titles of the royalties. The final effort was a potsherd with a similar but (inevitably) broken and incomplete inscription. The series as a whole con-jured up a pleasant picture of members of the Roman imperial family of the various centuries, all at once fiercely possessive and concerned about rank and titles, picnicking regularly in London's mediaeval city ditch.

So much by way of diversion. Other factors besides the difficulties of the available labour-supply contributed to uneconomical working. I have said that there was no way of getting obstructions removed in the early years, before rebuilding started. There were occasions when the pursuit of a particular problem involved the wasteful business of moving spoil and débris back and forth between cellars to get access to them. The investiga-tion of the Cripplegate fort defences required this to be done in Noble Street and at Aldermanbury Postern, to mention only two sites; and it was exasperating that with a small force we should have had to waste time and money shifting about large quantities of brick-rubble which were due to be removed anyway. Bomb débris was much more abundant in the cellars than might at first glance appear and in a number of places we moved a good deal of it, in Cheapside and elsewhere, clearing 'lanes' in order to put down trenches, if not actually dumping it into neighbouring cellars. In some areas its quantity was such that it completely defeated us. Even on sites which were open and available the extent of the area actually excavated was generally controlled by limitations of space in which to put excavated soil;

and here again double-handling had often to be undertaken. The temple of Mithras (p. 98) perhaps provides the best example of this. The first excavation of the building was carried to a point at which there was no room for more excavated material—indeed, the situation became positively dangerous, with the only access to parts of the site along narrow planks over cuttings which were feet deep in water. The 'public' character of the building could at this stage be guessed at; but further progress was impossible until the site was cleared by the developers. The consequence was the loss of precious months during which the temple and its surroundings might have been submitted to a more thorough examination in less distracting conditions than those that finally prevailed.

This, as the *Financial Times* recognised in one of the more balanced comments made during the later Mithras sensation, was the basic problem: lack of means, both facilities and money, to cope with this and other situations at the most opportune time. The real importance of the difficulties here catalogued, however, lay not so much in their wastefulness as in their effect on the excavation results. The consequence of being able usually to examine only a very small part of each available area was that it was seldom possible to produce much in the way of a plan. This was particularly the case with the buildings of timber and other perishable materials which seem to have predominated on the bombed sites that were available to us. Not enough can be seen of their post-holes and other features to lead to even a tentative reconstruction of their outline; one outcome of this must be that we shall always know much less about London than we do about many of our smaller stone-built Roman towns. This is a serious defect for which we shall be much criticized in the future and during all these years I have not been able to lose sight of it.

I think it may be fairly claimed that we did our best to make the most productive use of our funds. In one year for exceptional reasons the proportion spent on labour-wages was only 75·5 per cent; in eight it was above 90 per cent; in the rest above 80 per cent. Overheads and trimmings were kept to a minimum. Being unable to afford a night-watchman and even with the friendly help of the police, we suffered a number of losses by theft of tools and equipment; and having had our huts broken into regularly during our first experimental year we saved by dispensing with them from then on, improvising shelters and storage-places as necessary on each site.

Our somewhat ramshackle equipment was often the subject of amused or critical comment from outsiders; I was embarrassed by it only when foreign visitors expressed surprise at finding the British conducting investigations into the archaeology of their historic capital city in this meagre way. As one of the first archaeologists to make use of graders and other soil-shifting machines during the war I found it easy to visualise from the beginning the sort of mechanical aids that would have speeded the work along. Many such exist in, or could be developed from, appliances already in common use in the world of building and civil engineering. The problem is one of the capital costs which most archaeological enterprises are unable to meet once they have covered the straightforward requirements of labour and so on. Recent years have seen some movement in this direction and more can probably be expected if with its increasing responsibility for 'rescue' excavations of threatened antiquities the Ministry of Public Building and Works brings the expertise of its technical departments to bear on the problem.

Turning now to the events surrounding the discovery of the Walbrook mithraeum, I must begin with expressions of gratitude to the owners, Messrs. Legenland, and the builders, Humphreys and Company Limited, for their generous and enlightened attitude towards this investigation. During these years site-owners and builders generally have been sympathetically inclined towards us and gave such help as they could, often with some inconvenience to themselves. The friendliness and hospitality of officials expressed themselves in frequent cups of tea, readiness to store equipment and so on. This and much else I recall gratefully; but it was owing especially to Sir Aynsley Bridgeland and his fellow directors that we were allowed exceptional facilities for the temple excavation. The circumstances in which the excavation began were described on p. 98. It has also been said (p. 106) that the existence of the building had been recognised long before its association with Mithras was established. The owners protected the site for us while demolition and clearance-work were carried out around it and allowed us to resume our investigations when the course of their operations made it possible for us to do so. It would be misleading to pretend that the presence of archaeologists was welcomed unreservedly by all the site-officials: this is thoroughly understandable. But while the damage to the Bacchus sculpture (p. 109) was due to the unwarranted interference of one individual, the rest without exception were very patient with us.

The possibility of a mithraic connexion first presented itself when the fragmentary statue of Cautopates was found just outside the south wall of the building. During the earlier work this stone had been seen projecting upside down from the side of a cutting to which George Rybot and Gordon Atkinson had devoted many week-ends. Work on this part of the site had had to stop after a time because of danger to the excavators and the stone had to be left in place until the area came to be cleared by the contractors, who generously consented to remove the lower deposits by hand, instead of by machine. It was at once gratifying and a relief when the suspicious-looking stone proved to be 'something'. My own stock rose perceptibly amongst the practical men by whom we were surrounded and the discovery eased the way for the further work that required to be done.

The subsequent events were sparked off by the finding of the head of Mithras, which came to light during the digging of a narrow cutting, thought at the time to be the last that would be made, the aim of which was to establish the eastward limit of the building as it approached the Walbrook Street frontage. This was on the morning of Saturday, September 18th. The head was photographed by one of those press-photographers who always seem to be about; the work closed down at lunch-time; and I departed for the country, where I did not see the picture that appeared in the next day's *Sunday Times*. It was this picture, apparently, that brought visitors to the site in such numbers on the Sunday; and I was horrified to have the first inkling of this from a photograph in the following morning's papers, which showed people roaming all over it and displaying what I could not help but regard as an unhealthy interest in some of its more fragile features.

And so, suddenly and without warning, Mithras had arrived. The excavation was given a further reprieve. Messrs. Humphreys decided that they would open the site to visitors in the evenings for a week and access to it was organised accordingly. Nobody knew what to expect: perhaps 500 people, it was thought. The police estimated the queue that wound round the streets at at least five times that figure. The queues continued on this scale throughout the week and in the diminishing hours of September daylight it became impossible for all the people to get in before darkness fell. The waiting crowd would not listen to the police and it was my task then to try to persuade them to go home. As I made my way along the queue a running argument, by no means all of it good-natured, would develop out of my exhortations. Frustrated would-be viewers demanded floodlighting and other facilities: the demands seem to me to be as unreasonable now as I thought them then. The climax in these nocturnal happenings came on Sunday, September 26th, when literally in the dark and photographed by flashlight the head of a deity, not then recognised as Minerva, was found. It was removed from the ground by my assistant (as she then was) and displayed to the still-waiting crowds outside by Norman Cook as he conveyed it to the safe custody of the Guildhall Museum. A banner headline in the local paper 'back home' dealt ambiguously with this event. 'WELSH WOMAN', it said, 'FINDS GOD' . . .

An atmosphere of excitement amounting at times to something approaching hysteria is not the most suitable one in which to conduct an orderly investigation, particularly when time-factors are involved. There were occasions when the archaeology was in danger of being pushed into the background by various external pressures. Though the evening openings came to an end after the first week there were many visitors during the day throughout the rest of the period. A sudden interest in archaeology flowered in unexpected places; close acquaintanceship with one or other member of the working party was often surprisingly claimed as the substitute for the passes by which the owners sought to control access to the site. Publishers who had not previously concerned themselves with archaeological books were suddenly agog to enter the field. Even one or two scholars allowed their judgment to be infected by the excitement. Inevitably there were the insatiable demands of the press, which sometimes seemed (and not for the first time) to be concerned more with disseminating news than with imparting information. The whole thing had a curiously nightmarish quality; and through it our small organisation had somehow to get on with the work, which was not made any easier by the fact that we were already suffering under the handicap of having (for reasons beyond the control of anyone there present) to use procedures that we would not have adopted willingly for a building which had endured a complicated history. Life would have been even more difficult without the help of a hard-working group of volunteers which included colleagues from the Guildhall and London Museums and a contingent, led by George Rybot and Gordon Atkinson, from Shell, of St. Swithun's House, across the street. The collaboration of the Ancient Monuments Department of the Ministry of Works (as it then was) in the preparation of a valuable series of measured drawings of the building in all its aspects lightened my labours considerably. Thanks are also due to the City Police for the skill and patience with which they dealt with what must have been, even for them, an unusual situation.

The correspondence that developed in the papers tended to focus from the beginning mainly on the controversial question of the permanent preservation of the temple; but there were interesting side-issues, a lot of irrelevancies, and even, at times, local patriotism and rivalries (usually Mithras-in-the-north versus Mithras-in-the-south). Reading the various contributions at the time one tended to feel detached, sometimes as an onlooker not directly involved, sometimes like some kind of specimen submitted to critical and not always favourable examination. I do not myself collect newspaper cuttings, but through the kindness of Mr. J. F. Ronderson of Canterbury, who made me a present of his scrapbook, I have been able to re-read—or often to read for the first time—much of what was written. One striking feature of the correspondence was the number of letters that it produced which though written with an air of authority were grossly inaccurate in matters of ascertainable fact. I find myself wondering how often people who write to the papers with equal assurance on subjects about which I know nothing are equally misinformed.

The demand for the preservation of the temple *in situ* arose at once with the finding of the head of Mithras on September 20th. It caused considerable anxiety in more than one quarter and gave me personally more trouble than the archaeology. Preservation would have meant large-scale replanning of the new building and there were various other factors—a deep sewer traversing the area was, I believe, one—which added to the difficulty and cost. The total estimate for all that was involved was £500,000. The situation was finally resolved by the decision of the owners to reconstruct the building on a convenient part of the area as near as possible to the original site. The reconstruction, which would cost, it was said, £10,000, was to await the completion of the new offices.

My own feelings about the proposal to preserve the temple on its original site were very mixed. Regarding it professionally as an archaeologist concerned to unravel its history, the structure itself was interesting, though many of its striking features were perishable and incapable of preservation as found. Its association with one of the most intriguing of all pagan cults, heavily enshrined in mystery and legend and linked in a hostile sense with the rise of Christianity, strengthened greatly its appeal to the imagination. Nevertheless, half a million pounds (which is a large sum in relation to that spent annually on the British antiquities service as a whole) seemed too high a price to pay for it, and I could have thought of a number of monuments on which collectively so much money might more profitably have been spent. The real trouble, of course, was the one with which the reader who has persevered to this point will already have been wearied. The whole thing came too late because under the stultifying conditions that govern archaeological work in the City there was no possibility of determining the true character of the building sufficiently in advance of the redevelopment to enable its preservation to be provided for. In fact, by the time that the temple was identified preparatory work on the site was already well advanced; and while at one stage I advocated preservation I could not help but sympathise with those who were reluctant to embark on all that would have been involved in making the necessary changes. There were many sweeping statements from self-appointed spokesmen on what 'the public' wanted and how 'the City' would react; but for those who have been directly involved in the tedious business of having to get money, or of trying to persuade unconvinced authorities that certain courses of action are desirable, proposals that ignore the practical issues operate as counter-irritants, but do little else unless their originators are prepared to support them by action. When it came to the point none of the newspapers was prepared to take effective steps over the appeal for funds that many of them agreed was necessary. Very little support was forthcoming from the City when the appeal for more money for the Council's work was actually made. There was no more marked indication of a positive attitude in the Corporation than there had been previously.

The decision of the owners to reconstruct the temple at their own charges was the last of a series of generous acts which, as I have said, was accepted as the answer to the problem of preservation. Unfortunately, it has to be recorded that the final result, now visible on the Queen Victoria Street frontage of Bucklersbury House, falls short of what it ought to have been.

My own part in this project ended in about 1959, when I was invited by the architects to comment on the proposals then being prepared. What happened after that I do not know, except that in the outcome my suggestions were completely ignored. The outline of the reconstruction is presumably accurate enough; apart from some irrelevancies (crazy paving, for instance, for all floors in the body of the building) the internal features, such as the variation in floor-levels, that gave the original such architectural quality as it possessed have been seriously maltreated. The result is virtually meaningless as a reconstruction of a mithraeum. It is exasperating that so much money should have been spent to such poor purpose. The necessary facts were available and had indeed been provided on the archaeological side; the Ministry of Works was apparently not consulted over the restoration, though its unrivalled experience and skill in such matters would, I feel sure, have been freely given. Someone, somewhere, I suppose, thought he knew better.

From having been a nine-days' wonder Mithras has receded into the past, except for those who contend with the aftermath of the excavation report. When I think of it now some aspects of it still puzzle me. The *Illustrated London News* reminded us at the time that the finding in Bucklersbury of the mosaic pavement now in the Guildhall Museum produced a somewhat similar reaction in 1869. In 1954 many of our visitors obviously came because they were genuinely interested, but the presence of others could only be accounted for on the basis of some kind of sensationalism. This was something to see; and they were going to see it—under floodlights, if necessary. Such attitudes did not absolve us from the duty of doing our best to help visitors to understand what they were looking at. We suspended explanatory placards with sketch-plans and brief descriptions along the hoardings so that people might read while they waited; and put labels on the various parts of the building to correspond with those on the plans. By these means those who came to the site got maximum value in terms of information from it and the heavily pressed excavators were saved at any rate the more obvious questions. But whether 'information' was what a lot of them wanted I am not at all sure; nor, by the same token, do I find it easy to believe that the numbers who thronged to Walbrook during that week came because of a genuine interest—whatever that may mean—in the 'past'.

I will readily confess that this scepticism has its origin—or some part of its origin—in a professional distrust of what has been called the public 'instinct'. It seems to me to be a phenomenon of uncertain and fluctuating value. Perhaps it is unfair to test interest by looking at the amount that our collecting-box produced on the site over this period. It is, nevertheless, in matters of money that one is brought face to face with the facts of archaeo-logical—and other—life. Estimates varied as to the number of people who visited the temple during the excavation and I do not know what reliance to place upon them. But if we assume 30,000—less than the figure quoted for *one* night by some newspapers—this number gave us about £250, a matter of 2d per head. (The figure was in fact a good deal less than that, for a number of the gifts consisted of notes.) Commentators were quick to point the moral. Public discussion of the proposal to preserve the temple *in situ* led to an unsolicited gift from an anonymous donor of £2,000 towards a preservation fund. The donor allowed the Council to keep the money for its general purposes when the preservation proposal was dropped. Thanks are here recorded for a generous benefaction which has materially augmented the reserve which has been created to meet the cost of preparing and pub-lishing the detailed excavation reports. A widespread appeal, made with professional assistance while the discovery was still fresh in the public memory, produced £6,000 (which included the above gift). Not an en-couraging result. The Corporation of London contributed £300. Its collec-tions had already been enriched by the owners' gift to the Guildhall Museum of the sculptures and other finds from the site.[1]

In one respect the Mithras affair had a somewhat worrying aftermath. It provoked anxiety in the minds of site-owners, who dreaded the possibility that any other discovery might lead to a further outbreak of public en-thusiasm, with disastrous consequences for their building programmes. For some time after 1954 it became necessary to give various undertakings in seeking to excavate particular sites, but owners and developers maintained their helpful attitude in this respect and permission was never withheld. David Langdon's cartoon in *Punch* of 6th October 1954 commented pro-phetically on this situation. It depicts an as yet untouched building-site with

---

[1] Later, under its rights over Treasure Trove, the Corporation paid £3,000, the antiquarian value, for the silver gilt canister (p. 114) which was declared Treasure Trove at a coroner's inquest held at the Bishopsgate Institute on 12 December 1958.

labourers and others about to begin operations. 'Start about here,' says the foreman, 'and the first man to find a Roman temple gets docked a quid. . . .'

The critical, if not disgruntled, tone of much of this chapter might well leave the reader with the impression that archaeological work in the City of London is a depressing business. This would be far from the truth. The City is an interesting place to be in and many of its diurnal inhabitants, met in pubs and elsewhere, are kindly, friendly and entertaining people. Its standards of hospitality, official and personal, are traditional. There are many places where a strong whiff of Dickens has survived two world wars and drastic physical reconstruction. Archaeologically speaking, many of the excavations were of the plodding kind, with excitement, if any, at a low pitch. In this respect London is no different from any other site; and in any case, excitement can be triggered off by events of a comparatively trivial kind (in terms of discovery). When the objectives are historical facts rather than either finds or buildings as such, a significantly sited common Roman coin which gives a date to a feature causes more elation than any more 'valuable' object less fortunate in its surroundings.

For excitement I suppose Mithras must be said to stand alone, but the emotions aroused there were not entirely inspired by archaeology. Though I was given a C.B.E. for it I do not try to conceal the fact that in the conditions of the time the discovery was in the nature of a fluke. As I have already said, I had no choice of where to dig (Fig. 22): there was no heaven-sent inspiration to guide the siting of the trench that revealed the temple. This will not have been the first occasion when good fortune in the matter of finds has brought credit independently of the manner in which the actual work was done. Though I hope that the excavation was well-conducted and that the conclusions that will be drawn from it in the final report will find acceptance amongst scholars generally, the controlling factors at Walbrook prevented the excavation from developing organically. The processes of recovering the successive plans of the building as it changed with the years and of elucidating their relationships could only be pursued piecemeal, as more parts of the site were made available. Since already almost half of its internal deposits had been removed in the first exploratory cutting, made in the early stages when the possibility of our doing further work on the site had seemed remote, there was never any hope of seeing any phase in the building's history whole. The challenges so presented had to be taken up, but always with an awareness that the rules to be followed were not those of archaeology.

It is for this kind of reason that I shall always rate the other important Roman discovery that was the outcome of this work—the Cripplegate fort —as archaeologically the more satisfying achievement. Here, too, of course, 'luck' played its part in the way in which the fort could not have been identified—or would have been more difficult to identify—if in consequence of the bombing the crucial areas had not been available to me. There are, however, two things that may, I think, fairly be claimed for the series of excavations by which the fort was revealed.

In the first place, at the technical level the investigation achieved its result by the application of strictly archaeological method to a jigsaw of evidence the various pieces of which only fell into place in a sort of slow climax when the work reached the fort's south-western angle in Noble Street (*9*: p. 21). I remember how the corner-turret gradually emerged beneath the floor of a cellar which was still 8 or 9 feet deep in bomb-rubble, how for some days if not weeks the explanation looked likely but was not certain, and how, when the turret could be finally accepted, the inconsistencies and uncertainties in earlier interpretations which had driven the investigation onward all disappeared.

The second point is that identification of the fort has helped to clarify so much else: the Roman defensive system, the dating (still tentative as it must be) of the city wall, the influence of the fort plan on the mediaeval city plan in the area and so on. This coherence, extending beyond the details of the excavation, is an eminently satisfying thing. It remains so in spite of an awareness of questions that can now probably never be answered because the evidence does not exist.[1] The questions are not only ones of Roman chronology: there is the teasing business of the association of Saxon activity with the fort area, particularly in the Addle Street–Wood Street sector of the interior (p. 204).

---

[1] It is incidentally not entirely true to say that evidence that might bear on these problems does not exist. Something might yet come from the deposits which underlie existing streets that still follow their ancient line—Silver Street or Noble Street in particular—though they will have been much disturbed by modern drains and other installations. I do not feel hopeful about the mediaeval burial-grounds, in which the graves probably go too deep.

There remains one other matter that seems worthy of comment and it is not unrelated in its way to the lessons inculcated by the Cripplegate fort investigation. It is a commonplace of Romano-British history that knowledge of it away from the scanty framework of historically recorded facts relies to a very great exent upon archaeological evidence. The fort is only one of a very large number of discoveries that emphasise the oneness of aim underlying the modern use of archaeological and recorded information.

For the post-Roman periods also the same processes may be seen to be at work. The Church of St. Bride, Fleet Street (p. 182), illustrates them very well in the marked difference between the structural history as established by the excavation and that based primarily on the early records which was produced by the late Mr. Walter Godfrey in 1944.[1] An even better example is provided by the study of the late mediaeval mansion known as Brooke House, Hackney, in which we collaborated with Mr. W. A. Eden and his colleagues in 1954–5. This work was fully published by the London Survey and has not therefore been described in detail in this volume.[2] Its relevance here is that it demonstrates that if the complete history of a building is to be recovered the approach to it must in many cases be by way of a combination of visible architectural features, recorded history and excavated evidence.

The excavation of Brooke House revealed early phases in the building's development which were not in themselves visible in the surviving structure, though their influence on that structure could be recognised when once their existence had been established. In the reverse direction it provided a warning to the excavator of the dangers that may attend too close reliance on an excavated plan as the basis for a restoration of the superstructure, for at Brooke House there were important changes in the actual buildings, studied architecturally, of which no trace at all appeared in the excavated plan. The sequence here illustrated (Fig. 53) makes these points: the report provides the details of the evidence on which it is based.

The significance of the Brooke House study from this point of view is that it demonstrates more completely perhaps even than Charterhouse (p. 175) the importance of a 'total' approach to the problems of a building's history. If this and the other examples in this book are anything to go by full understanding of many mediaeval buildings would seem ideally to

[1] See W. H. Godfrey, *op. cit.*, footnote, p. 182 above.

[2] *Survey of London*, Vol. XXVIII, *The Parish of Hackney: Part One: Brooke House* (1960).

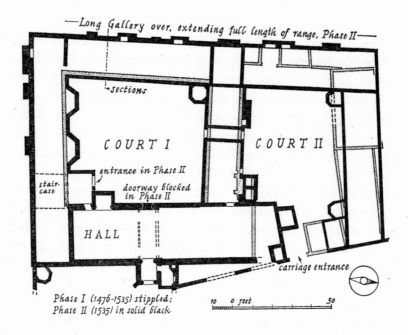

—Long Gallery over, extending full length of range, Phase II—

←sections

COURT I

COURT II

entrance in Phase II

stair-case

doorway blocked
in Phase II

HALL

carriage entrance

Phase I (1476-1535) stippled;
Phase II (1535) in solid black

10   0 feet   50

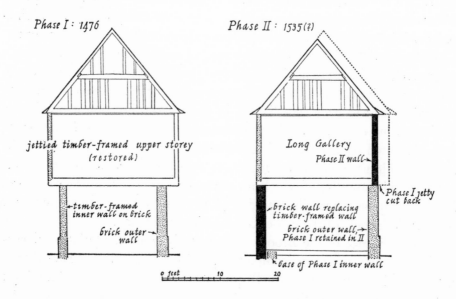

Phase I : 1476

jettied timber-framed upper storey
(restored)

←timber-framed
inner wall on brick

brick outer →
wall

Phase II : 1535(?)

Long Gallery

Phase II wall←

←Phase I jetty
cut back

←brick wall replacing
timber-framed wall

brick outer wall, →
Phase I retained in II

←base of Phase I inner wall

0 feet   10   20

53. Brooke House, Hackney: *above*, plan of the buildings as excavated; *below*, sections through the west wing of Court I, showing changes in the superstructure incompletely reflected in the plan.

demand attention to the possibility of evidence below, as well as to the evidence above, ground. But this, in the nature of things, is an ideal that will rarely be realised. It need worry no one whose interest is in visible architectural style for its own sake, though he may ponder what he may have lost; it is likely to depress those who are concerned to elucidate historical processes. Herein lies the justification for the pursuit of much unlovely detail. It is essential to the study of the past, seen whole, making its contribution to the understanding of the four- and five-star monuments (of which London still has a number) that are—in this context—the past's crowning achievement.

THE ROMAN AND MEDIAEVAL LONDON
EXCAVATION COUNCIL

The Rt. Hon. the Lord Mayor of London

VICE-PRESIDENT
The Rt. Hon. Lord Balfour of Burleigh

OFFICERS AND EXECUTIVE COMMITTEE

Chairman:
Professor Sir Ian Richmond (*Council for British Archaeology*)

Vice-Chairman:
N. C. Cook (*Guildhall Museum*)

Hon. Director of Excavations:
Professor W. F. Grimes (*University of London*)

Hon. Treasurer:
C. E. Denham

Hon. Secretary:
R. A. Woods (*Bank of England*)

G. C. Dunning
Sir E. G. M. Fletcher (*Hon. Legal Adviser*)
F. J. Forty (*Institution of Civil Engineers*)
Professor S. S. Frere
J. A. Giuseppi (Assistant Hon. Treasurer 1947–50; Hon. Secretary 1950–7)
Dr. D. B. Harden (*London Museum*)
J. F. Head (Hon. Treasurer 1947–57)
A. H. Oswald
P. K. Baillie Reynolds
Sir Ronald Syme (*Society for Promotion of Roman Studies*)
A. J. Taylor (*Chief Inspector of Ancient Monuments, Ministry of Public Building and Works*)
The late Miss M. V. Taylor (*Administrators of the Haverfield Bequest*)

PRESENT AND FORMER MEMBERS OF THE COUNCIL

The late Dr. J. Allan
Dr. W. Godfrey Allen

242

A. B. Ashby
Miss E. Bright Ashford (*London Society*)
The late Sir Harold Idris Bell (Chairman, 1946–52)
The Rt. Hon. Lord Blackford
The late The Rt. Hon. Lord Bossom
Commander G. Bridgmore Brown, R.N.R. (*London and Middlesex Archaeological Society*)
The late Sir George Burt
Esmond Burton (*Vintners' Company*)
The late D. A. J. Buxton
The Rt. Hon. Lord Catto (Vice-President 1955–57)
The late Rev. M. P. Charlesworth
The late Sir Alfred Clapham
The Rt. Hon. Lord Clitheroe
The late Dr. Philip Corder (*Society of Antiquaries of London*)
The late A. C. Dabbs
Dr. Norman Davey
Major L. M. E. Dent (*Grocers' Company*)
Dr. F. W. M. Draper
W. A. Eden (*London County Council*)
H. Farrar (*London County Council*)
P. Graves
A. H. Hall (*Guildhall Museum*)
Professor C. F. C. Hawkes
The late C. J. Holland-Martin
Edward Holland-Martin (*Fishmongers' Company*) (Joint Hon. Treasurer 1947–53)
G. R. Hughes (*Goldsmiths' Company*)
Sir Thomas Kendrick (*British Museum, British Academy*)
Dr. K. M. Kenyon
The late J. H. MacDonnell (*London County Council*)
John Makower
The late Sir James G. Mann (*Society of Antiquaries of London*)
I. D. Margary (*Royal Archaeological Institute*)
The late Henry Martin
The Very Rev. W. R. Matthews, Dean of St. Paul's
R. L. Moreton (*Haberdashers' Company*)
Sir Godfrey Nicholson
The late B. H. St. J. O'Neill (*Chief Inspector of Ancient Monuments*)
T. F. Reddaway
G. V. D. Rybot
E. A. Schalch (*City of London Real Property Co. Ltd.*)
The late W. Shepherd-Barron (*Port of London Authority*)

LIST OF SUBSCRIBERS TO THE FUNDS OF THE ROMAN AND MEDIAEVAL LONDON EXCAVATION COUNCIL 1946–62

£26,300 H.M. Government (through the Minister of Works)
£2,750 Bank of England
£2,000 An anonymous donor
London County Council
£1,050 Church of St. Bride, Fleet Street
£950 Lloyds Bank Ltd.
£550 The Corporation of London
£350 Society of Antiquaries of London
£255 Westminster Bank Ltd.
£250 Midland Bank Ltd.
National Provincial Bank Ltd.
Mrs. Smith Trust
£210 National Geographic Society
£200 Corporation of Lloyd's
Goldsmiths' Company
Grocers' Company
Imperial Chemical Industries Ltd.
Mercers' Company
£150 Barclays Bank Ltd.
Morgan, Grenfell & Co. Ltd.
£131 M. Makower & Co. Ltd.
£113 Martins Bank Ltd.
£105 Anglo-Iranian Co. Ltd.
Linoleum Manufacturing Co. Ltd.
Shell Petroleum Co. Ltd.
Whitbread & Co. Ltd.
£100 The Rt. Hon. Lord Catto, P.C.
Drapers' Company
Lazard Brothers & Co. Ltd.
I. D. Margary
Mrs. Fraser Parkes

Royal Exchange Assurance
Sun Life Assurance Society
Unilever Ltd.
£96 Cutlers' Company
£75 N. M. Rothschild & Sons
Standard Bank of South Africa Ltd.
£70 Wilmot Breeden Ltd.
£62 District Bank Ltd.
£55 City of London Reconstruction Advisory Council
£52 National Bank of Scotland
Sun Insurance Office Ltd.
£50 Alliance Assurance Co. Ltd.
Clothworkers' Company
Haverfield Trust
London Assurance
Miss B. Neville
Port of London Authority
Prudential Assurance Co. Ltd.
Salters' Company
£46 Carpenters' Company
£39 Professor Jocelyn Toynbee
£37 Coutts & Co.
Merchant Taylors' Company
£35 Browett, Taylor, Robertson & Martin
Leathersellers' Company
£31 Miss K. M. Kenyon
£30 Sir Albert Gladstone, Bt.
Glyn Mills & Co.
£27 Kleinwort Sons & Co. Ltd.
£26 Commercial Union Assurance Co. Ltd. and Associated Offices

Farriers' Company

The Institute of Actuaries

Legal and General Assurance Society Ltd. and Associated Offices

Liverpool & London & Globe Insurance Co. Ltd. and Associated Offices

P. A. Mayer

North British & Mercantile Insurance Co. Ltd.

Royal Insurance Co. Ltd. and Associated Offices

Spectacle Makers' Company

Swiss Bank Corporation

£25 Bank of London & South America Ltd.

Baring Bros. & Co. Ltd.

Caledonian Insurance Co.

Eagle Star Insurance Co. Ltd.

The Employers' Liability Assurance Corporation Ltd.

Guest, Keen & Nettlefolds Ltd.

The London & Lancashire Insurance Co. Ltd. and Allied Companies

L. Marchant

The Northern Assurance Co. Ltd. and Subsidiary Offices

Phoenix Assurance Co. Ltd.

Reckitt & Colman Holdings Ltd.

The Royal Bank of Canada

M. Samuel & Co. Ltd.

The Times

£21 Alexanders Discount Co. Ltd.

Atlas Assurance Co. Ltd.

British Mutual Bank Ltd.

Miss de Beer

Helbert Wagg & Co. Ltd.

National Bank of Australasia Ltd.

Sir C. Whitaker

£20 Fishmongers' Company

Founders' Company

National Bank of New Zealand Ltd.

Orient Steam Navigation Co. Ltd.

Vintners' Company

£19 Hudson's Bay Co.

£16 J. E. Broad

Matthew Clark & Sons Ltd.

N. Cook

Dr. N. Davey

Innholders' Company

National Bank Ltd.

Sir Frederick Tidbury-Beer

£15 R. Renfield

£14 Sir Alan Barlow, Bt.

£13 City Literary Institute

The London Fellowship

Saddlers' Company

£12 A. E. Benfield

A. H. A. Hogg

£10 Associated British Picture Corporation Ltd.

Balfour Williamson & Co. Ltd.

Bank of New Zealand

Barclays Bank, D.C.O.

The British Oak Insurance Co. Ltd.

The Builder Ltd.

Butchers' Company

L. Cadbury

Mrs. Chown

Coachmakers & Coach Harness Makers' Company

G. G. Davies

William Deacon's Bank Ltd.

The Dean & Chapter of St. Paul's

Mrs. C. Dowman

John Fowler & Co. (Leeds) Ltd.

Miss B. Graham
Arthur Guinness, Son & Co.
  (Park Royal) Ltd.
Guinness Mahon & Co.
M. S. Giuseppi
E. J. W. Hildyard
Coleman Jennings
London & Middlesex Archaeo-
  logical Society
A. K. McCosh
Miss Amy Neville
Mrs. Ringrose-Wharton
David Sassoon & Co. Ltd.
Singer & Friedlander Ltd.
Stationers' & Newspaper
  Makers' Company
W. Stebbing
Colonel C. E. Temperley
Turners' Company
The Union Bank of Australia
  Ltd.
£9 H. M. Taylor
£8 P. Corder
Sir Gerard Clauson
Miss Rose Macauley
T. Rayson
H. H. Robinson
£7 Sir Russell C. Broch
Dr. Joan Evans
Institute of Bankers, Scotland
C. H. Moore
H. J. Randall
£5 Mrs. Acworth
Lord Airedale
Arbuthnot, Latham & Co.
  Ltd.
Barbers' Company
J. C. Beaston
Leopold Behrman Ltd.
J. Bellingham
Leonard Bingham
E. J. Borrajo

C. J. Bowlby
Bowyers' Company
C. J. Branchini
F. E. Bray
British Archaeological Associa-
  tion
Brown, Shipley & Co. Ltd.
P. R. Buchanan & Co.
H. Busbridge
J. Chadwick
Professor Gordon Childe
City Livery Club
F. J. Collins
W. C. Crocker
Currys Ltd.
Lady Davson
J. P. Droop
Mrs. Duthie
Mrs. M. Egerton
Major P. Fletcher
W. H. Fraser
Gillett Bros. Discount Co. Ltd.
Gold and Silver Wyre Drawers'
  Company
A. Gravely
W. Grey
W. F. Grimes
Guild of Freemen of the City of
  London
Miss Hall
Harrison & Crosfield Ltd.
Mrs. Hatton-Wood
Mrs. M. Hencken
H. O'N. Hencken
E. Holland-Martin
F. Kdia
Legal & General Assurance
  Society Estates Department
Mrs. Lesley Lewis
The London Society
Mrs. V. McIvor
Maclaine Watson & Co. Ltd.

Manchester Guardian & Evening News Ltd.
Miss E. G. Marriage
Lt.-Commander J. Martin
Miss E. Minet
E. A. Moore
National Bank of Egypt
National Savings Committee
Sir Frank Newnes, Bt.
North Thames Gas Board
The Orient Bonded Warehouses Ltd.
Orpington Historical Society
Plumbers' Company
R. Powell
S. Prestiges
F. Gordon Roe
Royal Archaeological Institute of Great Britain and Ireland
D. T. Sanger
Joseph Sebag & Co.
Skilbeck Bros. Ltd.
The Viscountess Swinton
J. S. Syme
Laurence Tanner
J. B. Tolhurst
W. F. Towers
Sir Frederick Whyte
Mrs. Wilson Harris
Charles Winn & Co. Ltd.

£4 Miss A. E. Hickson
The Hon. Mrs. Dorothy Hood
Miss E. M. Mackenzie
Lord Nathan
C. Ralegh Radford

£3 John Allan
Blackburn Society of Antiquaries
Miss B. Blackwood
Boots (London) Camera Club
H. J. A. Bosanquet

Brentwood & District Historical Society
Mrs. F. Coston Taylor
George M. Davies
Professor Margaret Deanesly
Sir E. de Norman
Dr. F. M. W. Draper
Dr. D. Ferons
R. J. H. Jenkins
Miss G. I. Matthews
Phoenix House Ltd.
Mrs. Riddel
Sybil Rosenfeld
Geoffrey Thompson
Sir Robert Young

£2 Miss Audrey Anderson
Freda Anderson
A. J. Arkell
A. M. Arnott
Association of Optical Practitioners
R. L. Atkinson
A. Ballingall
Mrs. Julia Barnett
Bedford Modern School Field Club
Esmond de Beer
Sir H. I. Bell
Berkshire Archaeological Society
Colonel C. J. Blaikie
Lady Briscoe
Briscoe & Co. Ltd.
R. L. S. Bruce-Mitford
C. A. Butt
G. H. Christy
City Literary Institute Historical Society
The Rev. P. B. Clayton
S. E. Cook
Stuart Cook
Corby, Palmer & Stewart

Cordwainers' Company
A. Edmunds & Co. Ltd.
Miss M. A. Ehrenfest
Dr. L. Evans
The Misses Foyster
Mrs. E. Giblin
Miss Rose Graham
F. A. Greenhill
Daphne Hereward
J. W. F. Hill
E. Holland-Martin (Balance of
  Roman London Fund, R. M.
  Holland-Martin, deceased)
Miss M. B. Honeybourne
M. S. F. Hood
Miss Winifred M. Hume
J. Gibson Jarvie
H. E. Jevons
Sir Thomas Kendrick
F. Knott
Langley London Ltd.
H. C. Lea & Co. Ltd.
Albert Lee
A. W. Lloyd
London & Cripplegate Photo-
  graphic Society
Lord Mackintosh of Halifax
J. McIntyre
N. Maclagan
S. J. Madge
J. P. Maitland
Mary J. Meyler
Midland Electric Manufactur-
  ing Co. Ltd.
National Bank of Greece and
  Athens
Newbury District Field Club
Nigel Nicholson
C. B. Oldman
A. Oswald
B. Rackham
T. F. Reddaway

Miss Rosenfeld
St. Angela's Secondary Grammar
  School, Wood Green
Wilfred S. Samuel
Miss Scouloudi
W. G. Shiell
C. O. Skilbeck
A. C. Smith
John Spencer
N. C. Stanford
Miss C. Street
Surrey Archaeological Society
A. Sutherland-Graeme
A. V. Sutherland-Graeme
Mrs. Sutherland-Graeme
Tandy Textiles Ltd.
A. E. Thomas
Miss J. Toynbee
Mrs. Travers
Trice & Co. Ltd.
Miss Turnbull
Turnbull Scott & Co.
Visitors to Volunteer Diggers'
  Site
William R. Warner & Co. Ltd.
M. C. D. Watson
G. A. Webster
Miss Whitmore
R. F. Whitmore
W. Williamson
Raymond Wilson & Co. Ltd.
Woolwich & District Anti-
  quarian Society
Professor F. Wormald
Russell Wortley
£1 Mrs. M. D. Adam
Mrs. K. K. Andrew
Gordon Atkinson
C. F. Bailey
N. Baird
The Rev. E. P. Baker
M. W. Barley

E. Barrand
H. K. Barron
J. & E. Birchenough
Viscount Bledisloe
Mrs. H. G. Bowling
C. M. Bradshaw
Miss D. M. Brasher
N. Brett-Jones
The Rev. F. L. Bridges
Hester Brown
Miss M. Burton
Peter Cadogan
Miss J. Cameron
A. F. A. Carlisle
R. Champness
S. Cheisman
Frank Christy
Clapham History Circle
Charles Clay
Colonel R. Collings-Wells
C. Corbett Fisher
Cow & Gate Ltd.
The Rev. Cyril L. Cresswell
K. A. C. Cresswell
Hon. Marjorie and Miss K. Cross
Mrs. H. L. Cubitt
H. V. Cusack
A. C. Dabbs
Miss M. A. Durrant
George E. Eades
W. Eden
Mrs. K. M. Edwards
J. M. Ehrman
C. D. Ellis
R. H. Ellis
Ethel Emslie
H. G. Everton-Jones
V. M. Falkner
H. W. Fincham
A. P. Fletcher
Sir Cyril Flower
Freight Express Ltd.

H. R. Fuerst
A. W. Gent
Sir William Gibson
C. W. Giffard
David Gorsky
Miss T. Gosse
G. G. Green
A. Graham
Dr. G. Graham
George Graham
Mr. and Mrs. T. G. Grimes
G. T. Hales
J. F. Hales
K. Hare
F. M. H. Harper
Mrs. Harrison
P. C. Harrison
Dr. R. H. Hayes
R. G. Healey
T. A. N. Henderson
Mr. Heriot
The High School, St. Albans
W. Thomas Hill
Historical Association—North
    London Branch
C. W. Hitchcock
Miss D. F. Hobson
H. R. Hodgkinson
S. Hodgson
Professor S. H. Hooke
R. W. Hutchinson
Joan Ivory
F. H. J. Jervoise
T. P. Jordeson & Co. Ltd.
W. R. Kent
Colonel Sir Edwin King
Miss B. Lacaille and Miss F. Clift
W. D. Lang
G. D. Langham
E. B. Latham
Miss A. E. Lawson
Miss A. Leach

G. B. Leach
Malcolm Letts
Elsa Lewkowitsch
Miss L. Lindsay
Dr. T. A. Lloyd
H. Lloyd-Johnes
J. K. Lotinga
Mrs. Charles Lovell
J. S. M. MacGregor
Lord Marley
Mr. and Mrs. H. Marshall
Harold Mattingly
Miss M. Mills
Miss Mabel H. Mills
V. J. Mills
Captain Frank Mitchell
Miss J. M. Morris
James M. Morris
The Rev. C. B. Mortlock
Lord Mottisloe
C. F. Moysey
R. C. Musson
F. R. D. Needham
Theodore Nicholson
Mrs. H. V. Norland
C. L. Norman
F. J. Okey
Mrs. E. Temple Orme
B. Oulton
G. E. Page
Colonel R. G. Parker
F. M. Peake
A. Preston Pearce
Harold Proctor
K. A. Pryer
Miss Ursula Radford
Miss Joan Ralli
Miss Joyce Reynolds
Sir Albert Richardson
A. J. Rickards
F. Campbell Rose

A. G. Russell
George Rybot
David Saunder
E. A. Schalch
G. Scott Thomson
Miss C. Seccombe
G. Senn
Gilbert E. Smith
John Stead
Alderman W. P. Stebbing
G. Stedman
L. R. Stevens
Mrs. Dorothy Stevenson
Michael Tapper
Miss E. Taylor
Mrs. M. Rowland Thomas
Mrs. Thornton
Air Vice-Marshal H. K.
   Thorold
A. B. Tonnochy
Miss Tyler
University School, Bexley
Mrs. Theo Wadworth
Waley & Wilbraham
G. M. Warren
N. R. Watson
Wedd & Owen
Miss K. Wells
Were & Wright Ltd.
G. H. White
John White
Williams de Broe & Co.
C. S. Willis
Miss Edith Wills
Ethel M. Wood
Dr. W. Wood
C. E. Worthington
Dr. C. Wright
Young & Rochester Ltd.
Sir William Younger, Bt.
Mrs. L. D. Ziegler

In addition to the above there was a large number of donations of sums of less than £1.

Index

Addle Street, 25, 29, 37, 159, 161, 239
Addle Street–Silver Street, original
    Roman street, 29
'Agas' map, 189
Aldermanbury, 24, 25, 26, 159, 162
Aldermanbury Postern (St. Alphage),
    22, 25, 47, 83, 86, 226, 228
Aldersgate, 43, 45
Aldersgate re-entrant, 15, 20, 21, 47,
    52, 65
Aldersgate Street, 29, 43
Aldgate, 45
All-Hallows-on-the-Wall, city wall and
    bastion, 65, 73, 82
Apothecaries' Hall, 53, 54
Atkinson, Gordon, 129, 134, 231, 232
Austin Friars, Roman features, 124–6

Bacchus (Dionysus), 109, 230
Balfour of Burleigh, Lord, 221
bank, internal, to fort or city wall, 17,
    19, 21, 33, 48, 49, 50, 69, 116, 166
Barber Surgeons' Hall, 20, 34, 66, 79, 90
Barber's Warehouse (Coopers Row), 84n
Barbican, 15, 27
barrack-blocks, St. Alban Wood Street,
    35, 37
Bartholomew Close, 198, 199
basilica (Cornhill), 42, 43, 204n
bastions, 27, 65ff, 75ff
    bastion 10 (Camomile Street), 77
    bastion 11 (All-Hallows-on-the-
      Wall), 73, 77

bastion 11A (Cripplegate Church-
    yard), 27, 71, 72–8, 82n, 91
bastion 12 (Cripplegate), 66, 71,
    73, 76, 84
bastions 12–14, 84, 91
bastion 13 (Barber-Surgeons' Hall),
    65, 66, 76, 79, 87, 90
bastion 14 (Castle Street), 17–20,
    47, 64–6, 68, 69, 73, 76, 79,
    84, 90, 118, 164
bastion 15, 21, 65–7, 76, 91
bastion 16, 77
bastion 19 (Newgate), 64
bastions, date of, 70, 75–8, 84
    eastern series, 65
    western series, 65, 67, 76
bastions, spacing of, 77
Beasley, Fred, 223, 225
Bermondsey Abbey, 174, 210ff
Bermondsey, Manor of, 210
Bethnal Green, 45
Billiter Square, 122–3
Bishopsgate, 42, 43
Blackfriars, 54, 61, 63
Blossoms Inn, Lawrence Lane,
    excavation, 135–7
bonding courses, 18, 47, 48n, 79, 81,
    82, 85n
Bonus Eventus sculpture, 110
Boudicca, 11, 38, 39, 123, 124
Bourton-on-the-Water, Gloucestershire,
    Saxon hut-pits, 157
Bread Street, 135

1. *Above (left)* WINDSOR COURT (*3*): mortar-mixing pit beneath fort bank, with gully of *intervallum* road and part of road-surface to left.

2. *Above (right)* WINDSOR COURT (*3*): back of the city wall, showing the foundation of the internal thickening inserted in the fort bank. On top of the wall as surviving is the false double levelling-course of roofing tiles, which does not penetrate the wall.

3. *Below* WINDSOR COURT (*3*): the double city wall behind Bastion 14. *A: face of fort wall; B: 'city thickening'; C: repair to wall (built against original straight joint), of uncertain date.*

4. *Above* NOBLE STREET (*9*): the south-west corner turret of the Roman fort, with, to right, the double wall curving towards it from the north and Roman city wall going westwards from it.

5. *Below* WOOD STREET (*12*): the external ditch at the south gate of the Roman fort, showing surviving holes for supports for bridge, with Roman road metalling on each side, broken by mediaeval pit on left and by modern stanchion-base on right.

6. *Above* ALDERMANBURY (*14*): the external ditch at the south-east corner of the Roman fort in course of excavation: mediaeval rubbish-pit with stake-holes for wattle lining in middle distance, coopered well

(Plate 72) towards rear.

7. *Below* ALDERMANBURY (*14*): the external ditch at the south-east corner of the Roman fort as finally exposed.

8. *Above* (*left*) ALDERMANBURY POSTERN (*16*): the angle in the street-line of (old) London Wall reflecting junction of fort and city walls at north-east angle of the former.

9. *Above* (*right*) FALCON SQUARE (*5*): stake-holes along line of lateral gully of *intervallum* road behind the north turret of the west gate of the Roman fort.

10. *Below* FALCON SQUARE (*5*): the west gate of the Roman fort as exposed in 1957, from the north.

11. *Above* NOBLE STREET (7): internal turret to south of the west gate of the Roman fort.

12. *Below* NOBLE STREET (8): the double wall near the south-west angle of the Roman fort, showing, in a break caused by a modern foundation, the 'city thickening' (B) resting against the fort wall (A).

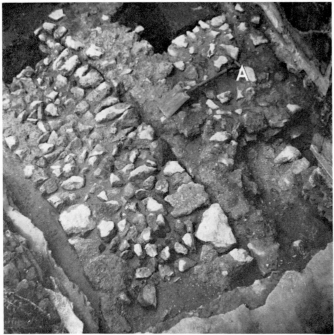

13. *Above* NOBLE STREET (*9*): the junction of the fort wall (A) and the city wall (B), with the culvert through the latter overlying the fort ditch.
(The fort wall, which can be seen approaching the modern wall in the background, is broken by a modern concrete foundation.)

14. *Below* (*left*) NOBLE STREET (*8*): the surviving stump of Bastion 15 (A), here seen to be toothed into the face of the Roman fort wall, behind which is the 'city thickening'.

15. *Below* (*right*) CASTLE STREET (*4*): arrow-loop, with blocked apparently mediaeval window-opening above, in face of Bastion 14.

16. *Above* CASTLE STREET (*4*): interior of Bastion 14 as finally excavated.

17. *Below* CASTLE STREET (*4*): Bastion 14 as visible above street level in 1966.

The features illustrated on Plate 15 *are to the right of the foot scale; another much mutilated mediaeval opening is visible at* (*A*).

18. *Above* CRIPPLEGATE CHURCHYARD (*1a*): general view of the surviving remains of Bastion 11a.

19. *Below* (*left*) CRIPPLEGATE CHURCHYARD (*1a*): the eastern abutment of Bastion 11a, with the patch (C) in the later city wall (B) above it; A: the Roman fort wall.

20. *Below* (*right*) BARBER SURGEONS' HALL (*2*): the junction of Bastion 13 (C) with the city wall. A: the Roman fort wall; B: the later (mediaeval) wall, for comparison with Plate 19.

21. *Above* (*left*) CASTLE STREET (*4*): section through the deposits inside Bastion 14, showing gravel floor (arrows) overlying the Roman city ditch, its inner end coinciding with the top of the Roman fort wall (extreme right) as surviving.

22. *Above* (*right*) CRIPPLEGATE CHURCHYARD (*1a*): the gravel floor inside Bastion 11a.

23. *Below* (*left*) NOBLE STREET (*8*): the inner face of the wall of Bastion 15 set in a recess in the wall of the Roman fort (right), with deposit under the rising foundation.

24. *Below* (*right*) CRIPPLEGATE CHURCHYARD (*1a*): the abutment of the wall of Bastion 11a with the Roman fort wall, here a straight joint, with the base of the foundation rising as with Bastion 15 (Plate 23).

25. *Above* ST. ALPHAGE (*17*): the mid-14th century wall face as first exposed in 1949, showing knapped flint and tile courses.

26. *Below* WESTMINSTER ABBEY: the north wall of the mid-14th century transept of St. Katherine's Chapel in post-war reconstruction, for comparison with the St. Alphage sector of the city wall.

27. *Above* (*left*) (OLD) LONDON WALL (*23*): one of a series of brick arches, apparently late mediaeval, built against the inner face of the Roman city wall (behind ranging rod).

28. *Above* (*right*) CRIPPLEGATE BUILDINGS (*18*): piled timber-framed structure (?wharf) on inner side of city ditch to the east of Cripplegate.

29. *Below* ST. ALPHAGE (*17*): the mediaeval city ditch: the line of the 17th century re-cutting is visible in the section about 2½ feet above the bottom of the first ditch.

30. *Above* CASTLE STREET (*4*): remains of the city wall (destroyed in 1957) immediately south of Bastion 14 (on left), showing mediaeval walling underpinned by modern brick.
(*Note: the lines purporting to mark embrasures in the wall-top are incorrect*).

31. *Below* (*left*) BUCKLERSBURY HOUSE (*44*): timber-lined gully in cutting to west of the Walbrook temple.
32. *Below* (*right*) BUCKLERSBURY HOUSE (*44*): Roman oak piles, with projecting from the face of the section on the right, remains of a plank floor carried on horizontal beams.

33. *Above* THE TEMPLE OF MITHRAS (45): general view of
the temple as finally excavated, just before dismantling,
from the north-east. Walbrook Street in foreground.
34. *Below* (*left*) THE TEMPLE OF MITHRAS (45): the
doorway in its original form in the first period.

35. *Below* (*right*) THE TEMPLE OF MITHRAS (45): general
view of west end, showing the apse, the block for the
support of the last altar (in front of ranging rod)
and in the south-western corner, the masonry block
overlying the well.

36. *Above (left)* THE TEMPLE OF MITHRAS (45): remains of joists and other timbers, perhaps supports for benches, mostly of the first phase of the building, in south aisle.

37. *Above (right)* THE TEMPLE OF MITHRAS (45): the north aisle wall as exposed in 1952, showing the wall of the first phase overlaid by the second phase lengths of wall between column bases.

38. *Below (left)* THE TEMPLE OF MITHRAS (45): timber features of the second phase, in bays 3 and 4 from the west. Also visible: the raised stonework on the sleeper wall (cf. Plate 37) of this phase, stumps of wooden posts, mostly later, and, in background, section through later floors of nave.

39. *Below (right)* THE TEMPLE OF MITHRAS (45): the longitudinal beam dividing the nave from the south aisle of the third phase.

The arrow indicates the make-shift altar (a former column capital) beneath the beam.

40. *Above (left)* TEMPLE OF MITHRAS (45): the north side of the temple at the west end, showing the remains of the longitudinal beam corresponding with that on the south (*Plate* 39). *A: the second phase aisle wall just appearing; B: a modern stanchion base.*

41. *Above (right)*: the final floor of the temple.

42. *Below (left)*: the west end of the temple showing, right, the accumulation of nave floors.

A: the risers of the steps of the first phase; B: 'pedestal' (set in intermediate floor); C: filling of the hole probably dug to remove second 'pedestal'; D: base for final altar.

43. *Below (right)*: aisle wall on south side with remains of setting for a column of the first phase and base of post of a later phase flattened on the surface of the wall.

44. *Above* TEMPLE OF MITHRAS (45): head of the god Mithras. (*Height* 14½ *inches*)
45. *Below* TEMPLE OF MITHRAS (45): Mithraic group representing the Bull-Slaying, found on or near the site of the Temple in 1889 and now in the London Museum. (17 *by* 20 *inches*)

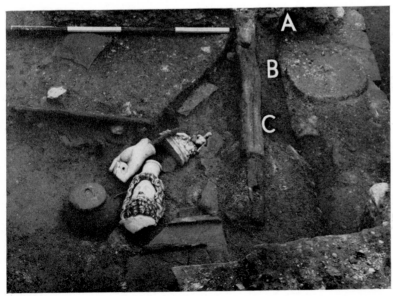

46. *Above* TEMPLE OF MITHRAS (45): head of the goddess Minerva. (*Height 10 inches*)
47. *Below* TEMPLE OF MITHRAS (45): the second group of marbles as uncovered in the ground.
(*A: position of the Mithras and Minerva; B: 'concrete pad' for arcade column of first phase;
C: end of north longitudinal beam of the third phase (cf. Plate* 40))

48-50. TEMPLE OF MITHRAS (45): the sculptures of the second group:
48. *Above (left)* head of the god Jupiter Serapis. (*Height* 17 *inches*)
49. *Above (right)* figure of the god Mercury with companions. (*Height* 10 *inches*)
50. *Below* gigantic hand. (*Length, including iron shank,* 14¾ *inches*)

51. *Above* TEMPLE OF MITHRAS (45): the god Bacchus
(Dionysus) with companions.
(*Height* 13½ *inches*)
52. *Below* TEMPLE OF MITHRAS (45): fragmentary
inscription (on a re-used marble panel) dedicated to
Mithras, from one of the later floors (6A) of the Temple.
The reference to the four Augusti (AV] GGGG)
fixes the date as A.D. 307-8
(12½ *by* 10 *inches*)

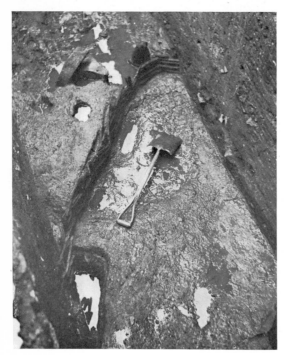

53. *Above (left)* GUTTER LANE (*25*): remains of a timber (?plank) floor.

54. *Above (right)* BLOSSOMS INN, LAWRENCE LANE (*41*): slots for wall-partitions.

55. *Below (left)* BUCKLERSBURY (*43*): view from above of Roman wattle 'fence' showing the relationship with the wattle lining of a mediaeval pit.

56. *Below (right)* BUCKLERSBURY (*43*): close view of the Roman wattle; in the background fragmentary Roman millstones.

57. *Above* (*left*) HONEY LANE (*40*): section showing (behind the left-hand scale) the accumulation of Roman deposits, cut through by a mediaeval rubbish-pit; projecting from the face part of a stone-built hearth, with post-holes in the exposed surface.

58. *Above* (*right*) HONEY LANE (*40*): part of a 'well' for a timber hut or room floor.

59. *Below* (*left*) HONEY LANE (*40*): Roman tiled hearth.

60. *Below* (*right*) FRIDAY STREET (*37*): Roman gully, originally timber-lined (cf. Plate 31), with on left at higher level, the foundations of a mediaeval building.

61. *Above (left)* ST. SWITHUN LONDON STONE (48):
section on south side of the church showing the edge of
the Roman street, with side-gully.
(*The natural surface is about six inches above the rule;
note A: stake holes (? for revetment of gully;
B: large post-holes, truncated by 18th century vault.*)
62. *Above (right)* ST. SWITHUN LONDON STONE (48):
tile-arched culvert beneath the east wall of the church,

opening into the side gully of the Roman road.
63. *Below (left)* CHEAPSIDE, SOUTH (38): top surface of
Roman street, broken by a post-Roman pit.
64. *Below (right)* UPPER THAMES STREET (32): the sloping
surface of the London Clay, interpreted as the slope to
the river in Roman times, on the north side of the
modern street.

65. *Above (left)* FALCON SQUARE (5): the blocking, of uncertain date, across the northern roadway of the west gate of the fort, partly removed to expose the foundation.

66. *Above (right)* FALCON SQUARE (5): the blocking of the southern roadway of the west gate of the fort, showing its abutment on the south turret of the gate. The arrow indicates the worn door socket.

67. *Below (left)* CANNON STREET (*Financial Times*) (35): north-south cutting showing Hut Pits in section, Pit I behind the further foot-scale, II behind the nearer, with a partly excavated mediaeval pit between.

68. *Below (right)* CANNON STREET (*Financial Times*) (35): the eastern portion of Hut Pit I as it survived beyond the section face.

69. *Above (left)* CANNON STREET (*Financial Times*) (*35*): Hut pit: II from the east. A-A: the enclosing gully, much broken by later pits.

70. *Above (right)* ADDLE STREET (*21*): part of a hut-pit, possibly Anglo Saxon, with two surviving post-holes, cut through in foreground by a mediaeval pit with wattle lining (behind rule): to the right of the rule a modern

foundation; behind it part of a mediaeval pit.

71. *Below (left)* CANNON STREET (*Financial Times*) (*35*): a mediaeval rubbish pit near the northern margin of the site with the wattle lining partly preserved. (*Scale = 1 foot.*)

72. *Below (right)* ALDERMANBURY (*14*): mediaeval coopered well (diameter *42* ins.).

73. *Above* NEVILLE'S INN (*3*): general view from the north during excavation in 1947, showing pits and foundations in course of clearing following the removal of modern concrete foundations.

74. *Centre* (*left*) NEVILLE'S INN (*3*): a mediaeval chalk-lined pit.

75. *Below* (*right*) NEVILLE'S INN (*3*): view from the east of the southern part of the site excavated in 1956, showing blocked staircase to cellar behind Falcon Square.

76. *Below* (*left*) NEVILLE'S INN (*3*): the staircase in Plate 75 with later wall removed, exposing surviving steps and much battered Reigate stone jambs.

77. *Above* (*left*) CHARTERHOUSE: the doorway of Cell B
in the Great Cloister, showing the serving-hatch,
from the outside.
78. *Above* (*right*) CHARTERHOUSE: the doorway of Cell S
on the east side of the Great Cloister, from the inside.

79. *Below* (*left*) CHARTERHOUSE: the serving-hatch of
Cell C from the outside.
80. *Below* (*right*) CHARTERHOUSE: the serving-hatch of
Cell S from the inside.

81. *Above* ST. BRIDE FLEET STREET: general view of the interior of the building.
Outlined in white, the Anglo-Norman church; in black, the 12th century 'square end'; A, A: 15th century arcade bases.
82. *Below (left)* ST. BRIDE FLEET STREET: burial, perhaps late Roman/early Christian, near the west end of the church.
83. *Below (right)* ST. BRIDE FLEET STREET: early mediaeval burials, east of the apse, cut through by the 'square end' (beyond trowel).

84. *Above (left)* ST. BRIDE FLEET STREET: view from east of western part of the internal long vault.
A, A: bases of walls of Norman tower, with relaid tiles between; B: original face of north tower wall; C: arch of staircase with 17th century brick filling.
85. *Above (right)* ST. BRIDE FLEET STREET: south-western angle column base in tower.

86. *Below (left)* ST. BRIDE FLEET STREET: north-eastern angle column base in tower.
87. *Below (right)* ST. BRIDE FLEET STREET: the moulded plinth of the tower at original ground level, exposed by the removal of the crown of the later vault, with foundations below partly masked by brick.

88. *Above (left)* ST. BRIDE FLEET STREET: foundation of a pier of the north arcade of the mediaeval church showing re-used column capital. Behind, the sleeper-wall of the north arcade of Wren's church, with remains of an earlier chalk-lined burial at its base.

89. *Above (right)* ST. BRIDE FLEET STREET: the complex of foundations on the north side of the church.
A: the first aisle; B: the north-eastern chapel;

C: the later enlarged aisle; D: wall of Wren's church.

90. *Below (left)* ST. BRIDE FLEET STREET: foundation of the west wall of the mediaeval church, cut through by the foundation of Wren's church on left.

91. *Below (right)* ST. BRIDE FLEET STREET: surviving fragment of the floor of the mediaeval church, the bricks and tiles crazed by the Great Fire of 1666.

92. *Above (left)* ST. ALBAN WOOD STREET (22): sill of the south door of the first church.

93. *Above (right)* ST. ALBAN WOOD STREET (22): the south-western angle of the nave of the late mediaeval church, showing the structural succession.
A: base of Roman wall; B: south wall of first church; C: foundation of later mediaeval pier; D: base of wall of 17th century church.

94. *Below (left)* ST. ALBAN WOOD STREET (22): base of later mediaeval pier with 17th century wall in background.

95. *Below (right)* ST. ALBAN WOOD STREET (22): the eastern end of the south-eastern chapel showing the foundation arch.
A: gravel of street of Roman fort; B: straight joint of chapel wall with south wall of church; C: base of foundation for respond of late arcade on south side of church; D: 19th century apse.